Dogs in My Life

The New Orleans Photographs of John Tibule Mendes

Edited by Bill Lavender

Introduction by John H. Lawrence

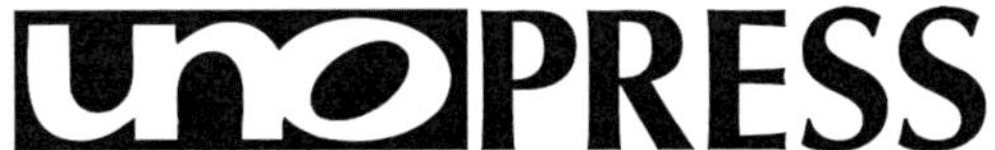

Printed in the USA

Library of Congress Control Number: 2009934538

ISBN: 1-60801-005-8
ISBN 13: 978-1-60801-005-9

Book and cover design by Kelcy D. Wilburn

Cover photo by John Tibule Mendes. 2003.182.533
[Uncaptioned. Little Miss Lucille Newlin and Mayor
Behrman welcome Rex at City Hall. February 19, 1917]

Back cover photos appear in the text on pages 68, 15, and 113.

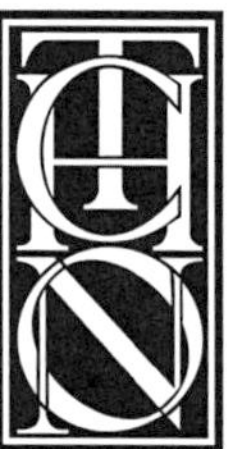

This collection was made possible in part by the cooperation of The Historic New Orleans Collection. The numbers in each photograph's caption refer to The Historic New Orleans Collection's accession numbers.

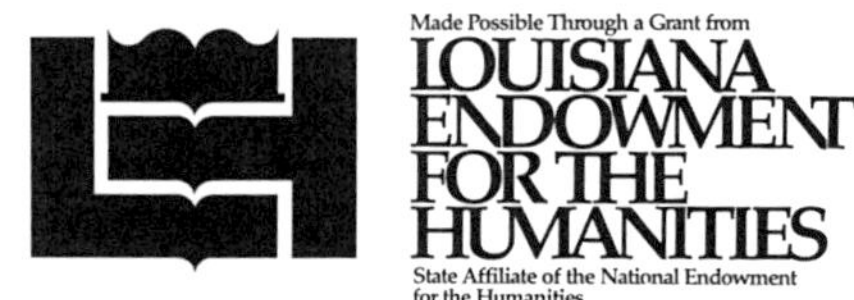

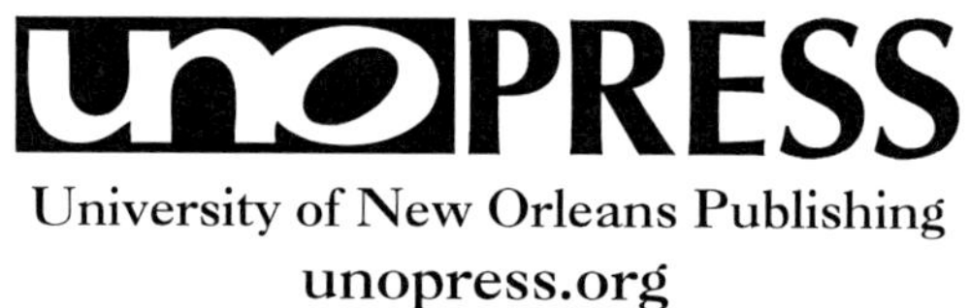

Acknowledgments

The editor would like to thank all the people who have contributed to this inaugural publication of the photographic work of John T. Mendes. First and foremost I want to thank the conscientious staff at The Historic New Orleans Collection and its Williams Research Center, along with Executive Director Priscilla Lawrence. Jessica Dorman, Director of Publications, supported the project from the beginning and facilitated the coordination among departments. Reference Assistants Daniel Hammer and Mary Lou Eichhorn were instrumental in making the materials accessible for this publication. Ms. Eichhorn also conducted research on Mendes family history and the subjects of many photographs. Jude Solomon, Associate Curator, along with intern Cath Cain, did much of the initial archiving of the negatives. Ms. Solomon and John Magill, Curator, were helpful with dating, identifying, and describing the subjects of Mendes's photographs. And of course John H. Lawrence, Director of Museum Programs, whose enthusiasm for the project has been inspiring, contributed the introductory essay.

At UNO Press, Kelcy D. Wilburn designed the book, a process that often seemed half detective work, half artistry. G.K. Darby first proposed the project to us and has been invaluable in his efforts to promote and set the stage for a successful publication.

Thanks also to John Kemp and the Board at LEH for their financial, logistical and moral support. Thanks to Nancy Dixon for program evaluation.

Besides John T. Mendes himself, no one bears more responsibility for this work than the late Waldemar S. Nelson. Mr. Nelson preserved the negatives following Mendes's death in 1965, carefully sheltering them for forty years before donating the archive to The Historic New Orleans Collection. Thanks to his dedication, this work is now able to be shared.

John C. Kelly, Library Archives Analyst II of the *The Times-Picayune*, provided citations and references pertaining to press coverage related to John T. Mendes.

Notes

Each photograph is captioned and marked with an accession number and date. Captions and date information are taken from Mendes's own labels, unless they appear in brackets, in which case the information has been inferred and added by the archivist. The numbers (in the form: 2003.182.xxx) are The Historic New Orleans Collection accession numbers for each individual negative.

The larger blocks of text are excerpts from *Dogs in My Life*, Mendes's self-published memoir. In the case of both this text and the photo captions, we have preserved Mendes's unique style of grammar and punctuation.

The memoir appeared in 1964, and the latest date on a photograph in the collection is 1929 (though undated photographs, based on their subject matter, are as late as 1932), so the memoir and the photographs are separated by some years.

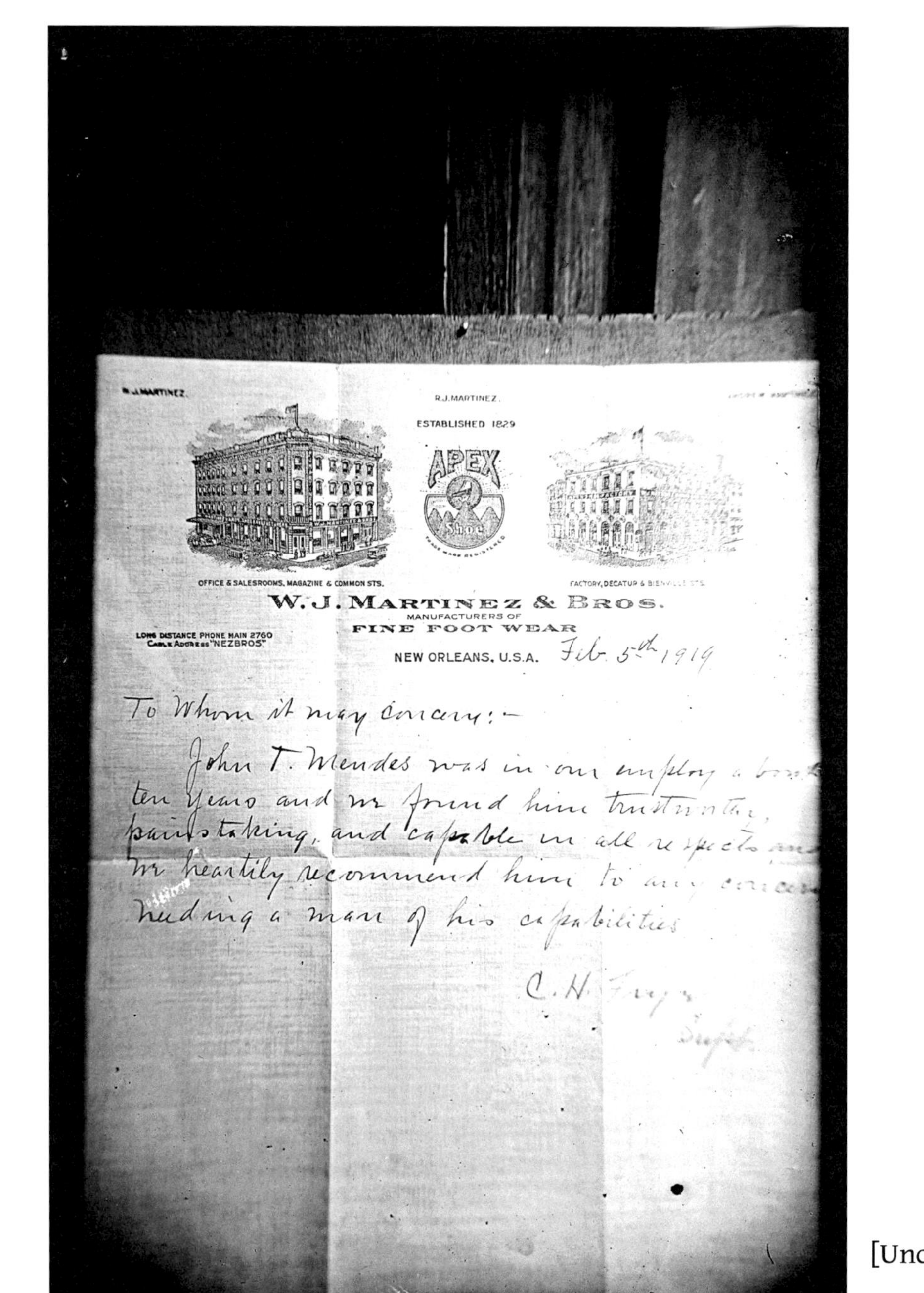

R. J. MARTINEZ.

R. J. MARTINEZ.

ESTABLISHED 1829

APEX Shoe

TRADE MARK REGISTERED

OFFICE & SALESROOMS, MAGAZINE & COMMON STS.

FACTORY, DECATUR & BIENVILLE STS.

W. J. MARTINEZ & BROS.

MANUFACTURERS OF

FINE FOOT WEAR

LONG DISTANCE PHONE MAIN 2760
CABLE ADDRESS "NEZBROS"

NEW ORLEANS, U.S.A. Feb. 5th 1919

To Whom it may concern:—

John T. Mendes was in our employ about ten years and we found him trustworthy, painstaking, and capable in all respects and we heartily recommend him to any concern needing a man of his capabilities

C. H. Fry

Supt.

[Uncaptioned]

2003.182.585
[1919]

Introduction

John H. Lawrence

Prologue

In 2003, Ken Nelson telephoned The Historic New Orleans Collection on behalf of his father Waldemar S. Nelson with the offer of donating a group of photographs that had been in the latter's possession for a number of years. After hearing the intriguing description of the pictures (documenting aspects of New Orleans during the "Roaring Twenties"), museum staff went to the Nelson home to view the materials: a quantity of several hundred glass negatives stored in a wooden packing case. The photographs were the work of John Mendes.

The weary crate had been reinforced with rope in order to better contain its weighty contents but, once unbound, revealed its treasure. Accompanying the negatives were two wooden tripods dating from the early 20th century. No camera was present. The photographs were gratefully accepted by The Collection, and, in the intervening years, they have been catalogued, scanned, and printed. This publication marks their first time in print as a collection.

The Nelsons had acquired the negatives with the purchase of a property adjacent to their home. The most recent occupant of that property had been John T. Mendes, who moved there in the summer of 1947. Mr. and Mrs. Nelson knew Mendes as their neighbor and were instrumental in helping him publish *Dogs in My Life* in 1964. *Dogs in My Life* recounts the series of pets that Mendes had throughout his lifetime. Underscoring his passion for dogs, Mendes was an ardent anti-vivisectionist and supportive of other causes that aided dogs. In 1947, The Hobson Press had published Mendes's first and only other book, *Bess, World War No. 1 War Dog*, which was a work of fiction.

Waldemar Nelson was able to piece together a sketchy biography of Mendes and provided a copy of this dossier with the donation. John Mendes was born in New Orleans and, from every scrap of evidence yet unearthed, lived his entire life in the city. A newspaper article from the World War I era (when these photographs begin) listed his name among those in his ward reporting for a physical examination at the draft board, but there is no indication that he ever served in the military. Perhaps his age (nearly 30), his being the only son of a widow, or other reasons, kept him at home. But aspects of the Great War, as manifested on the home front, did provide subjects for his camera. Mendes was a lifelong bachelor and lived with his mother until her death in 1942. He had a sister, Regina, who lived at least part of her life away from New Orleans. His mother's visit to Regina for one week, Mendes writes, is the only time that he was ever out of his mother's company.

Howard Jacobs, a columnist for *The Times-Picayune*, wrote on May 21, 1965, of Mendes's passing two days earlier: "Mr. Mendes was a genuine humanitarian in a crass and materialistic world, and his death serves a valuable and wistful link with the past." In a similar vein, Hermann Deutsch of *The States-Item*, in his column of March 29, 1965, referenced *Dogs in My Life* by writing: "What [Mendes] turned out was not literature, but... it was the sort of intensely human document, simply told, one finds only now and then, but remembers because reading it is so very moving an experience."

The Photographs Of John Mendes

When John Tibule Mendes (1888-1965) exposed the earliest dated negative in his archive (February, 1916), he was partaking of a photographic tradition that had begun in New Orleans some 76 years earlier, when Jules Lion produced and exhibited the first photographic images (using the daguerreotype process) in March, 1840. Though photography had made enormous technological leaps in this brief existence— both in equipment and image-forming materials— Mendes's approach to using the medium had less, perhaps, in common with practitioners who worked in 1916 than those working in 1878. This latter year marked the commercial perfection and introduction of the gelatin dry-plate process (a ready-to-use light-sensitive emulsion on glass), replacing the cumbersome and messy wet-plate process that had held sway for the previous two decades. Such plates were invariably exposed in a tripod-mounted camera which had extendable bellows and interchangeable lenses. More important is that their ready-to-use character permitted the photographer to approach picture-making with an attitude that could be adjusted while the scene was unfolding. While they still tethered the photographic process to a tripod, the prepared plates offered a possibility of risk-taking. When compared to the wet-plate process, variants of a picture could be made fairly rapidly. The archive, in its entirety, indicates that Mendes made variant exposures of many different subjects.

The notes recorded on the paper sleeves that held his negatives indicate some familiarity with photographic darkroom practice and interest in technique. One note identifies reticulation (though misspelled), the "shocking" of the gelatin surface of the plate caused by an extreme shift in temperature going from one chemical bath to another (94). Another note indicates a double-development of the plate, first with pyro (pyrogallic acid, a staining developer) followed by "special development" (46).

Mendes's equipment contrasted with that used by mainstream amateur snapshooters of his day, who tended to use hand-held cameras. Those devices possessed simple dedicated lenses and a limited capacity to adjust shutter speed. They produced negatives on flexible film. By eschewing this equipment, in form if not intent, Mendes was emulating the serious hobbyist and professional photographers who lived and worked in this era. In a life of some 77 years, Mendes seems to have devoted only a dozen or so years to photography, a conclusion based on the surviving photographic record. In his self-published autobiography (*Dogs in My Life*, 1964), the references to photography are sparse and exclusively mentioned in connection with photographing dogs. Indeed, a number of photographs in the present publication do include canine subjects.

No hard evidence exists that Mendes ever established a professional practice, but the world of New Orleans professional photography of his time is worth noting nonetheless. In examining the Soards' city directories for New Orleans between 1916 and 1929, one finds a fairly consistent number of professional listings for photographers (between 32 and 39, depending on the year) and a wide geographic distribution of their businesses throughout the neighborhoods of New Orleans.

If surnames can be taken as a valid indicator of ethnic heritage, a virtual League of Nations was represented. Some appearing during this fourteen-year period include: Bedou, Bellocq, Bertrand, DeBrueys, Dunn, Foletti, Franck, Fritch, Harvey, Hitchler, Krause, Lillenkohl, McCormick, Moore, Moses, Odiorne, Paddio, Pons, Scordill, Teunisson, and Whitesell. Though several of these individuals and firms are firmly ensconced in regional, national, or international photographic histories, many of the era's practitioners are virtual unknowns. The specialties of these men (and the occasional woman), when they had specialties, varied greatly: portraiture, soft-focus architectural views, industrial subjects, and weddings, to name just a few. Mendes, a visual omnivore, embraced a range of material that hinted at personal interests but never quite announced them. His gaze was not only straight ahead, but up and down, left and right. The diversity of his subjects (whatever the impetus to select them) and his own discerning (and often elegant) eye make these photographs both interesting and compelling.

One of a handful of signed photographs in the archive (64) is of a dog. The setting of this picture clearly relates it to another (37), made more in the vein of news photography, showing Mr. and Mrs. Elwood Lloyd arriving at a Mississippi River landing via canoe in July of 1916. This episode may have been connected to Lloyd's talk, "A Voyage of Friendliness," given for the Louisiana Historical Society at the Cabildo of the Louisiana State Museum on August 3 of that year. Perhaps this picture was submitted for publication and for that reason is signed. But the dog accompanying them (seen in Mrs. Lloyd's care, 36, 37) and solo (64), clearly captivated Mendes; though the plate is signed, it is difficult to imagine mainstream commercial sale of that image.

Regardless of the disposition of the Lloyd series, Mendes seemed to have some predilection for "newsy" events. Other photographs falling into this category are those of General John Pershing's visit to the city (70); an outdoor speech by Louisiana governor John M. Parker (84); the exploits of daredevil Bill Strother (the "Human Spider") ascending the wall of the Hibernia Bank building (24); the land reclamation on the shore of Lake Pontchartrain near Spanish Fort amusement park (22); and the North Broad Street pumping station (91), a structure virtually on Mendes's front doorstep. The demolition of two architectural landmarks, the New Orleans Cotton Exchange (110-114) and the St.

Louis Hotel (46-47), would have been of general public interest. Perhaps even the champion pig (48) could have commanded a column or two under the right circumstances. Whether these photographs were taken for their newsworthiness or not, Mendes did seem to have a fascination with the fourth estate. He avers having over 150 letters to the editor published in his lifetime, and both the release of *Dogs in My Life* and Mendes's death the following year prompted coverage in the New Orleans dailies.

In his memoir, Mendes reveals in words (the book is without illustrations) possible clues or references which might provide background for some of the photographs. We learn that he worked as a packer for the Maison Blanche department store on Canal Street. At least some of the photographs appear to be taken from the roof of this building, completed in 1908, which until 1921 would have been one of New Orleans' tallest (103). He mentions his mother's job as a city Playground Supervisor, and a number of patriotic pageants and other parades featuring children are probably the projects of that municipal agency (26, 27, or 66, 67). It is tempting to conjecture that the interior view (57) is of his North Broad Street residence. The view on page 16 is undoubtedly made from the front porch of that home. Given his extremely tight circle of social contacts, one may speculate on the subjects of certain portraits. That on page 40 could well be a self-portrait, the position of the hands perhaps holding and hiding the cable release to the camera's shutter. The chair does resemble a home-made version of a Morris chair that Mendes mentions in passing. Might the portrait of the woman on page 41 be his sister, Regina? And given its identifiable setting of the house next door to Mendes's, the portrait on 107 may well be his neighbor Elvia (Mrs. John W.) Schroeder. Would the answers to these questions make the pictures less or more satisfying?

That in his writing Mendes is practically silent concerning his interest in photography may be puzzling, but it doesn't detract from the interest that the pictures hold for today's viewer. The day-to-day activities of New Orleanians from nearly a century ago hold attention because they present familiar things (e.g., Mardi Gras, children at play, street life) in ways that no longer seem familiar. Traditions endure, but surroundings change, and the ensemble of city life changes, too. People as well are different, and those differences may be measured either individually or socially by the yardstick of Mendes's pictures.

American photographer Garry Winogrand (1928-84) was correct in stating that "there is nothing as mysterious as a fact clearly described." Despite what we make of them today, an underlying premise of factual recording is the foundation of Mendes's pictures. The cryptic nature of their creator adds to the mystery partly because as viewers we wish to know not only "what" and "where" but "why." The photographs are his method of inquiry, the examination of a personal universe measured not in light years, parsecs, and the timelessness of space, but in city blocks and a handful of years.

John H. Lawrence
The Historic New Orleans Collection

Dogs in My Life

No human being on this Earth, once trained, could have been cleaner than Our dogs. With death only a short time away I have known they wanted me to carry them to the yard, and I did so.

All of the dogs I write about were true, loyal, and fine companions for my Mother and I. They were all affectionate, and required, and got a lot of love. The "Dogs In My Life" helped me to keep away from bad associations, and lead a clean life. At 76 years of age I have never got into any kind of trouble outside of my own home. Although my life was a hard one, working out for low wages, I being a poor person always, my beloved Mother, and Our dogs helped me to know supreme happiness. — To them I owe a debt of gratitude. I want the Reader of this book to understand fully that a short Chapter about a dog does not imply less love for that particular dog but a set of circumstances was the direct cause.

I also want the Reader to know this: I would not for any amount of money offered to me, sold or given away any dog I ever owned, and I am sure my Mother shared my own feelings absolutely.

As to whether I should have revealed things about my, and my Mother's dogs in this book I am sure, if such a thing were possible, all of Our dogs would give their consent freely.

I sincerely hope this book will do some good for dogs, and cats, and the Animal Creation.

- *Dogs in My Life*, Preface

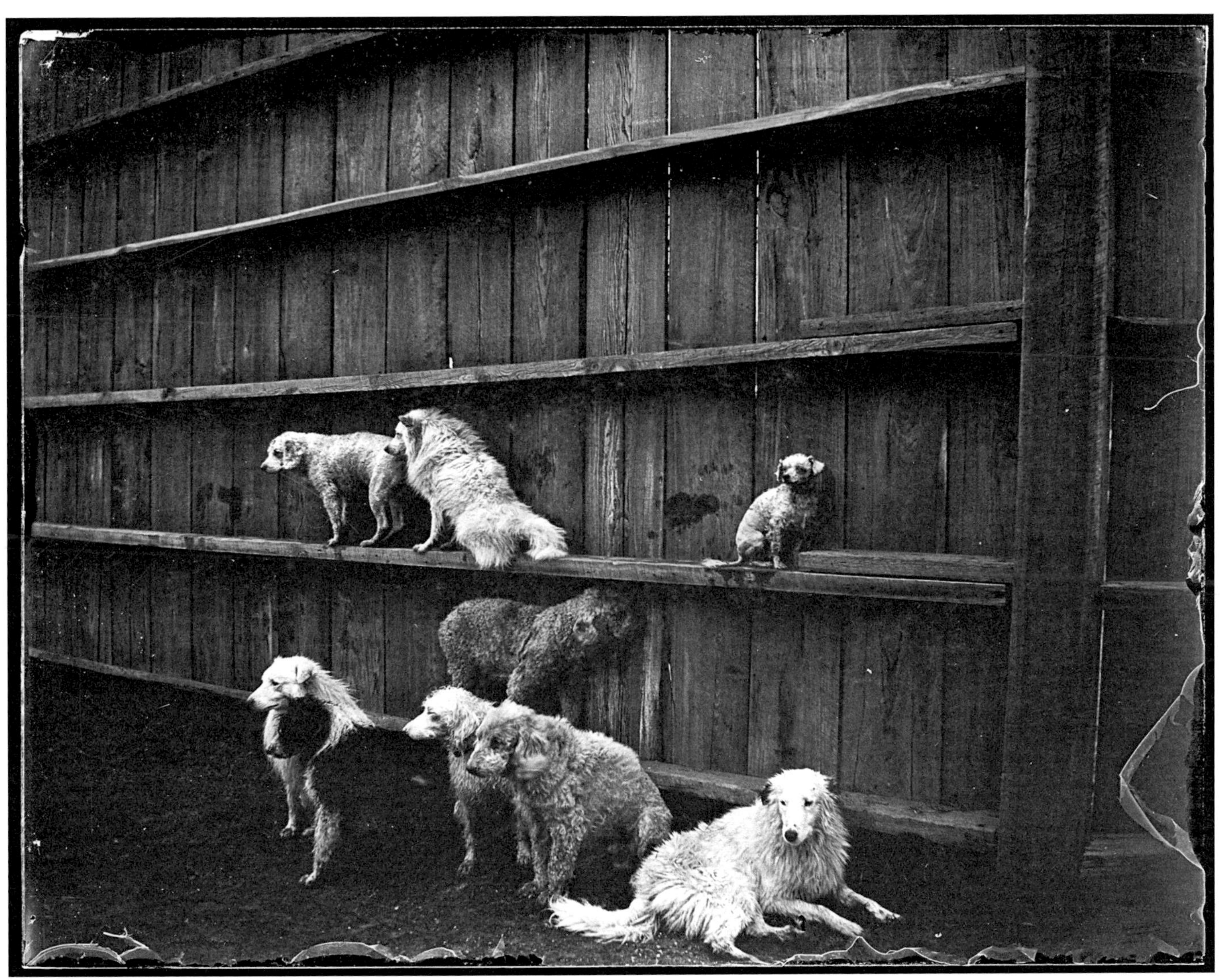

Gentry Bros. Shows. Nine dogs, one that was struck by clenched fist of man attendant Second row center. (The dog was hit in the face)

2003.182.189
April 21, 1919

I never finished what was known then as the "Third Reader." I secured my first job in the early 1900's when I was about 13 years old. The place was a small Dry Goods Ladies Ready-to-wear articles shop, on the 1200 block of Canal street.

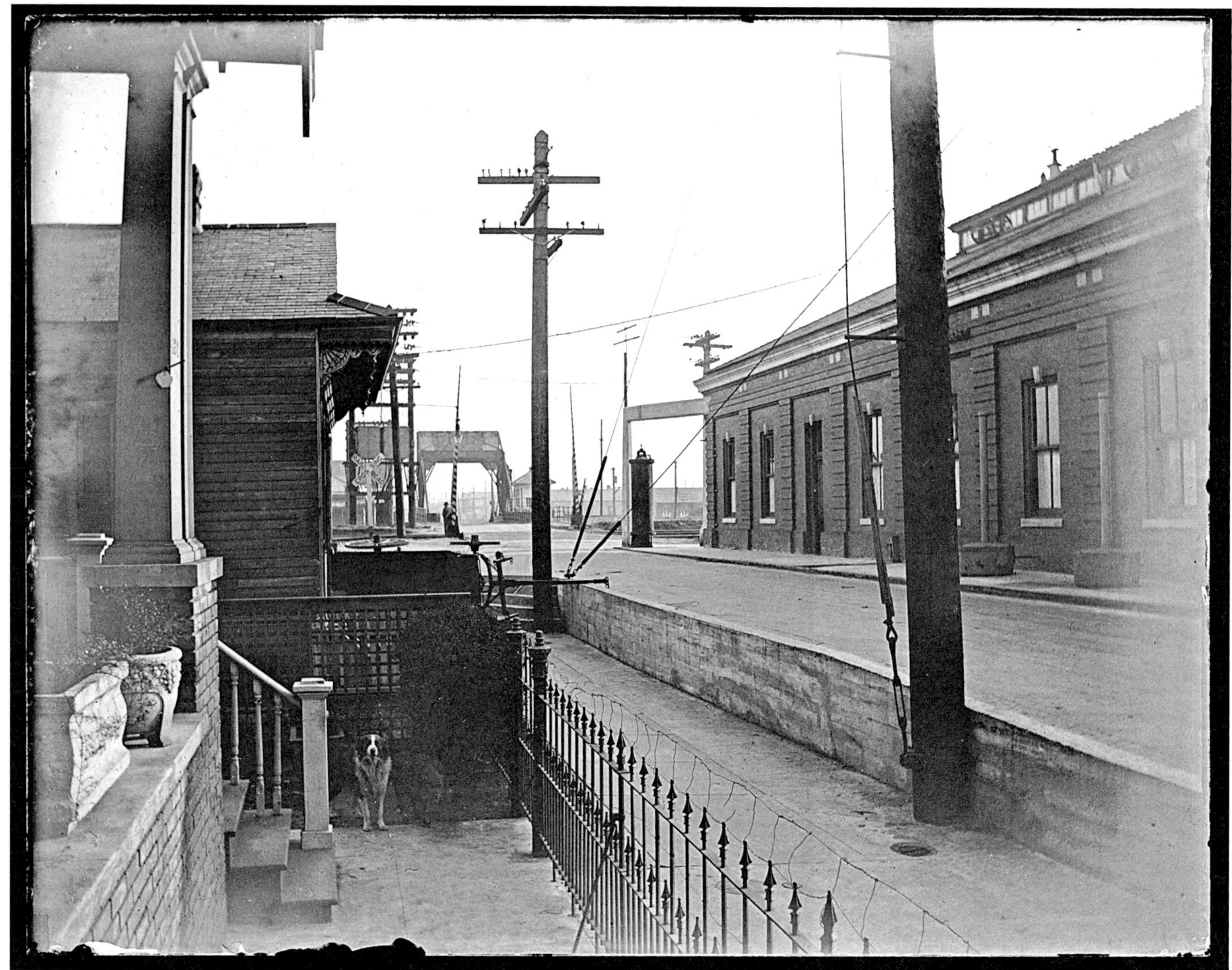

Taken from front steps to show overturned wagon

2003.182.248
March 1920

Taken from Pickwick Club

2003.182.6
March 7, 1916

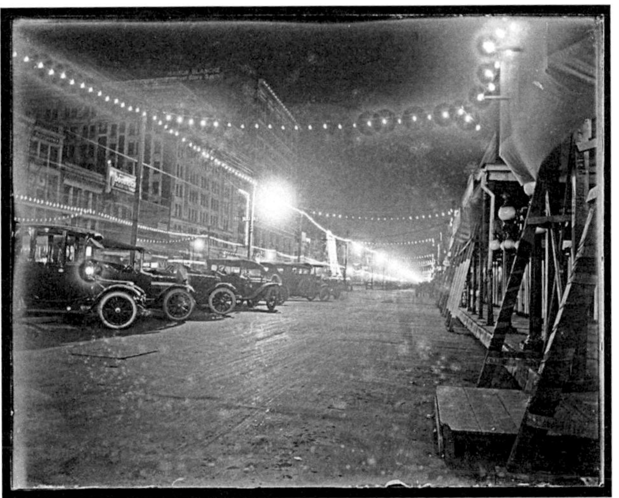

My hours of labor were from 8 A.M. to 6 P.M. every day except Sunday, and the wages was $1.50 per week. I helped about the store, and when my "boss" did some house-to-house peddling carried two full suit cases. While the salary looks pitiably small as compared to that earned today, let me show what could be done with 25 cents. For a family of three, like us, and a dog, and a cat, we could eat a good dinner for that small sum of money, like this:

> — Half of a nickle of red beans, and rice (.05); one pound loaf of good bread (.05); slice of pickled pork (.05); a pat of real butter (.05); quart bottle of Jumbo (soft drink) (.05); an onion, salt and a piece of natural ice to cool the Jumbo, lagniappe (free); the wood to cook the beans and rice on an iron stove (free) — picked up in the street.
>
> \- *Dogs in My Life*, 2

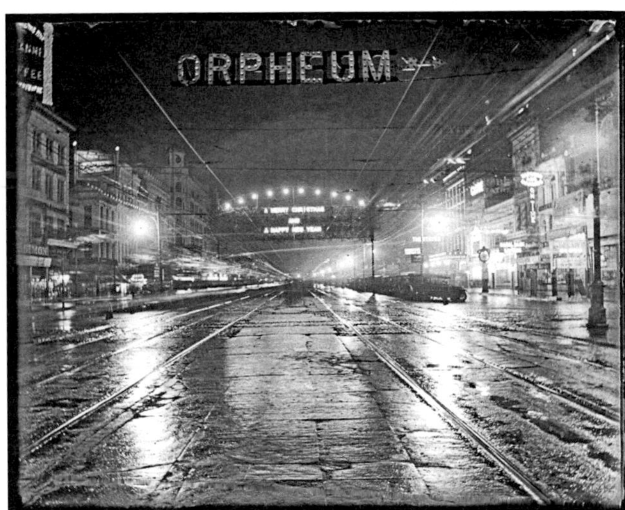

Canal St. looking towards the Merry Christmas sign. [Exposure] About 20 minutes

2003.182.71
December 1916

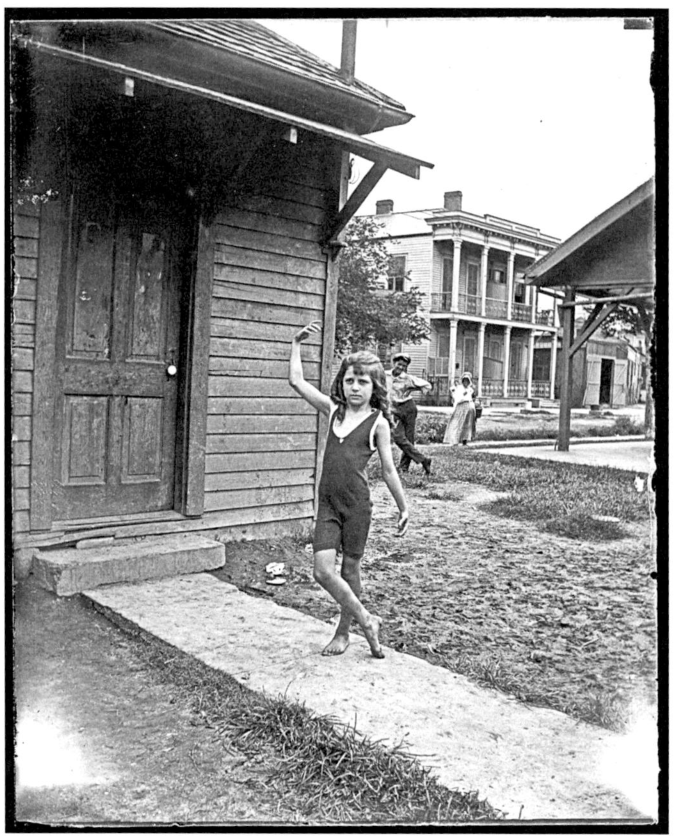

Little girl in bathing suit

2003.182.314
June 1923

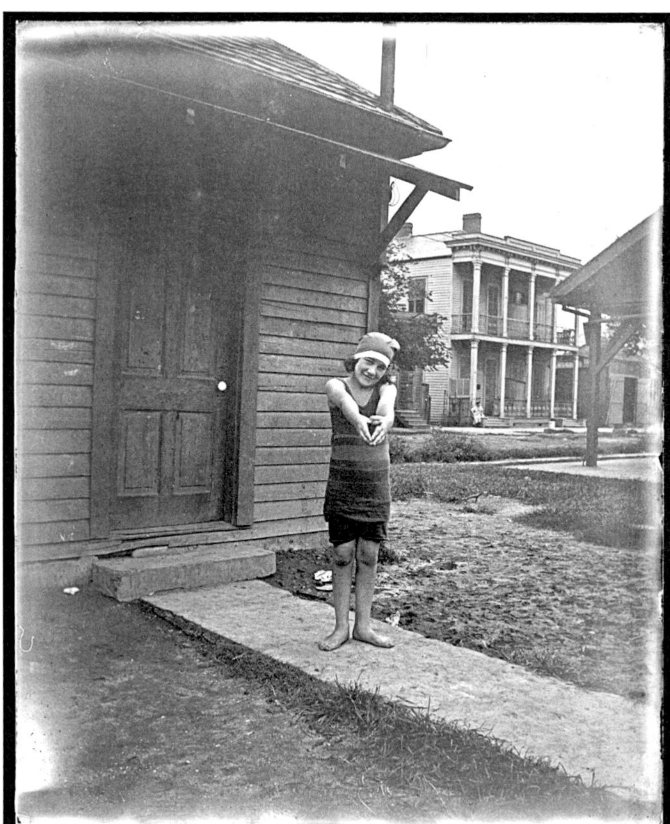

[Uncaptioned]

2003.182.316
June 1923

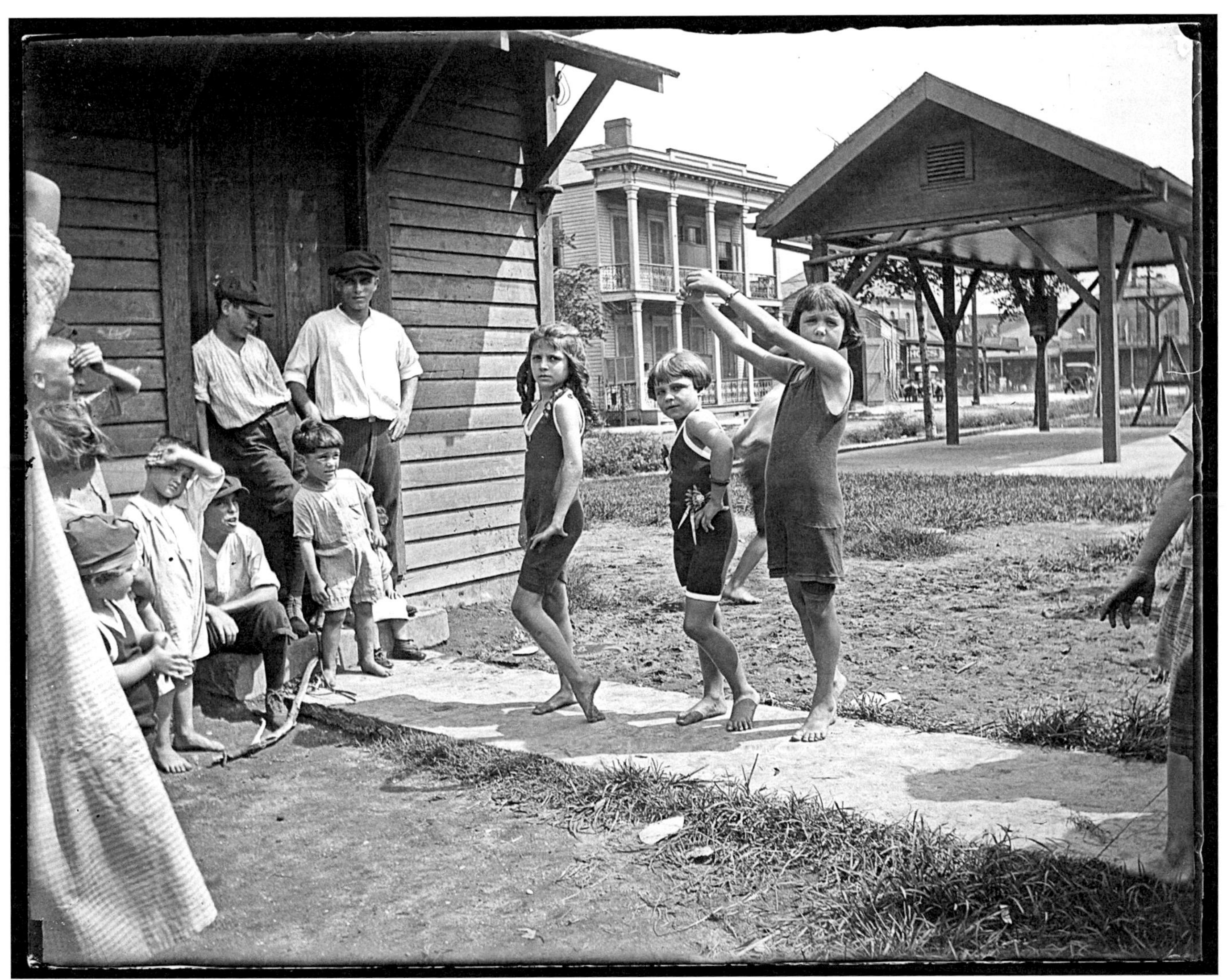

[Uncaptioned]

2003.182.470
[June 1923]

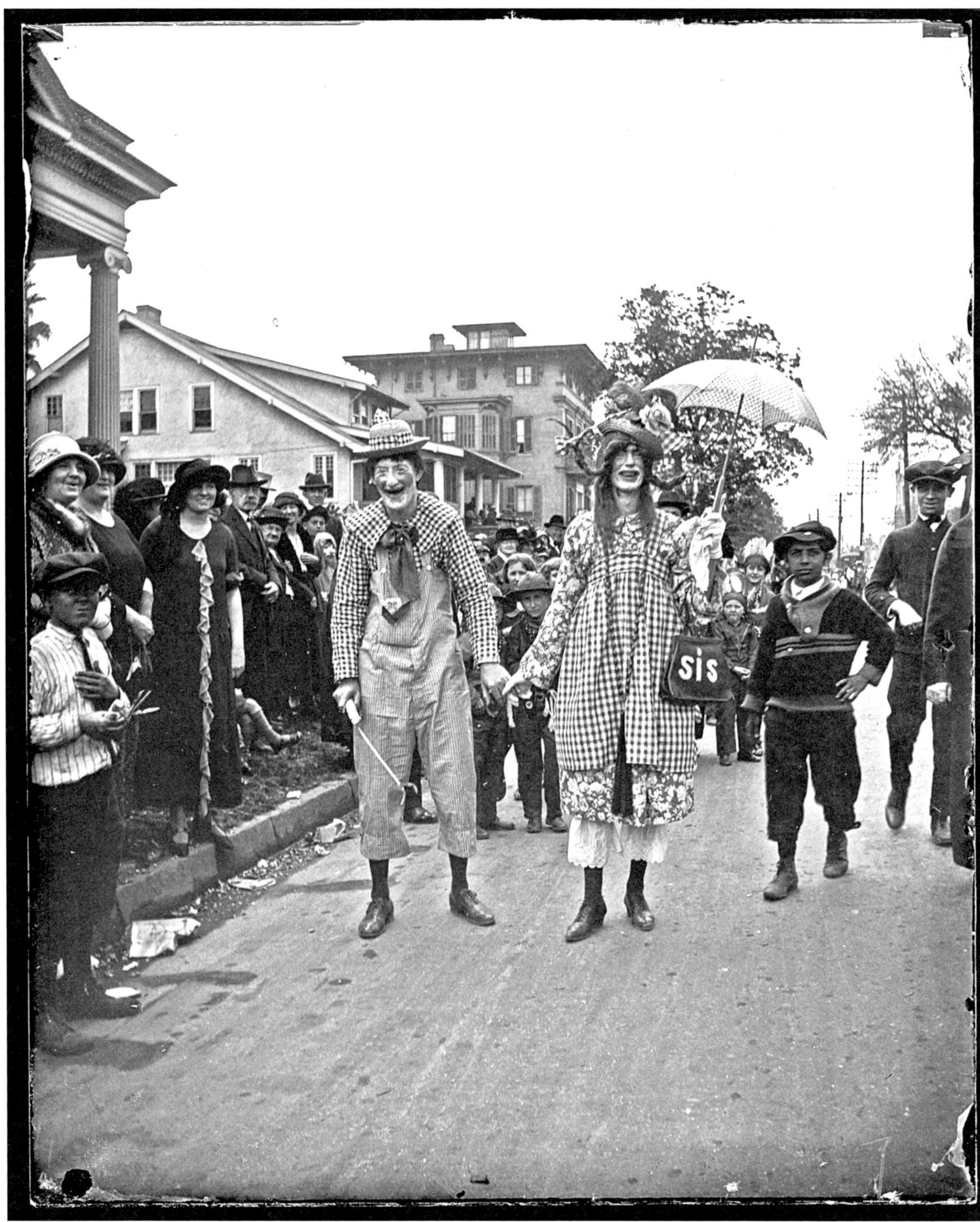

Two County Maskers
W.H. Holmes
1129 8th Street

2003.182.327
March 4, 1924

Archbishop Shaw
Blessing Front of New
Sacred Heart Church

2003.182.324
March 2, 1924

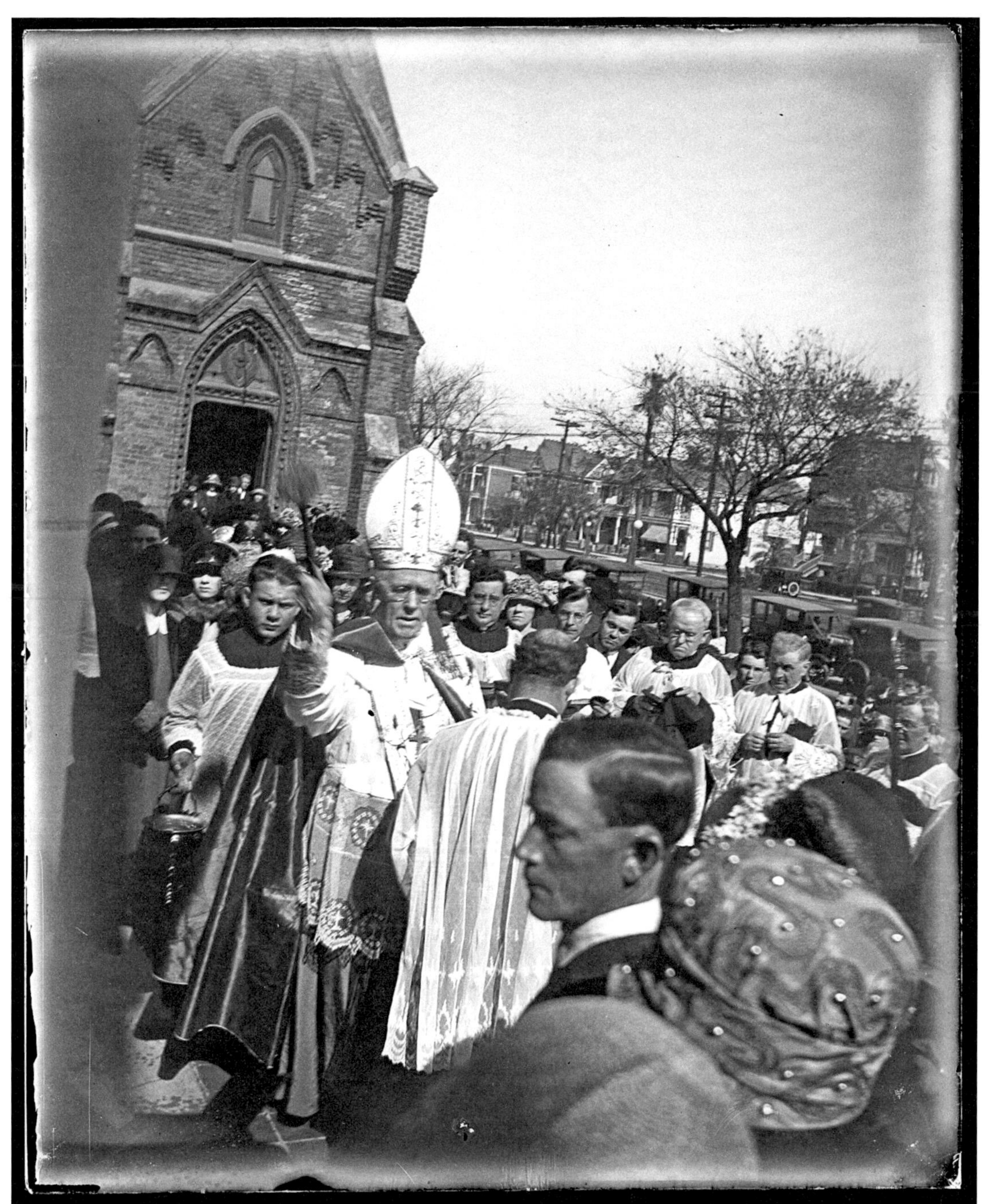

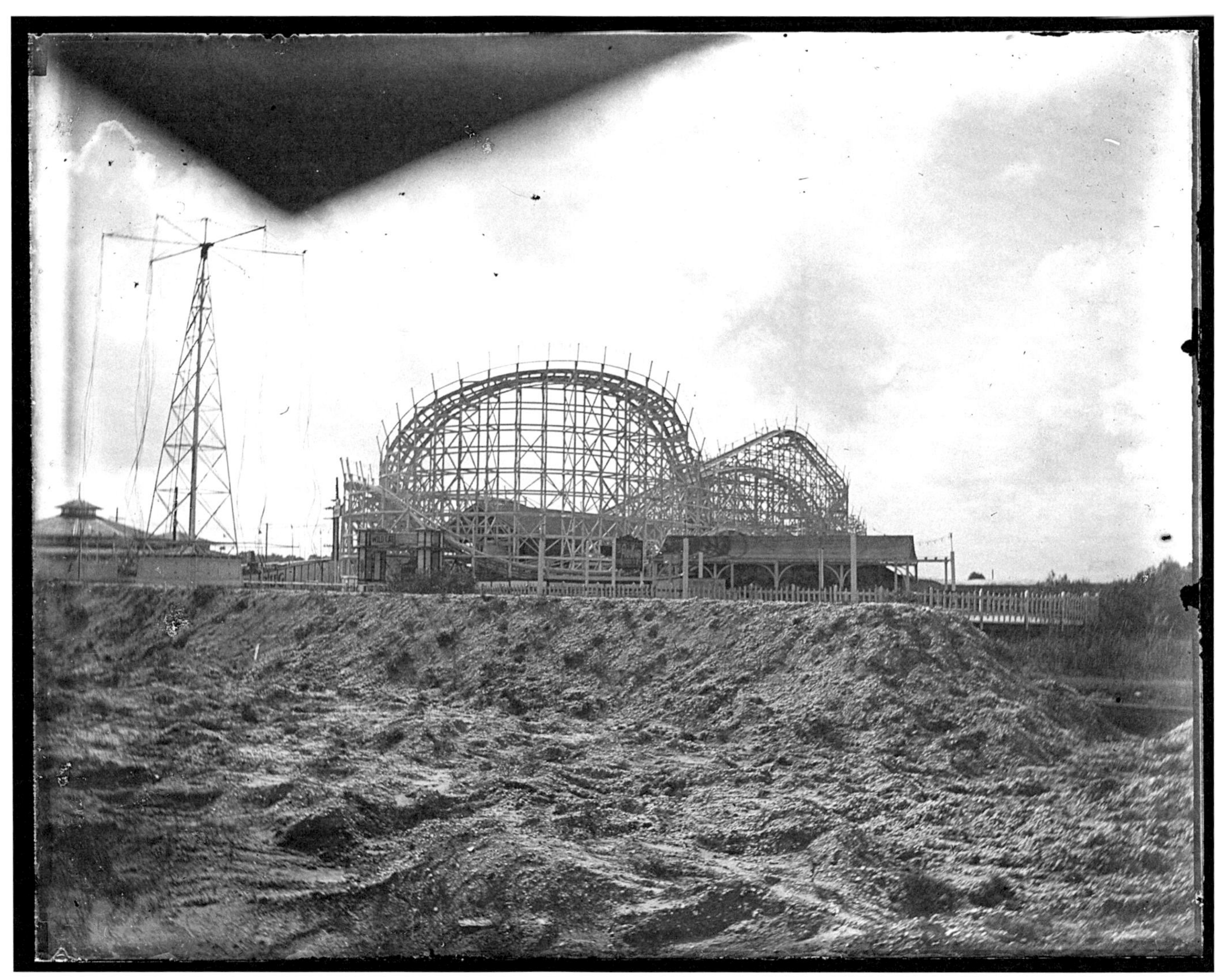

[Uncaptioned. Spanish Fort Amusement Park.]

2003.182.421
[ca. 1926]

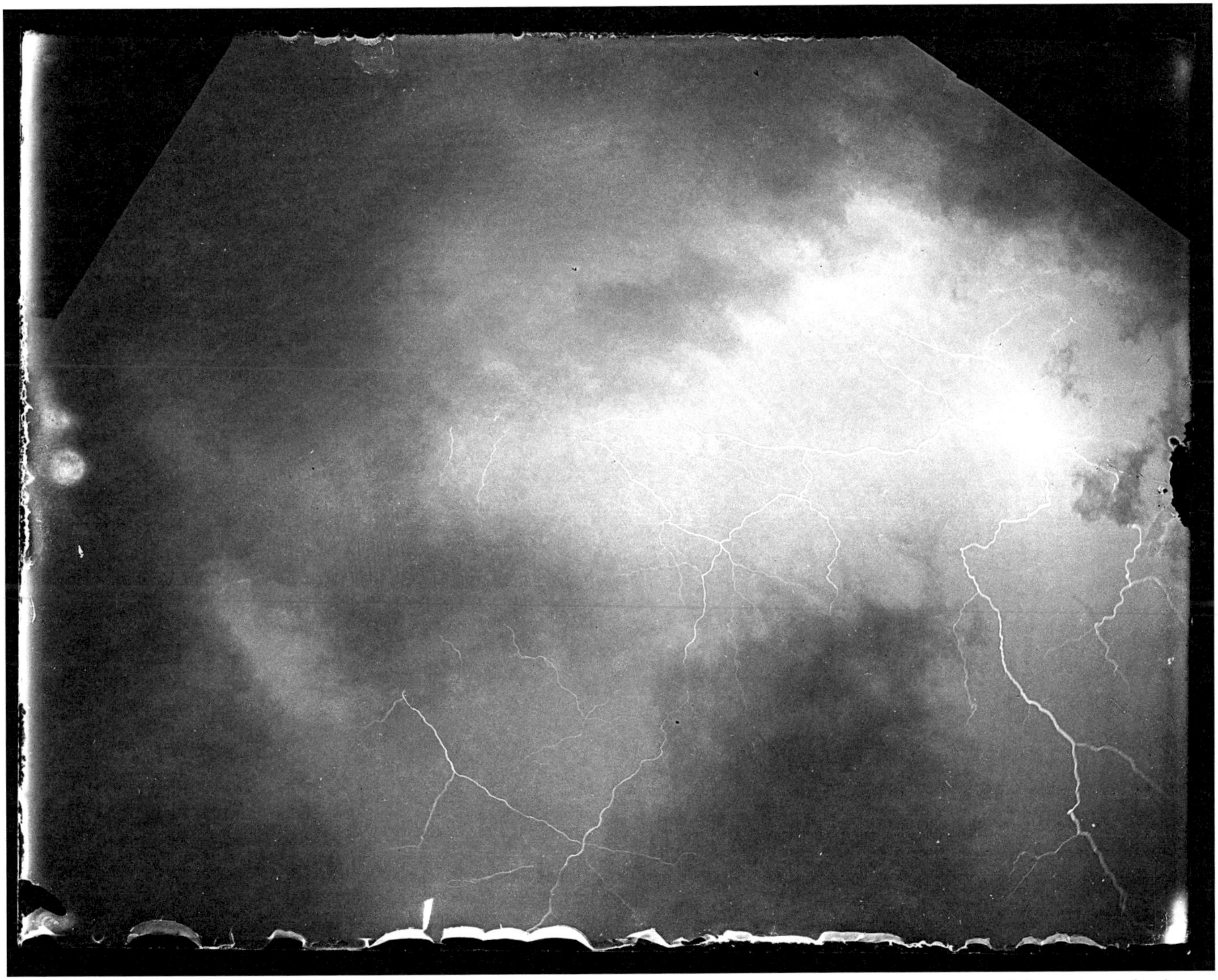

Lightening Flash

2003.182.31
June 24, 1916

Bill Strothers walks to a window on the 7th floor of the Hibernia Bank

2003.182.195
April 22, 1919

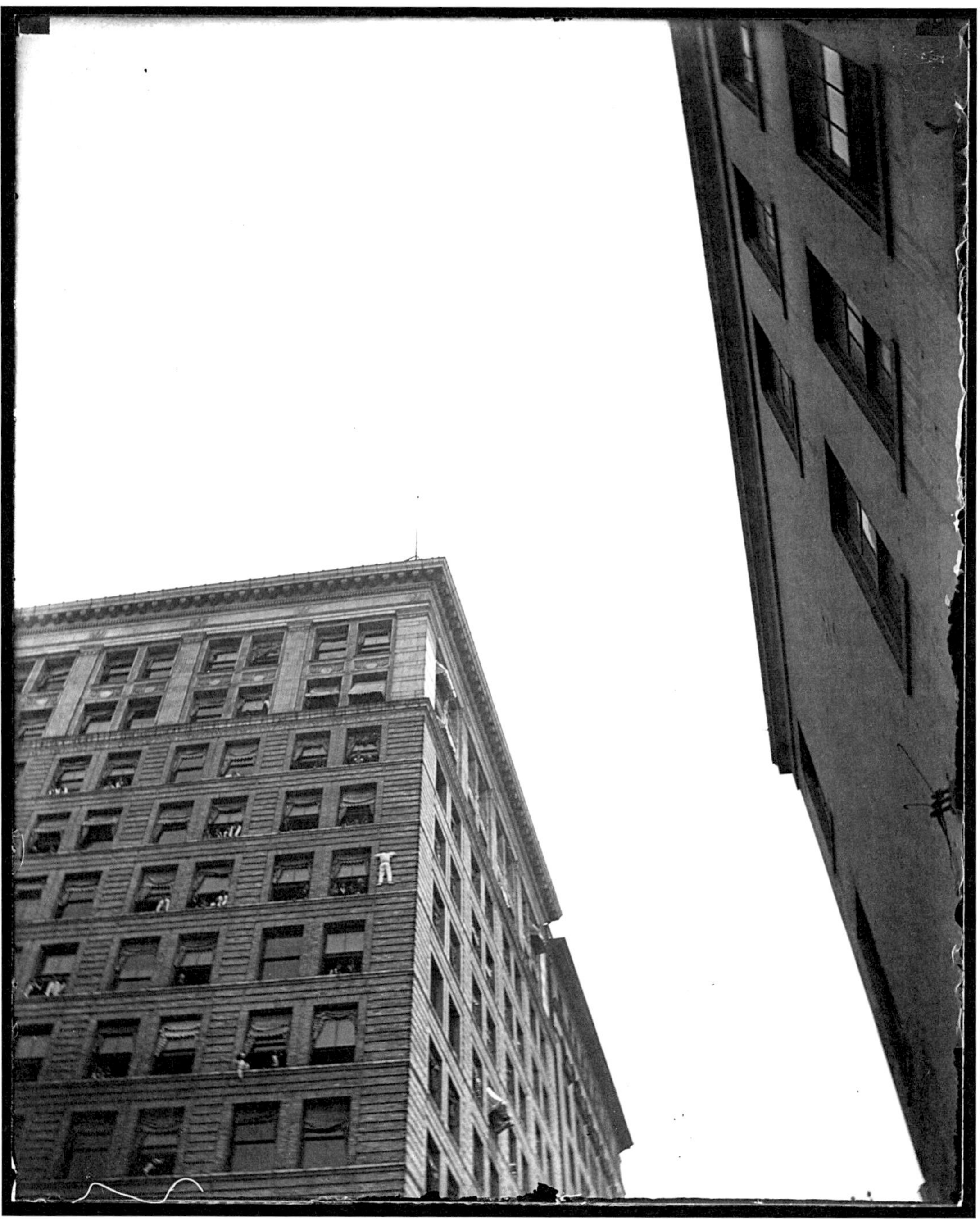

This Veterinarian who had been “treating” my dog suggested that if I would allow him to give Elsie “an injection” it would “quiet her,” and she would “surely wake up feeling better.” After hesitating a while, having to make the decision myself, since she was MY dog, I consented.

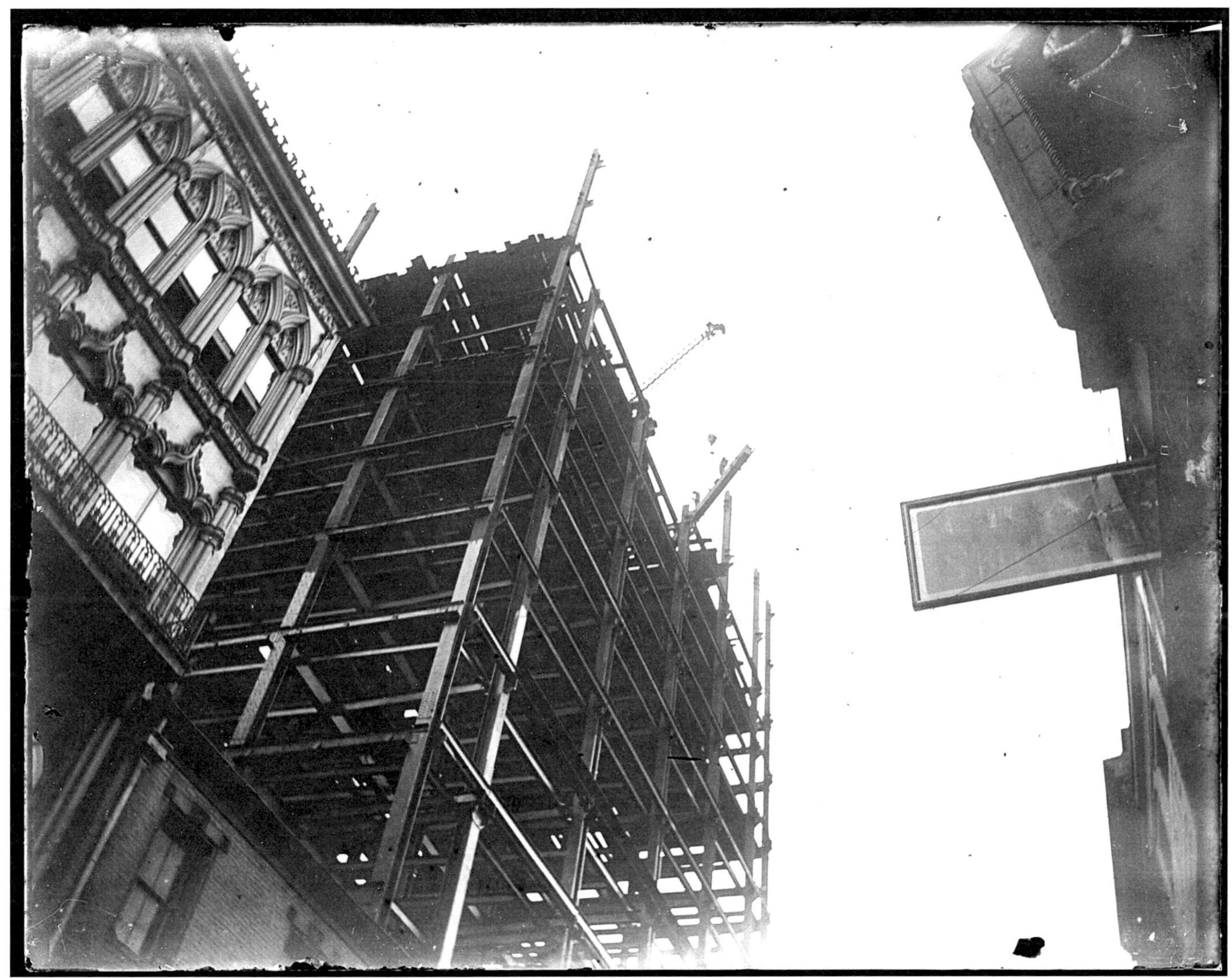

Structural steel workers riding up on beam

2003.182.306
1920

(I am positive my dear Mother never suspected what that Veterinarian was going to do). Sitting beside my beloved Elsie, entirely ignorant of that "Vet's" real intent, she died, having lived only six short years. (Note: Not even in her life time my Mother never did know (and I've told only one person after her death) how near I came to bodily injuring that Veterinarian.

- *Dogs in My Life*, 14

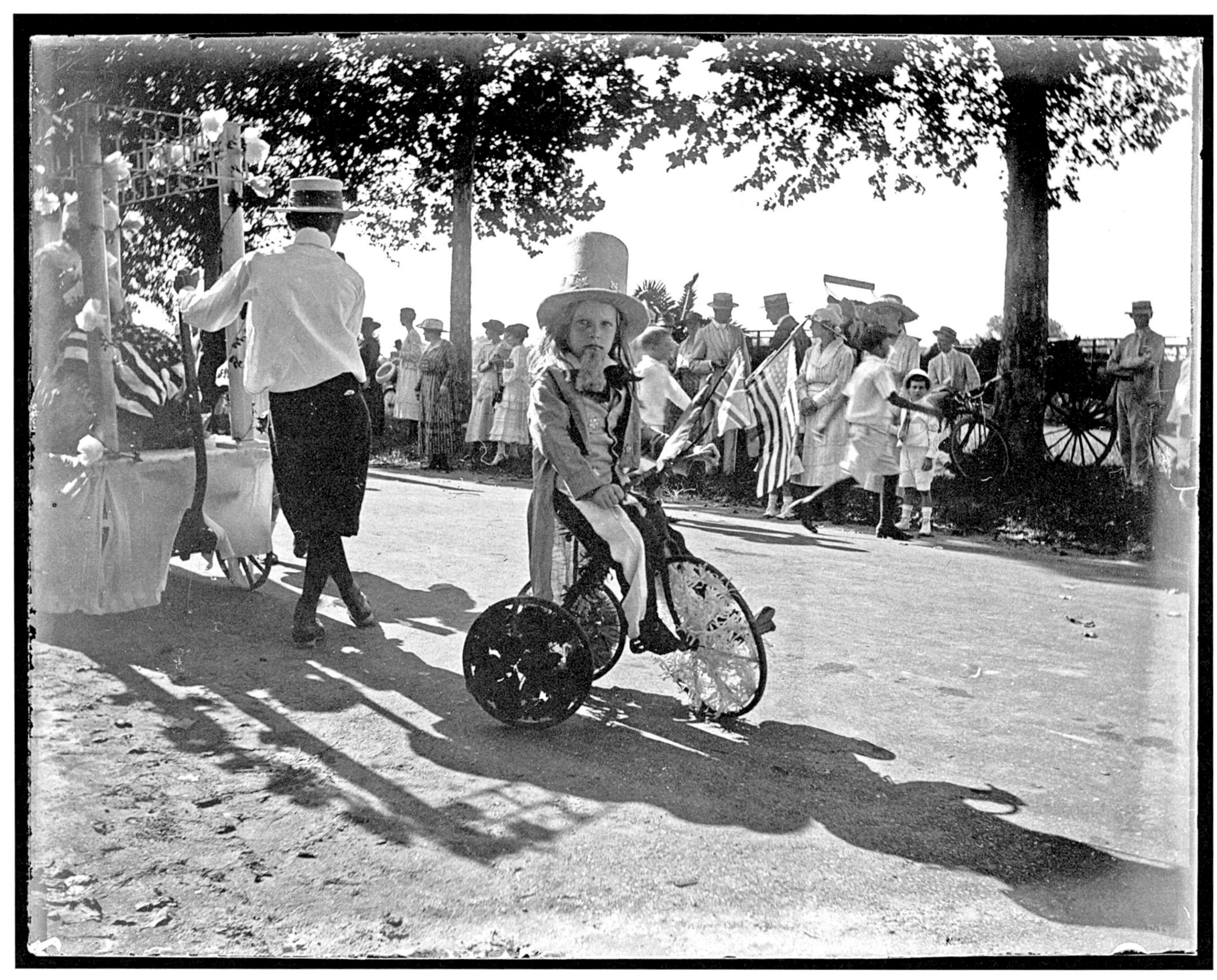

[Uncaptioned. Children's parade float.]

2003.182.385
[ca. 1916]

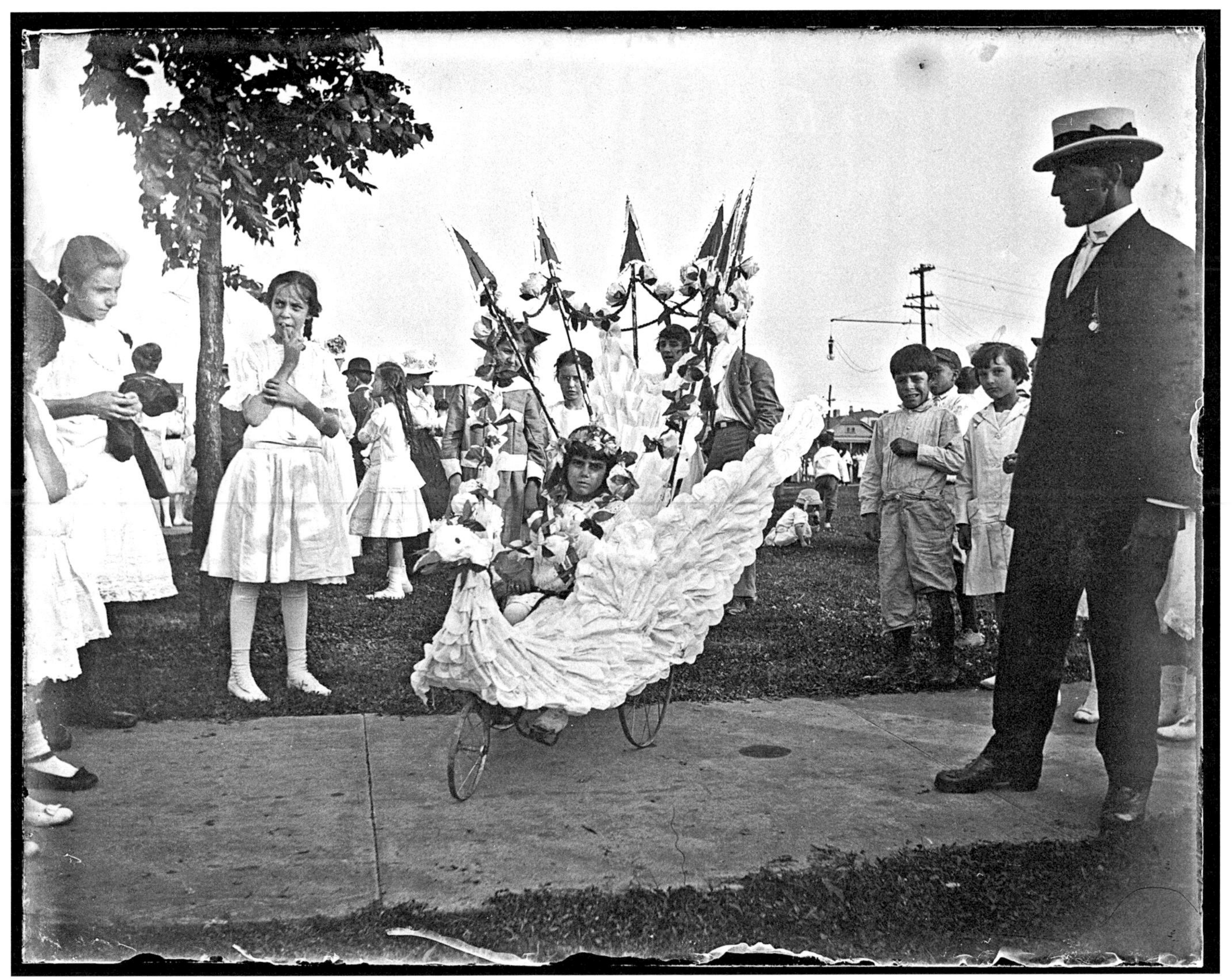

White bird tricycle. Taylor

2003.182.99
May 13, 1917

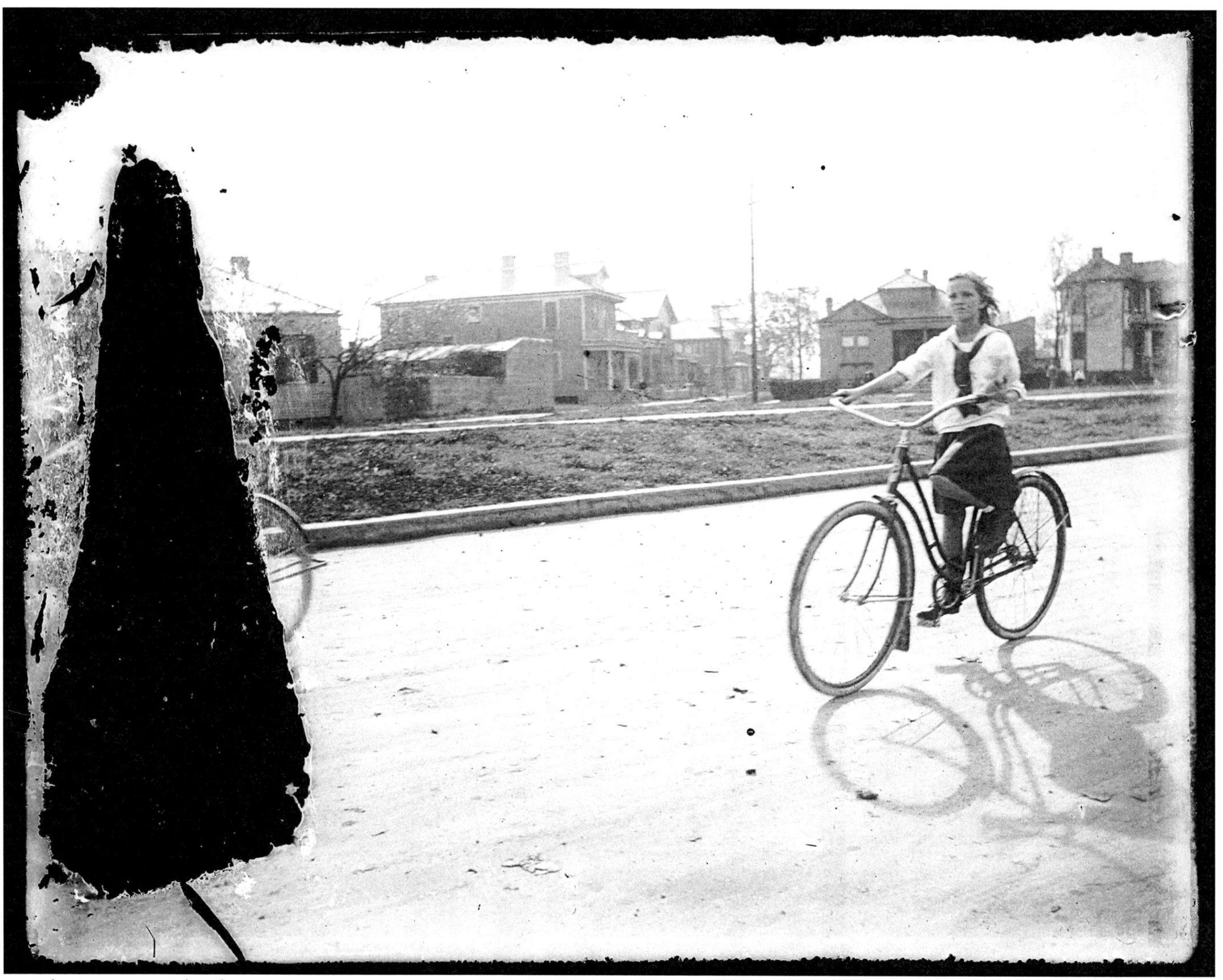

2nd Picture with Plate Camera
Girl on Bicycle

2003.182.404
[ca. 1916]

When Our last dog died my Mother, and I agreed, for several good reasons, not to take into Our home another dog. She was in her sixties, and I had passed my fortieth birthday. We lived alone, and did not have any close relatives, or distant, for that matter, who ever came to see us, or we had ever spoken to in many years. [...] In time of need we did not have any close personal friends to call on for aid. [...] And so we planned not to take on any extra responsibilities. So much for Our well laid plans.

- *Dogs in My Life*, 27

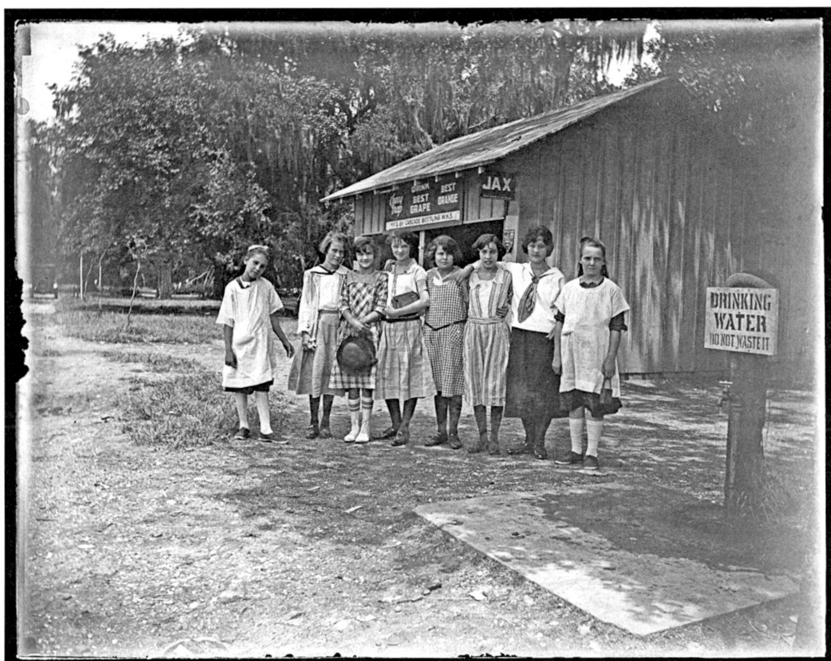

Groupe Cleveland Playground girls. City Park Picnic.

2003.182.310
June 23, 1923

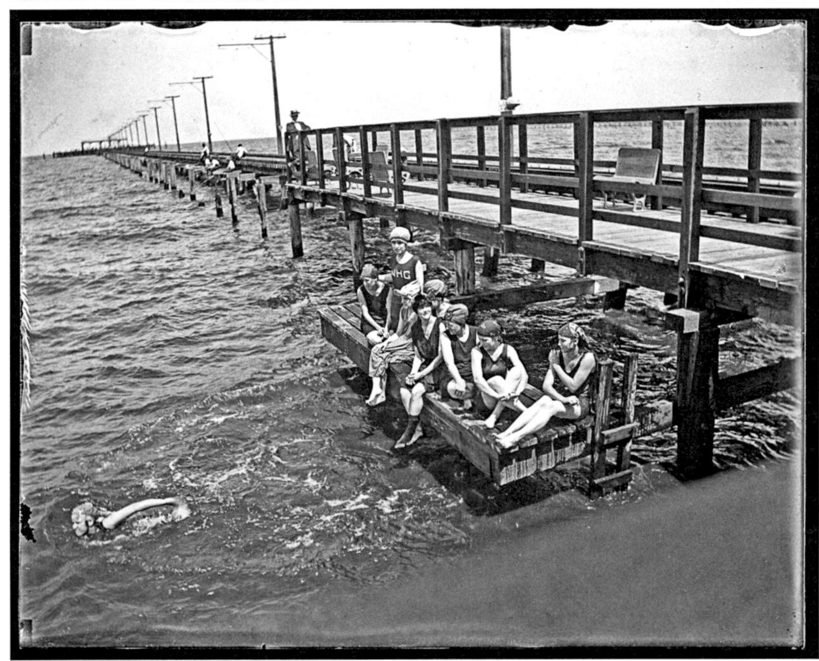

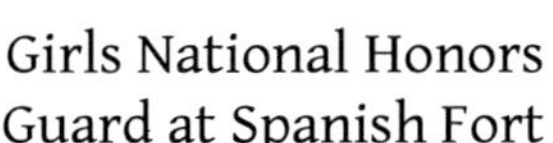

Girls National Honors Guard at Spanish Fort

2003.182.47
September 15, 1916

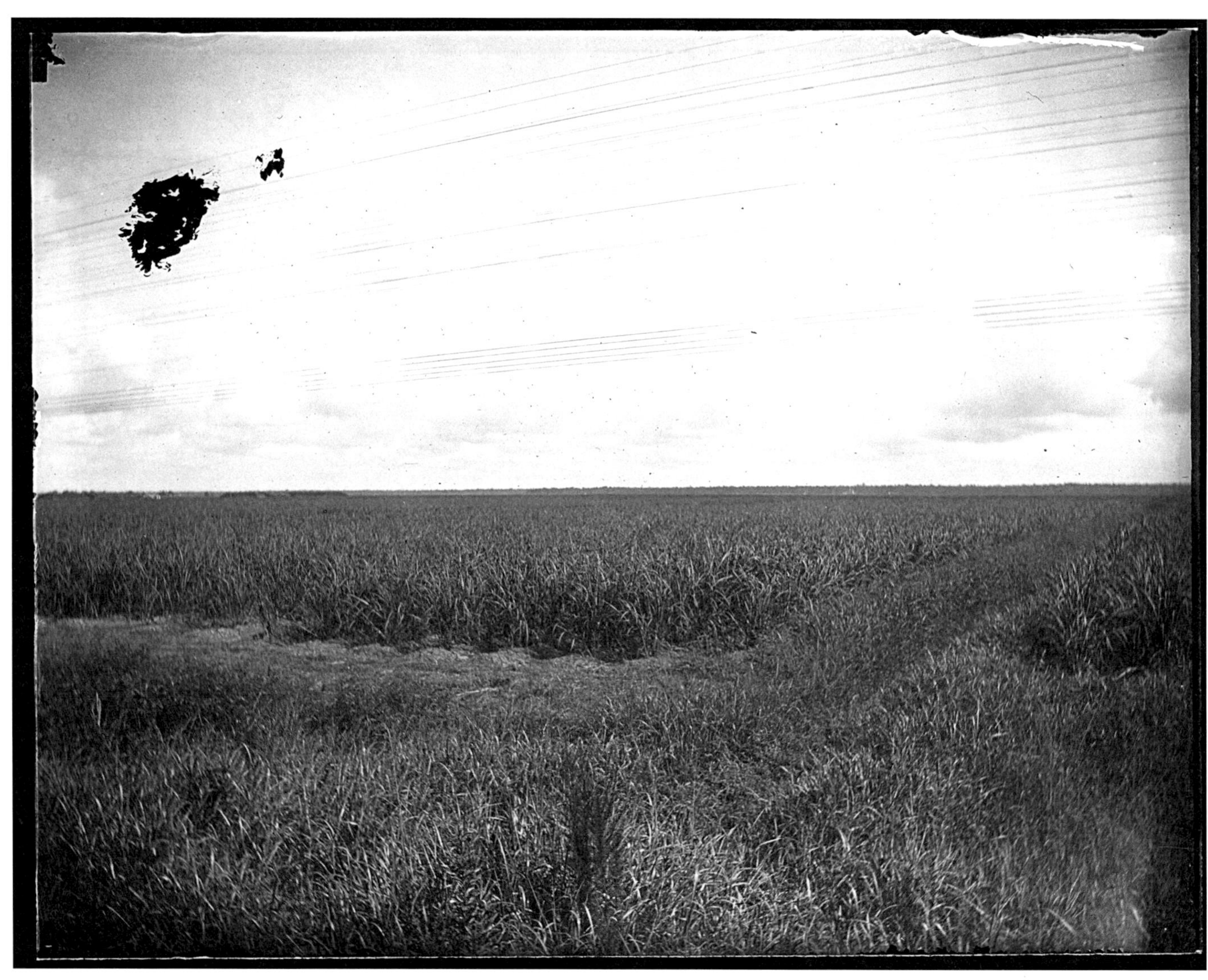

[Uncaptioned. Sugar cane field.]

2003.182.465
[ca. 1925]

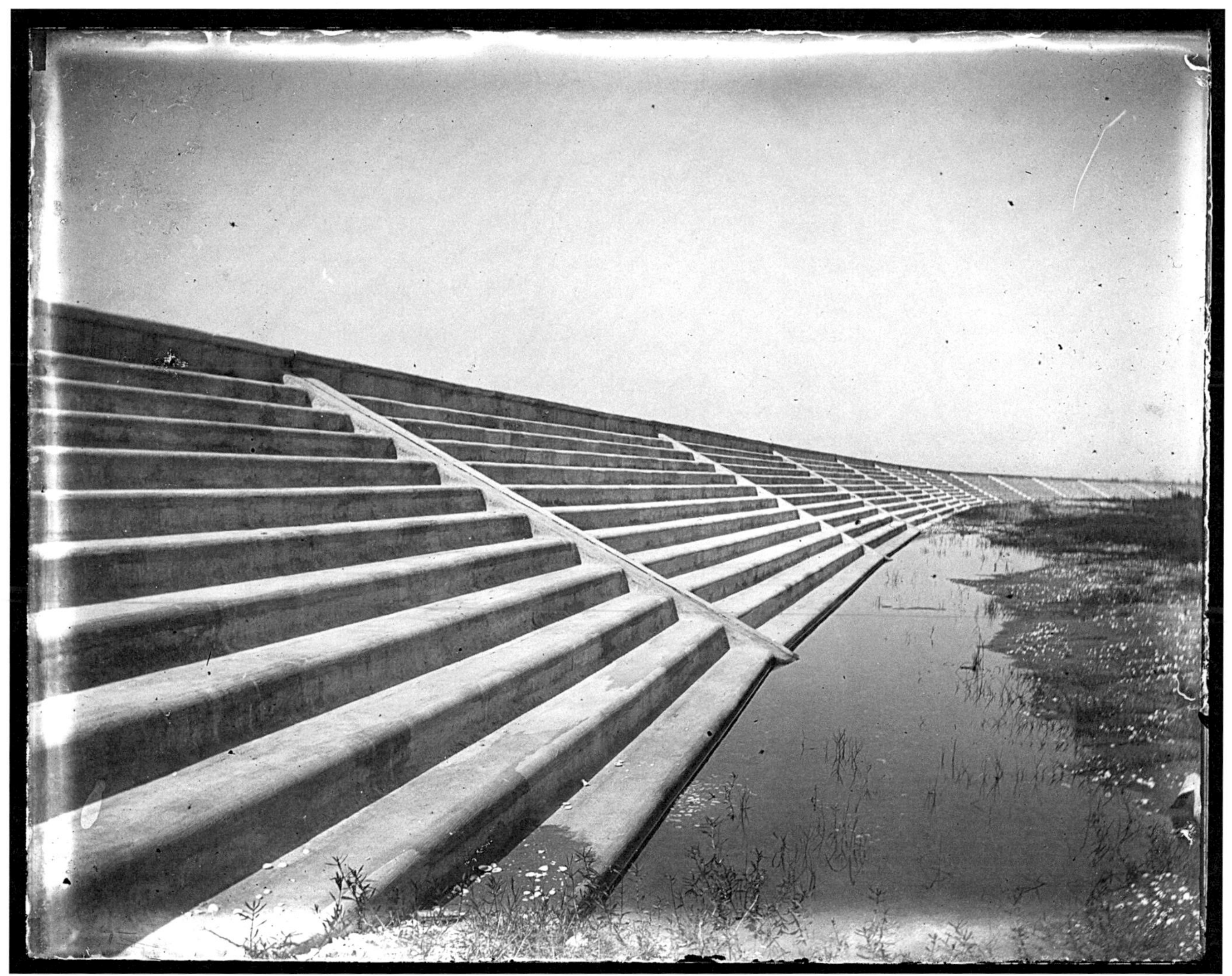

[Uncaptioned. Newly constructed Lake Pontchartrain seawall.]

2003.182.384
[ca. 1930]

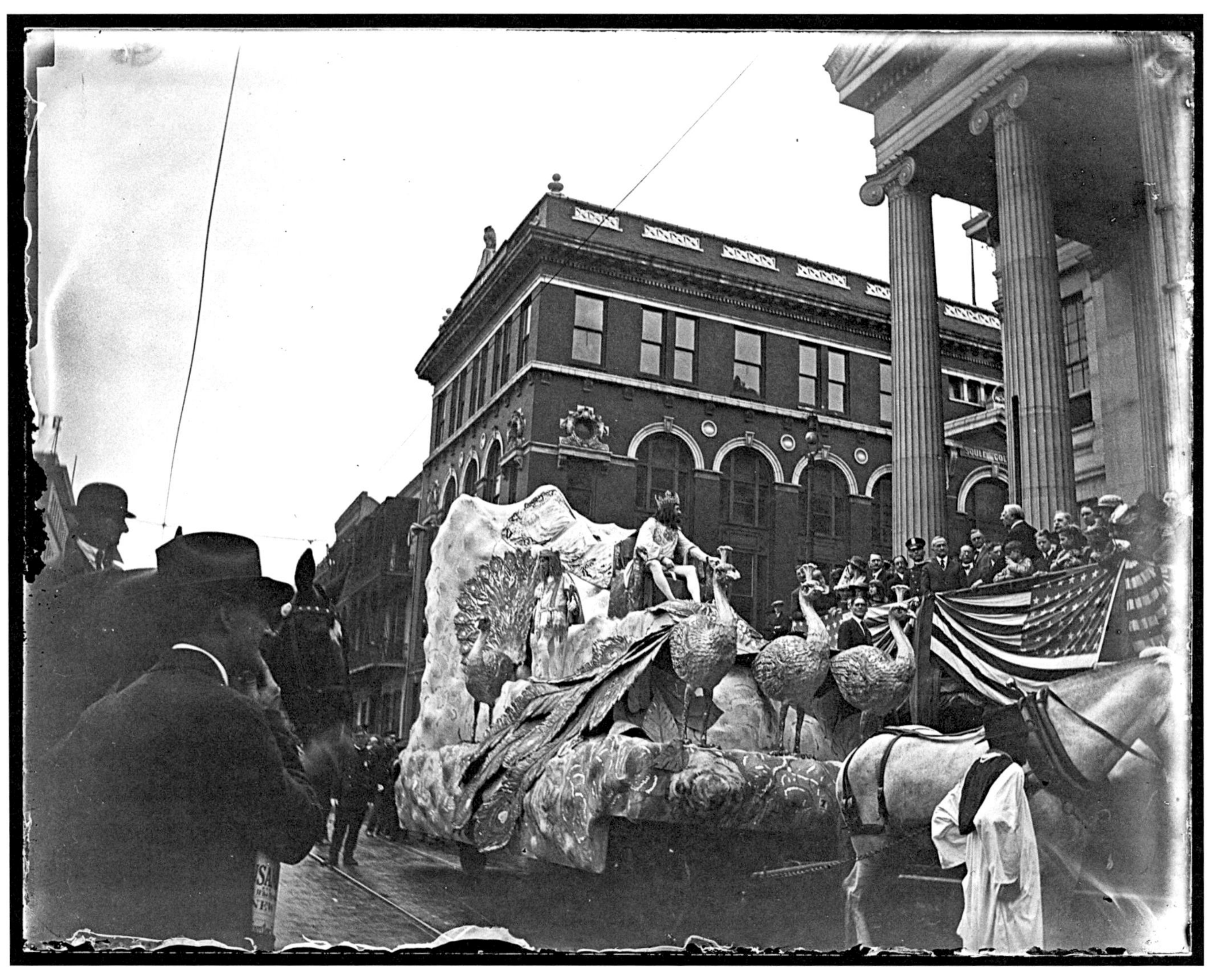

[Uncaptioned. King's float at Gallier Hall.]

2003.182.433
[ca. 1920]

[Uncaptioned. Rex Parade, “Cleopatra’s Barge,” Mardi Gras Day.]

2003.182.416
February 21, 1928

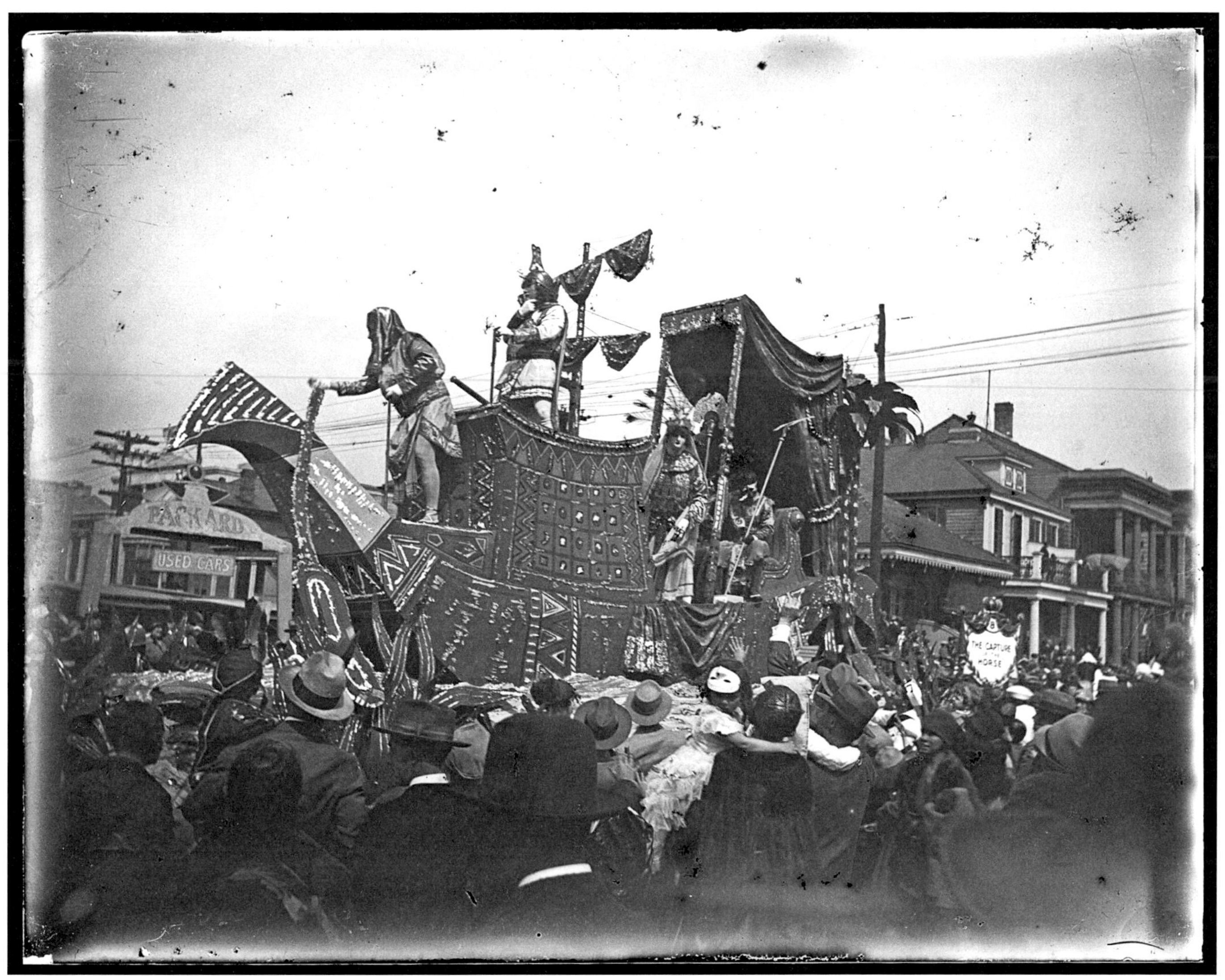

Raining,
August 8,
1:15 pm

2003.182.41
August 8, 1916

The eating habits of Jerry did not always follow the general pattern of Our other dogs. Like all Our other dogs we fed Jerry what we eat ourselves, with extra meat for him. [...] Of candy he liked we gave him small amounts — but he got some always. In the morning, when in good health, Jerry liked to eat coffee, and bread. We would fix a cup of coffee, with sugar, and condensed milk (some times Mother would use a little of her cows milk), and with toasted, and buttered bread we would dip the bread into the coffee, and feed Jerry piece by piece.

- *Dogs in My Life*, 32

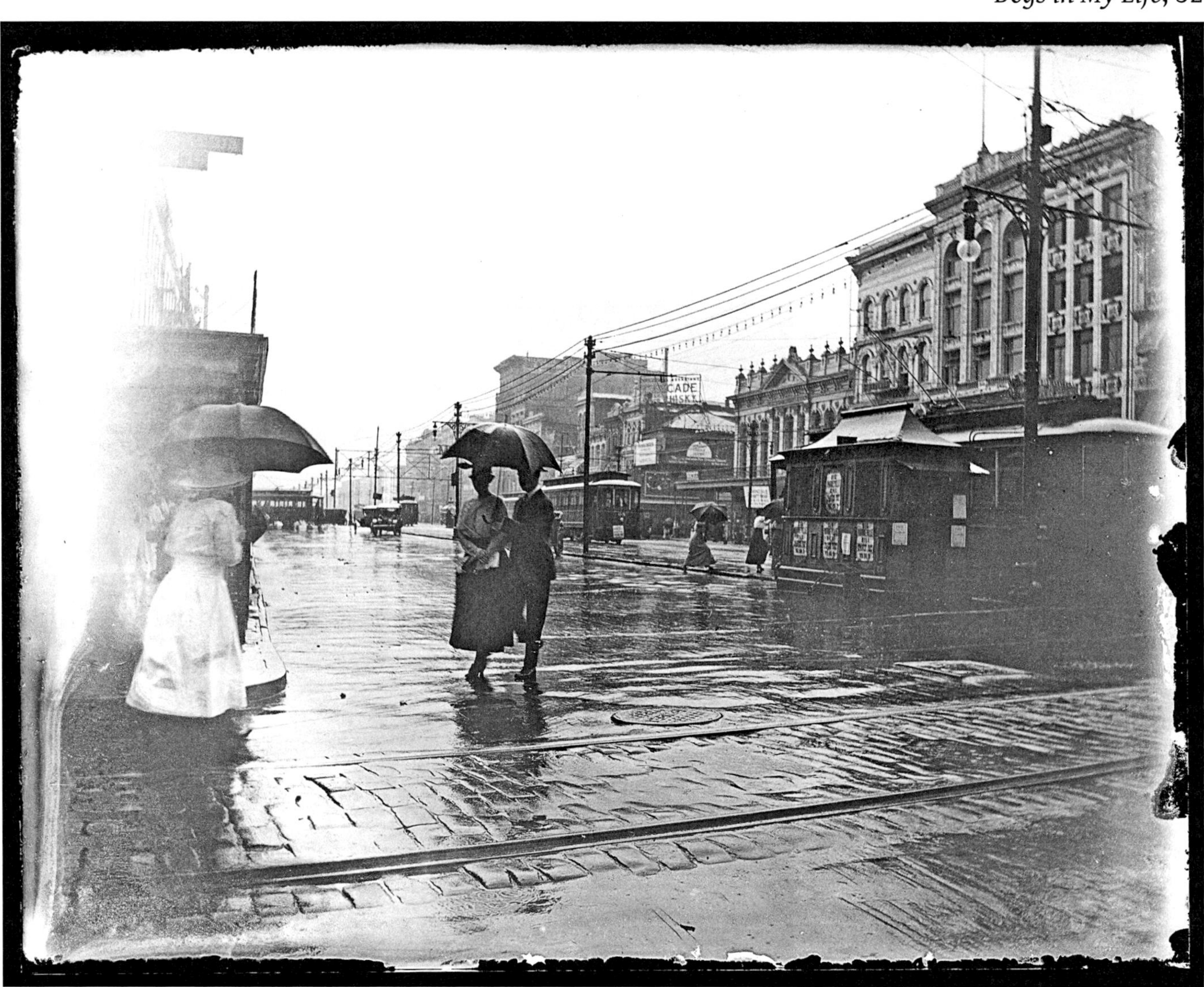

More Ring Signs

2003.182.295
1920

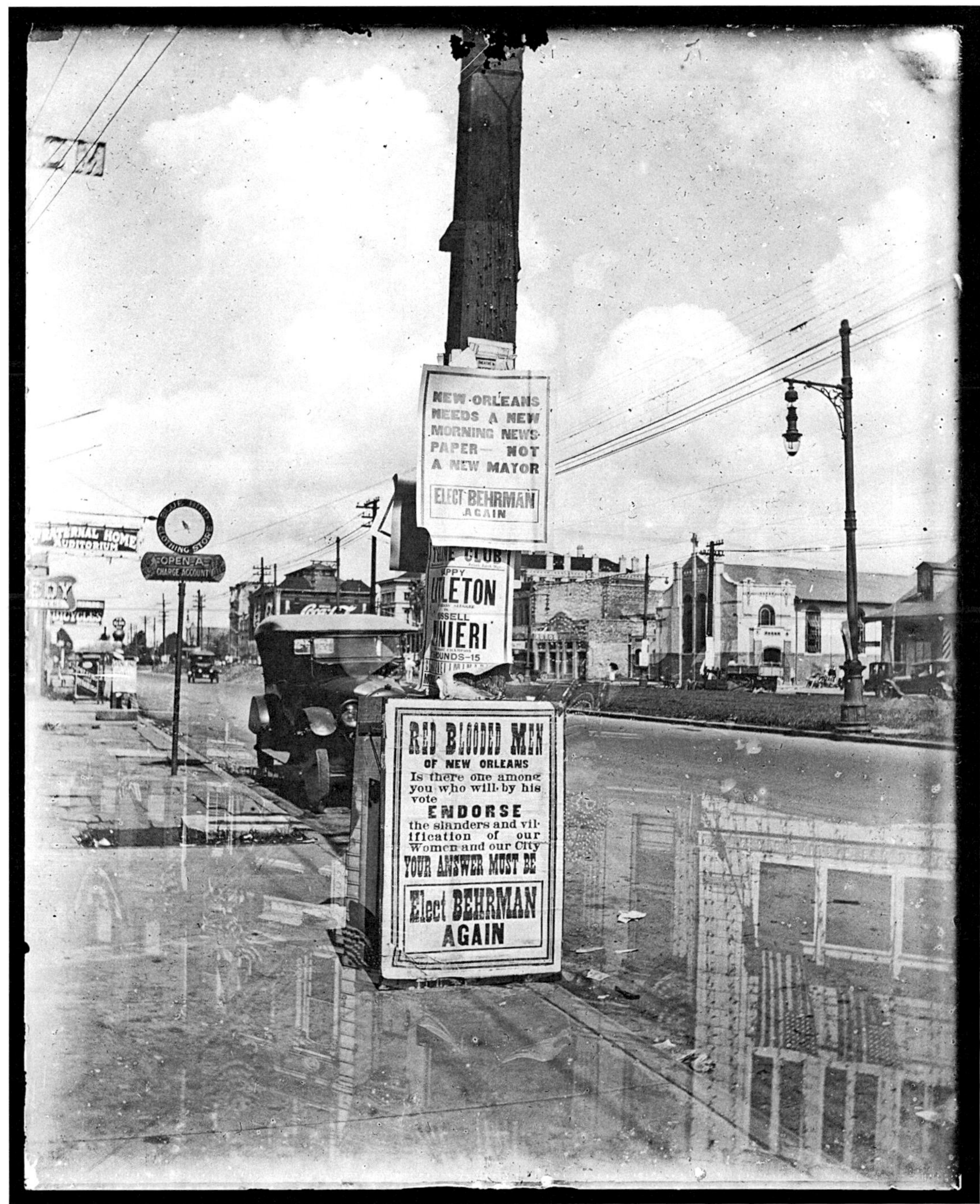

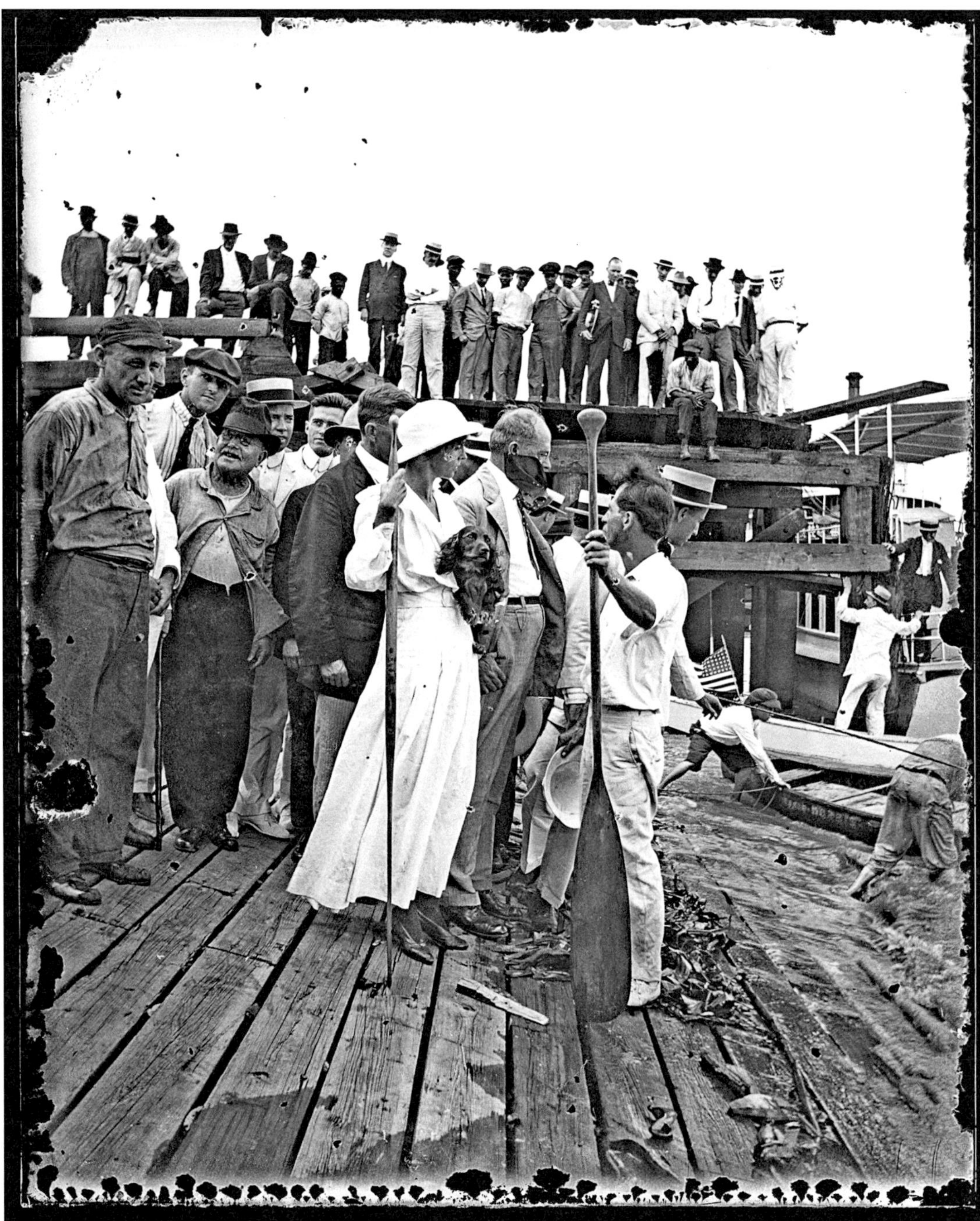

Elwood Lloyd and wife after landing (dog seen)

2003.182.148
July 28, 1916

Mr. and Mrs. Lloyd in Canoe

2003.182.42
July 28, 1916

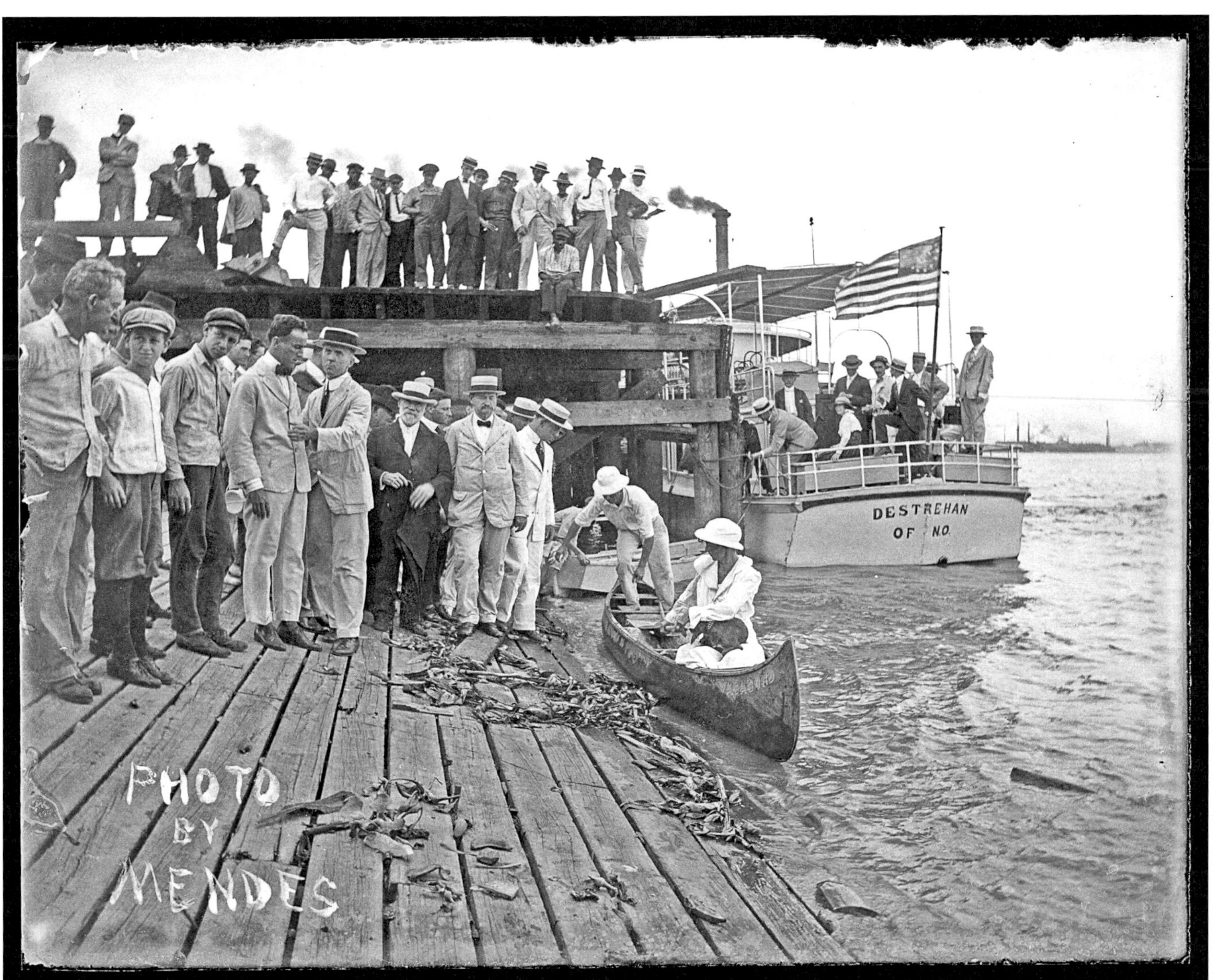

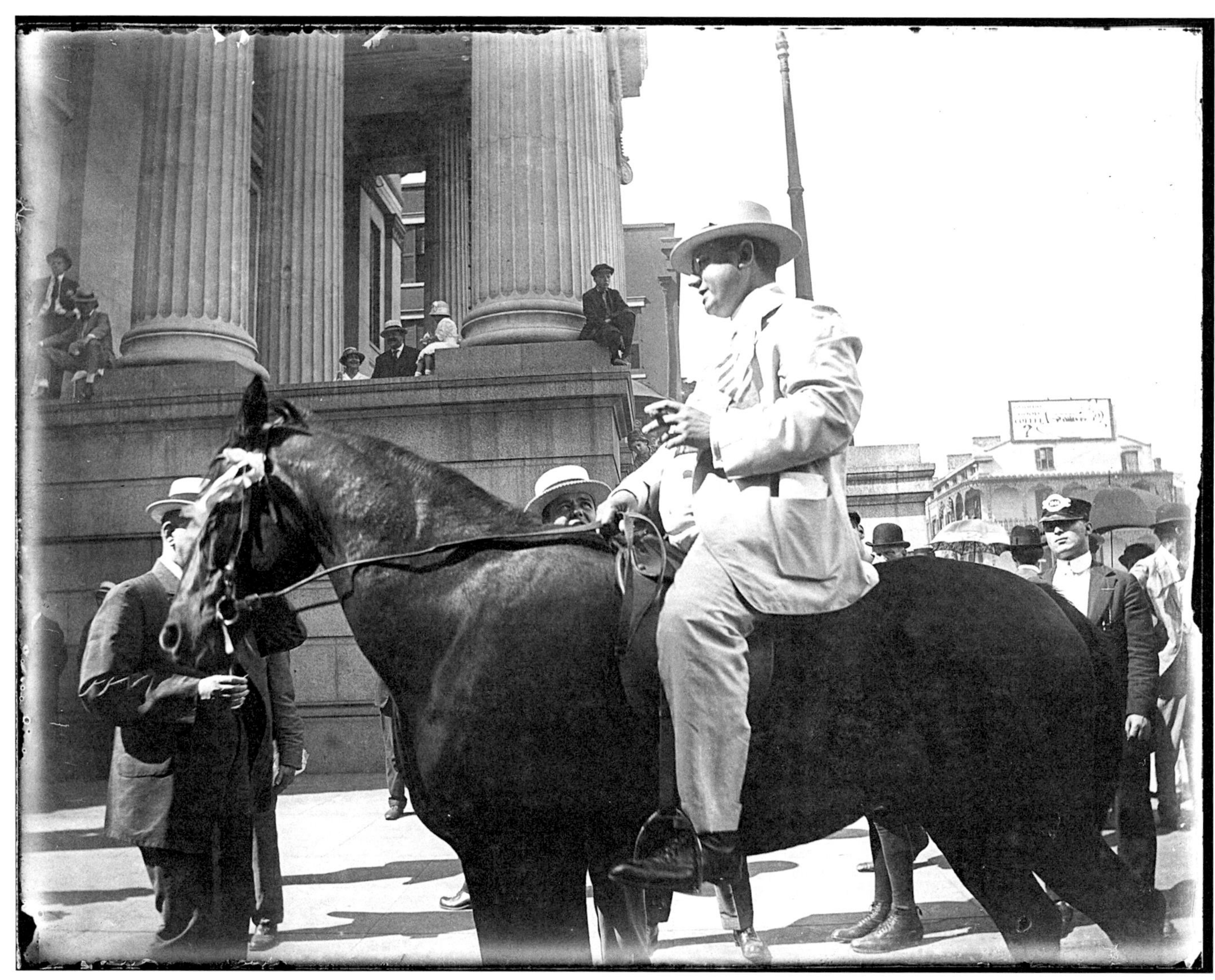

L.Di. Benedetto on horseback

2003.182.23
May 7, 1916

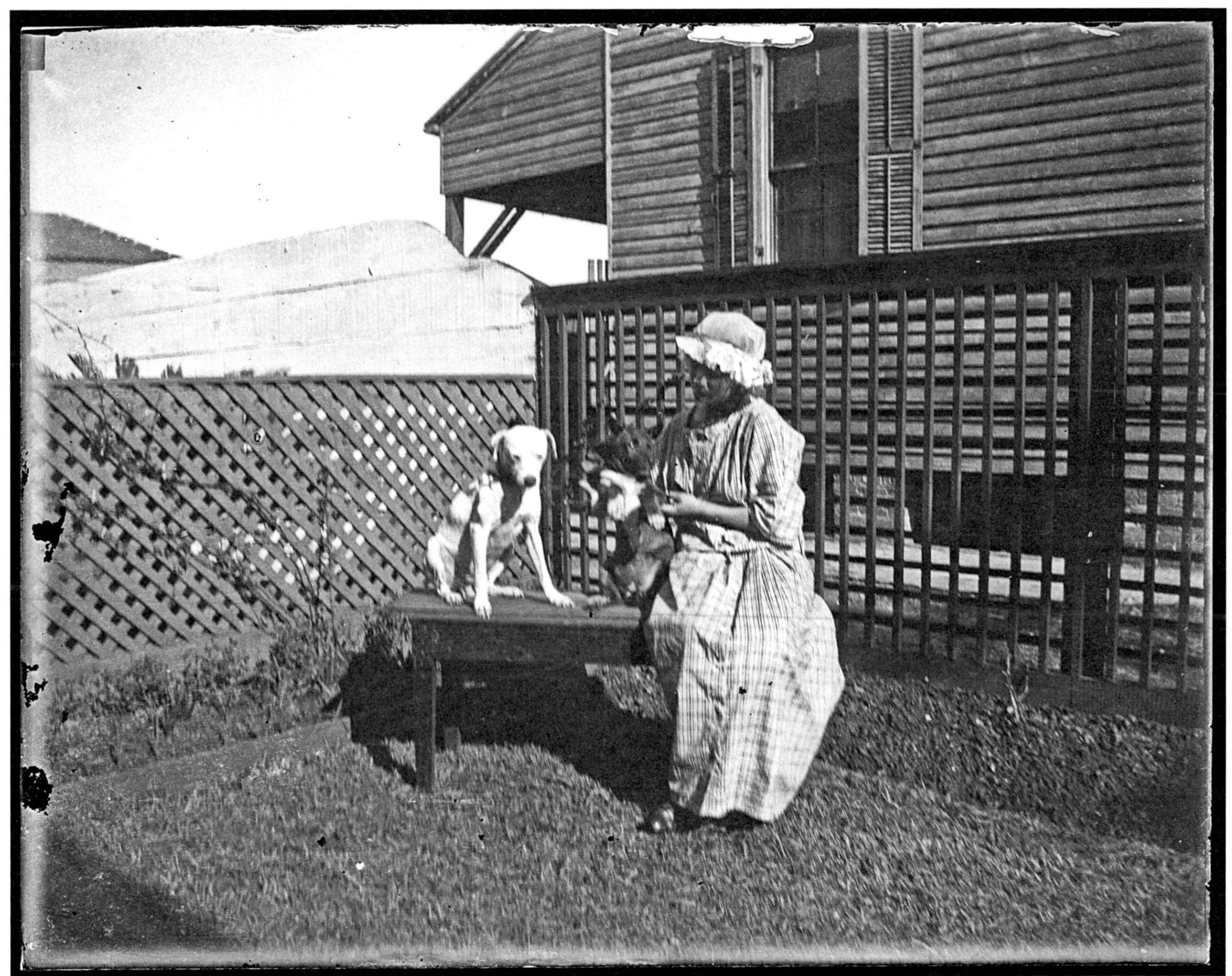

[Uncaptioned]

2003.182.478
[ca. 1921]

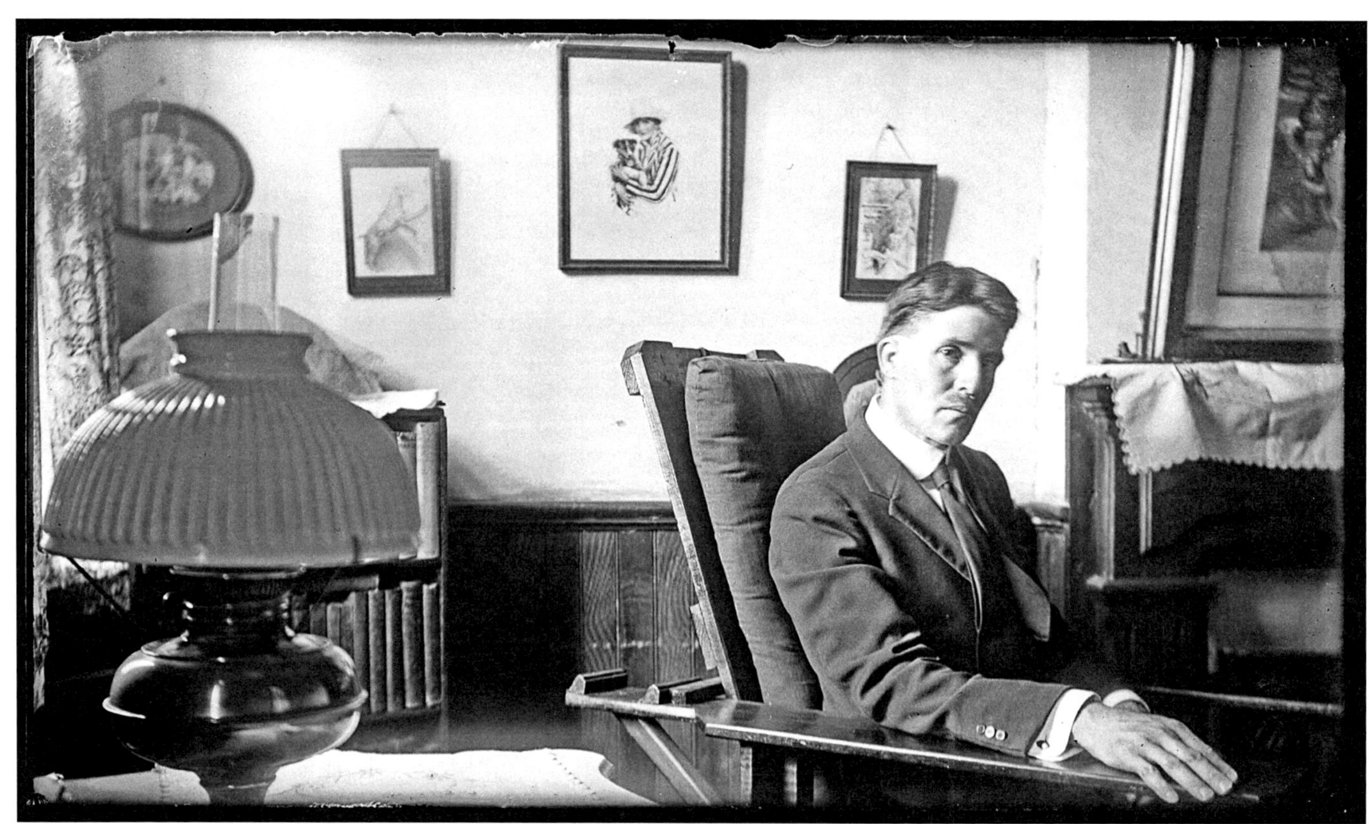

[Uncaptioned]

2003.182.603
[ca. 1921]

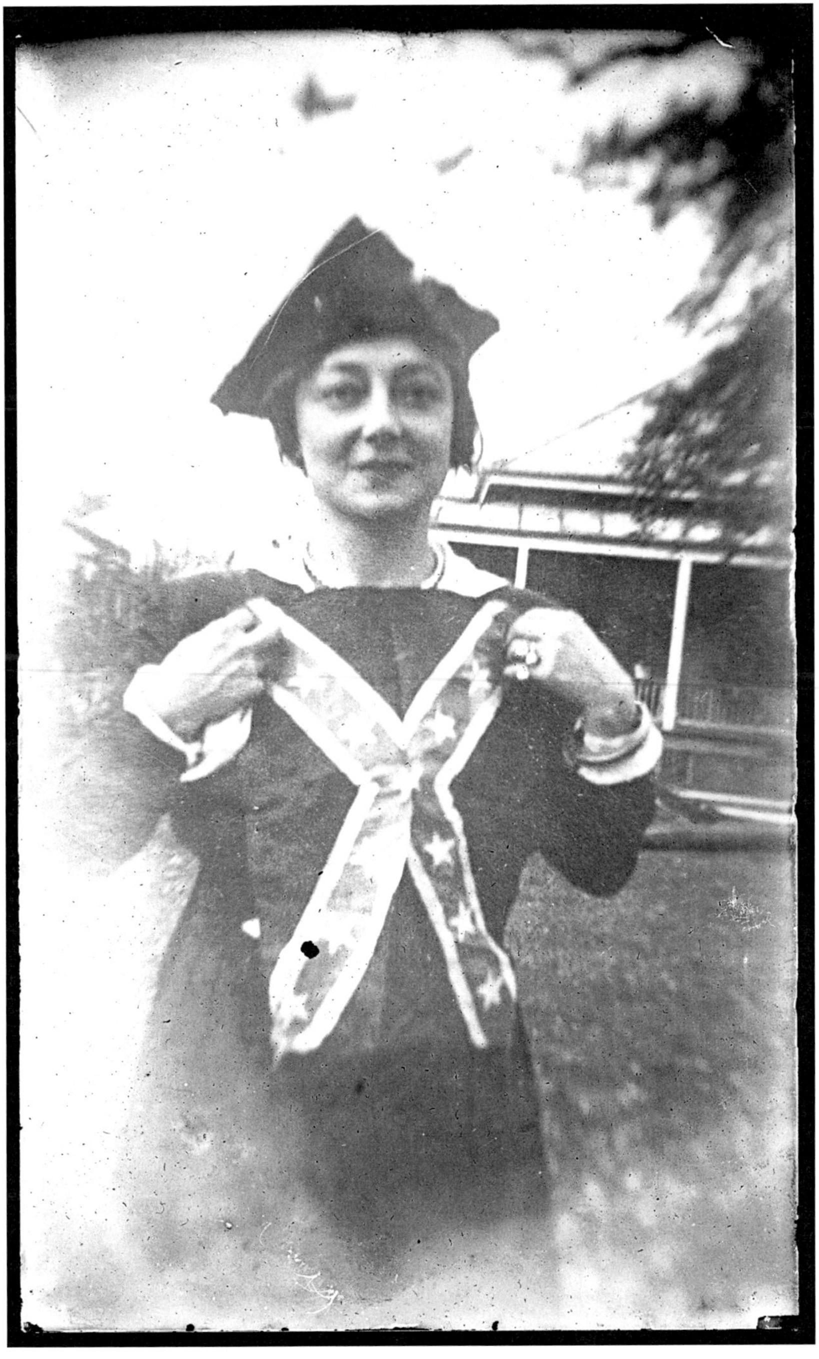

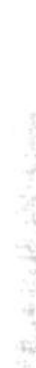

[Uncaptioned]

2003.182.573
[ca. 1921]

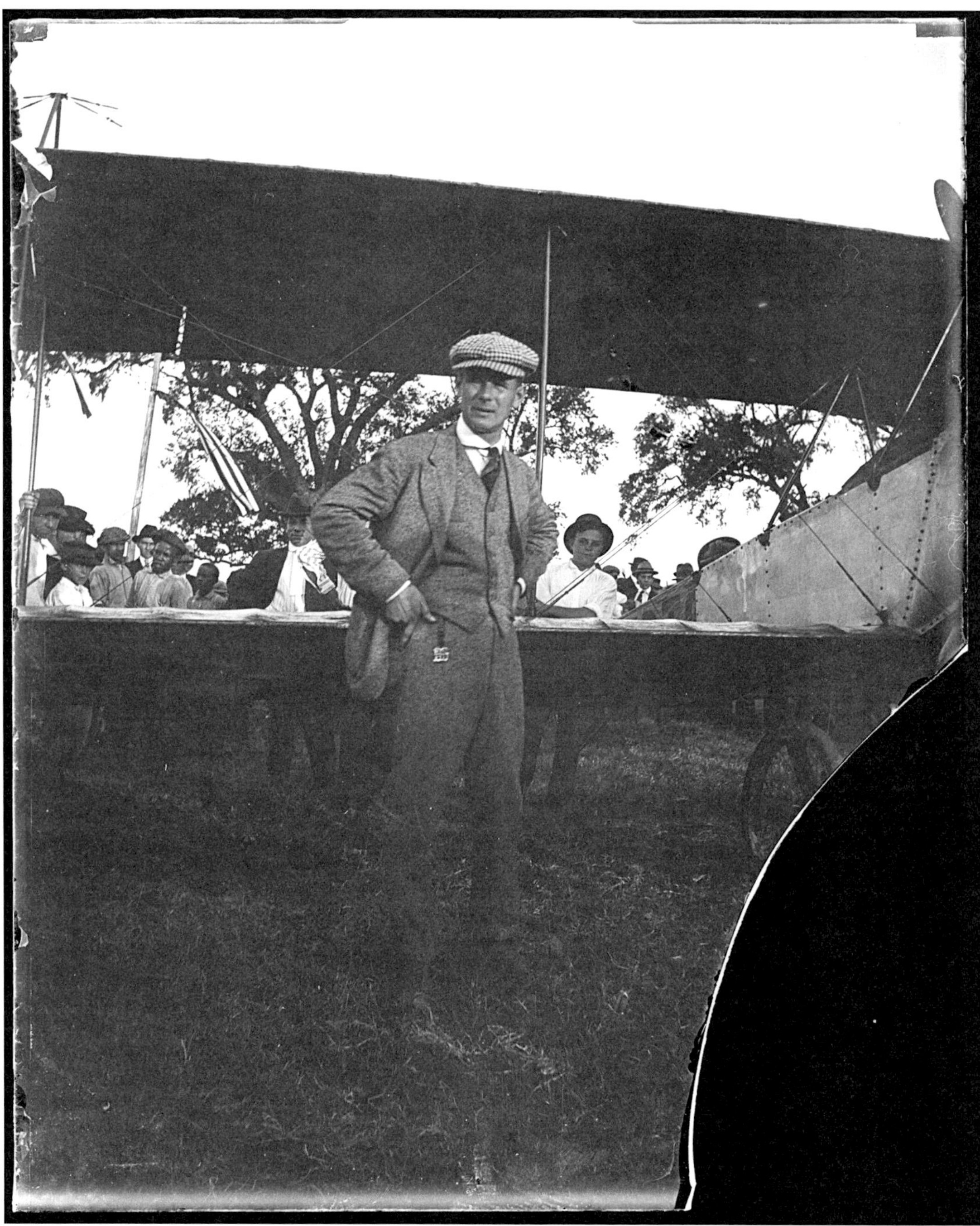

Louis Gertson

2003.182.53
November 11, 1916

Two Girls, employed by [?] who is trying to make a trip around the World in an Auto

2003.182.307
1920

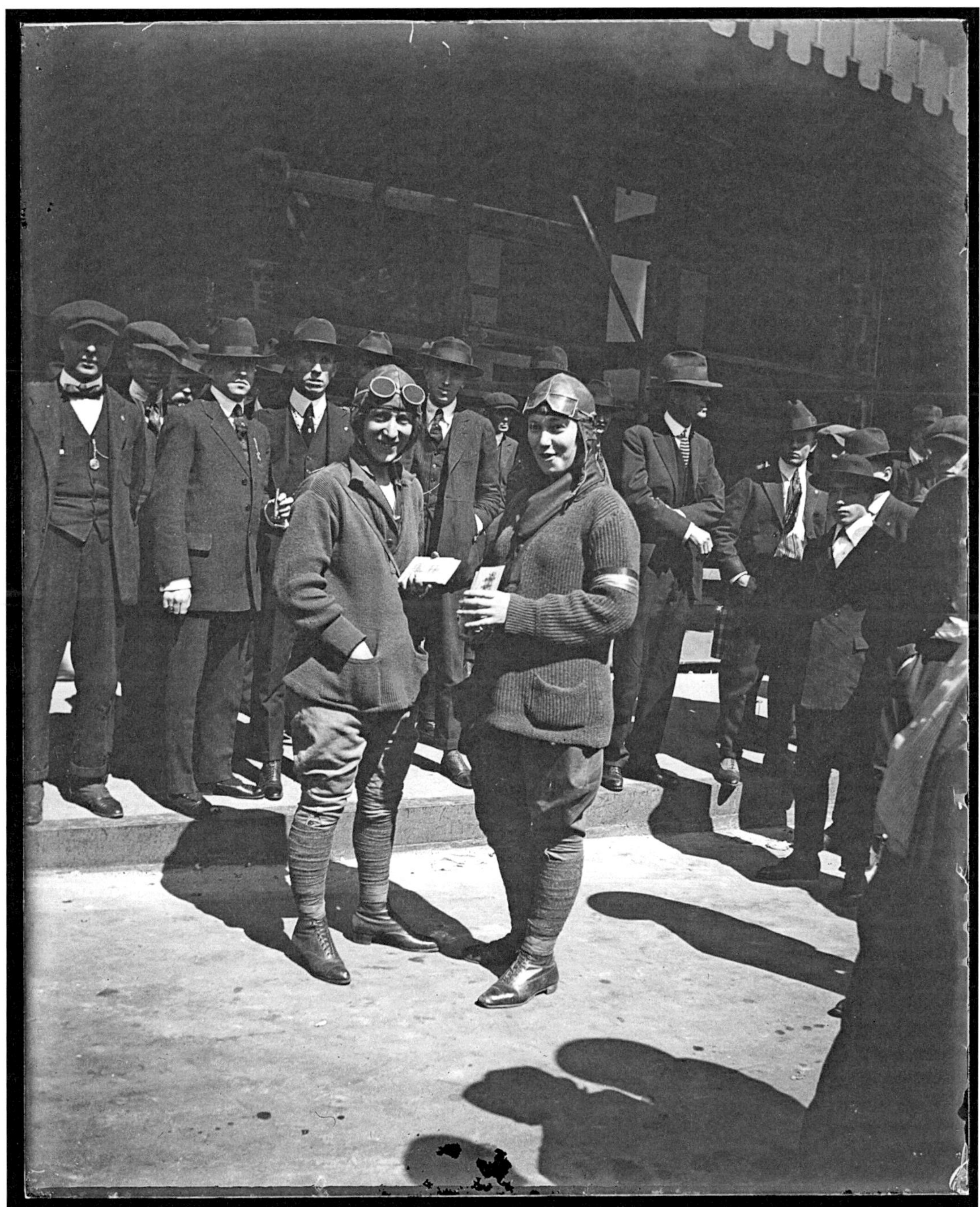

[Uncaptioned. Howard Ave. at Lee Circle.]

2003.182.513
1928

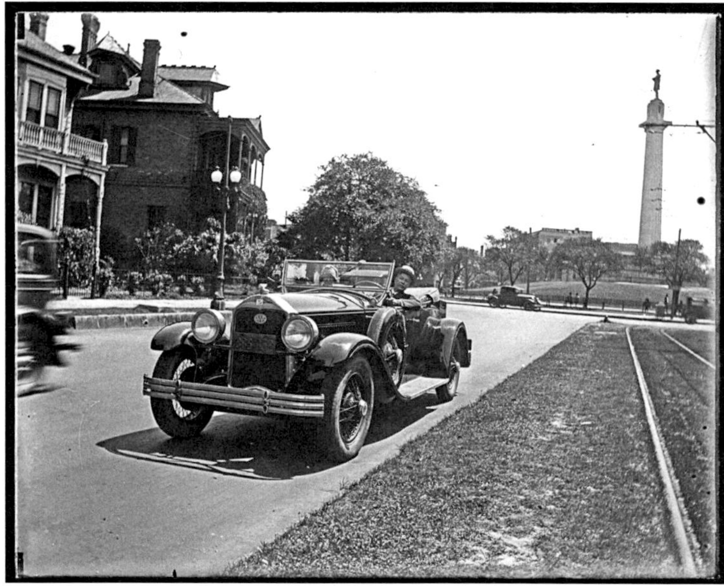

Early in 1932 my Mother became suddenly seriously sick, and I rushed her to a Private Hospital on Tulane Avenue by her doctor's orders where she lay on her back for seven weeks. Jerry had to go back outside Our rooms, but at that time he had not been used to living inside. He had his comfortable Dog House on the fenced in, roofed gallery, to rest or sleep in, the shed, and the freedom of a large yard. After feeding Jerry, and myself in the morning I would leave home at 7:30 A.M., ride Public Service to the Hospital, see my Mother, and then again ride to my place of work. I would punch in at 8:30 A.M. I would go home for lunch, feed Jerry, and go back to my job — Trolley cars. I would get off from my work about 6:05 P.M., and go, and stay with my Mother until 8 P.M. or later. [...] (Although she wanted me to be with her as long as possible she had a mother's consideration, and concern, and knew I was tired, and most times urged me to leave her earlier than I ever did.) I would go home to get a grand, and affectionate welcome from Jerry. He was a great comfort to me. Then Jerry, and I would eat our late supper or dinner. [...]

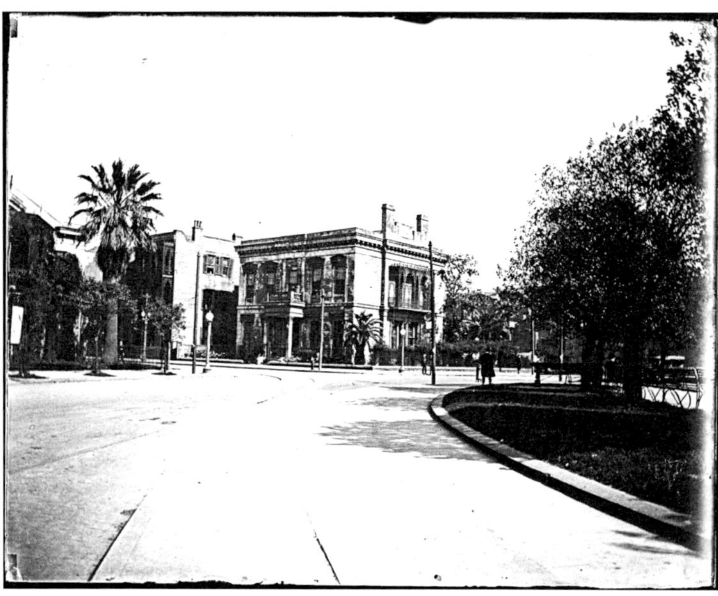

Mansion Lee Circle

2003.182.241
February 1920

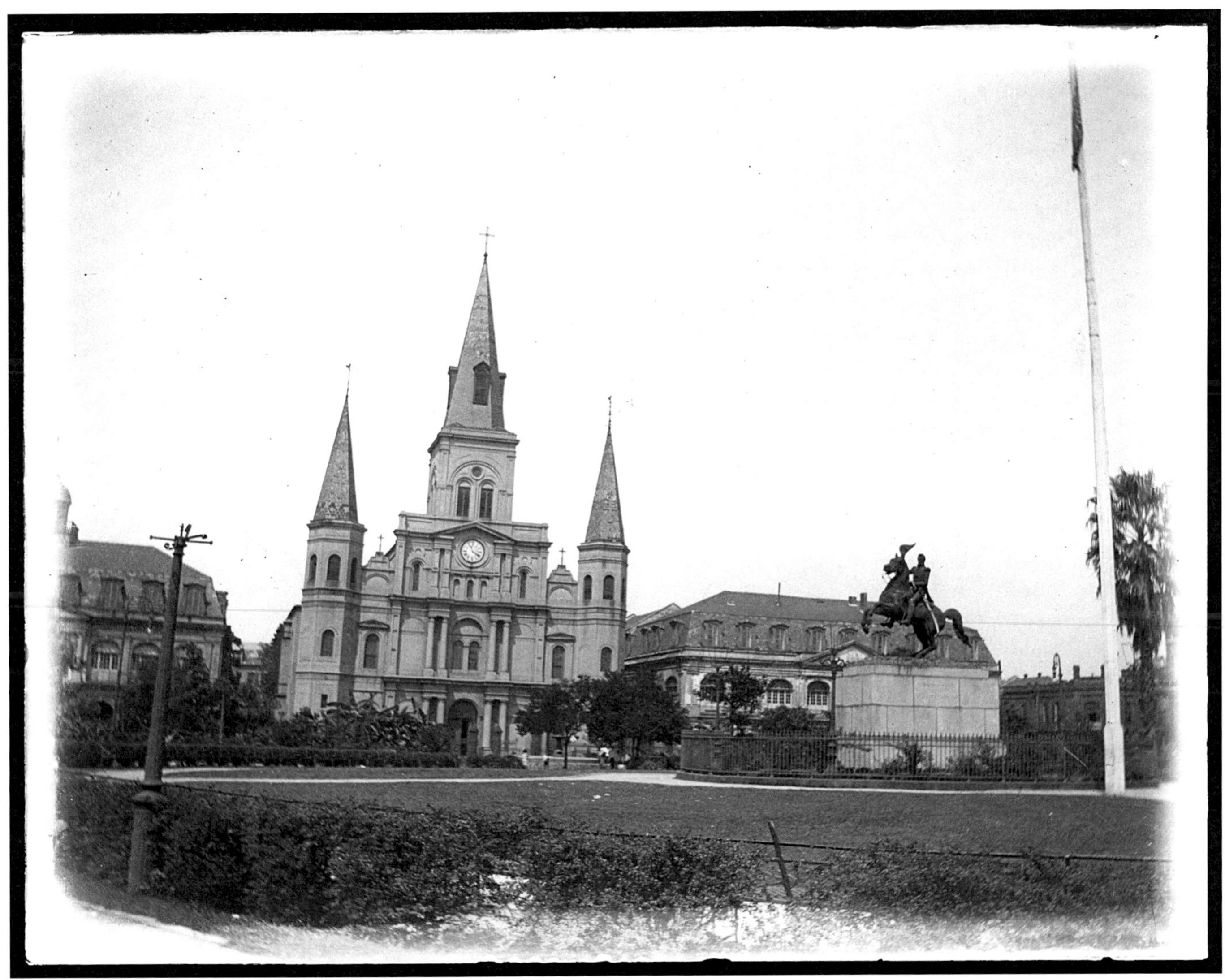

St. Louis Cathedral

2003.182.386
1925

Jerry was a great power for good in those dark days, for I had never lived away from my home, and Mother in all of my life. Of course I hated to leave Jerry all alone all of those long hours but I could not help that. I had no one to help me. This was the first separation of Mother and I since she had gone out of town, for less than one week, to visit my older sister in another city.

- *Dogs in My Life*, 33-34

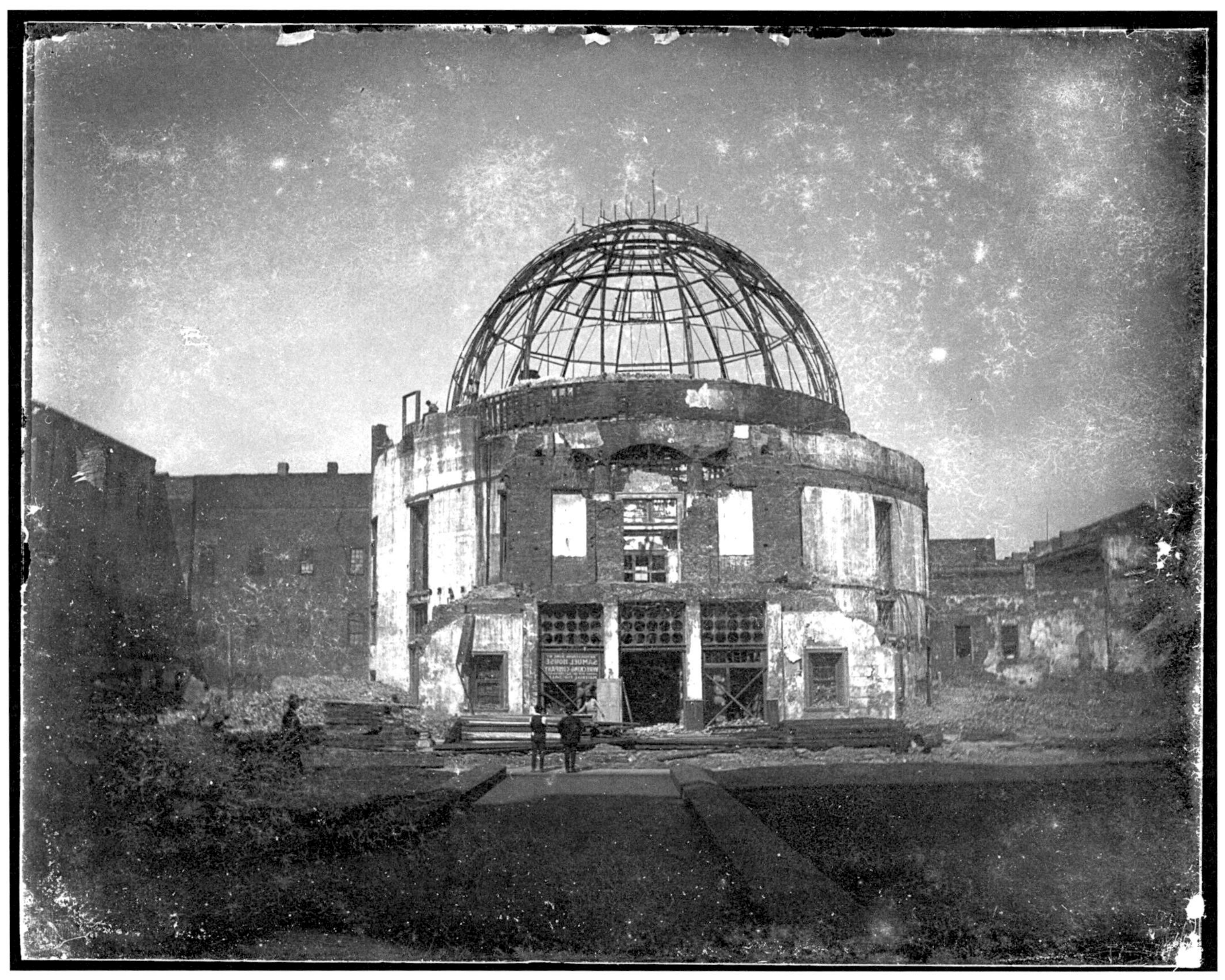

St. Louis Hotel Dome. [Photographer's] Note: This negative was partly developed in Pyro and then in Special Developer.

2003.182.133
1916

Front Entrance
St. Louis Hotel
being demolished

2003.182.11
May 1916

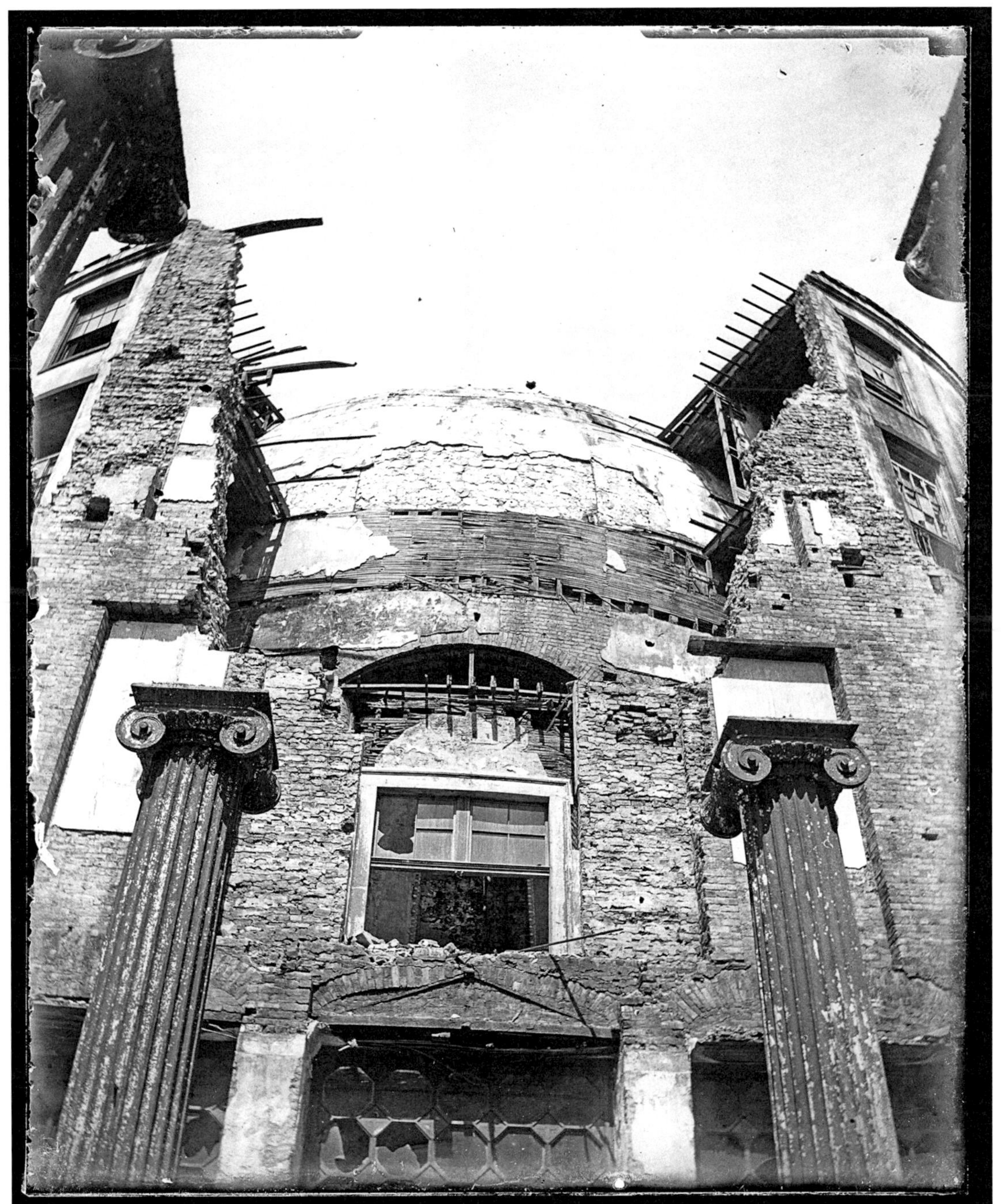

E. J. McCall. Hog that weigh 890 pounds.

2003.182.54
November 11, 1916

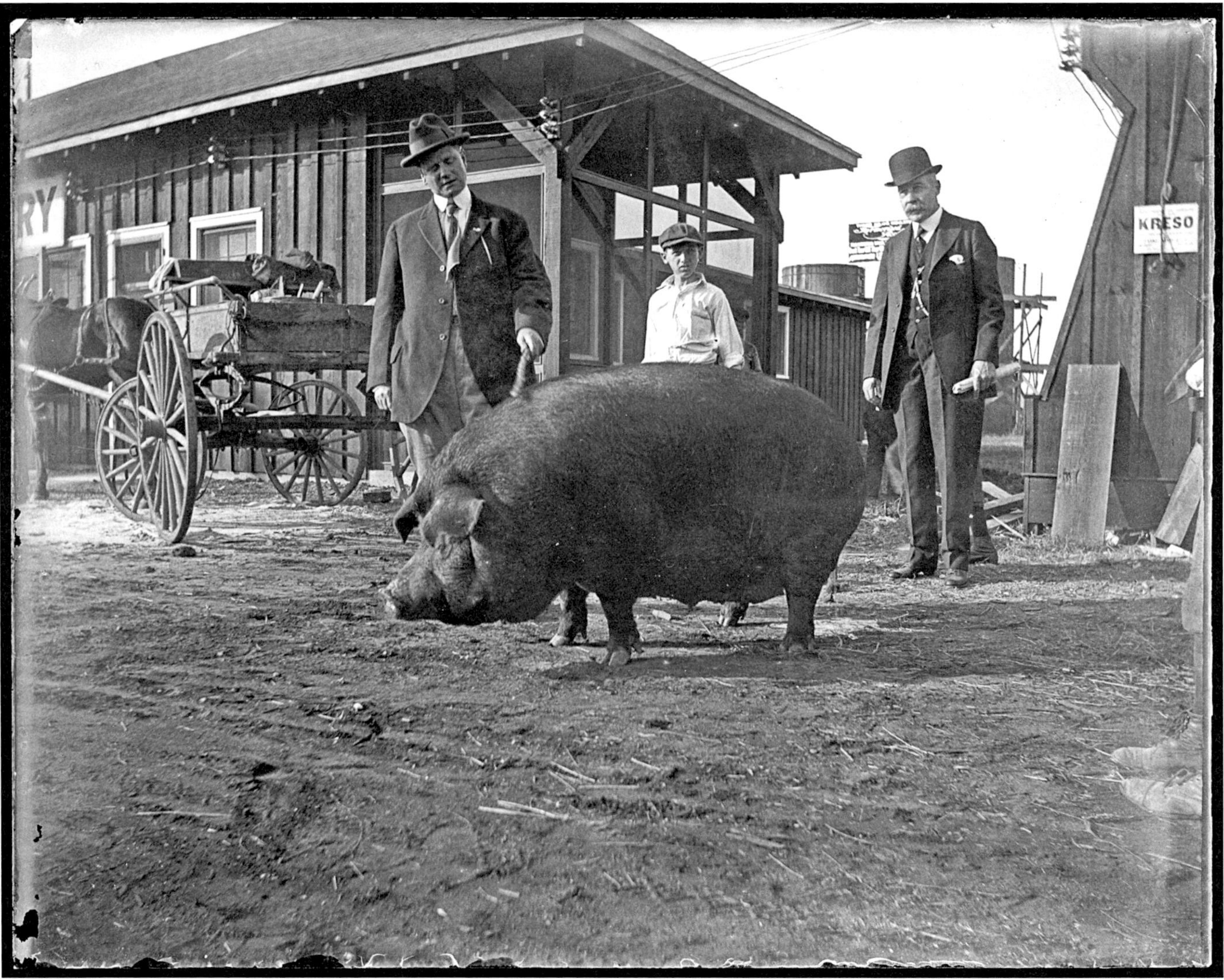

Mr. Murphy with pony

2003.182.18
February 1916

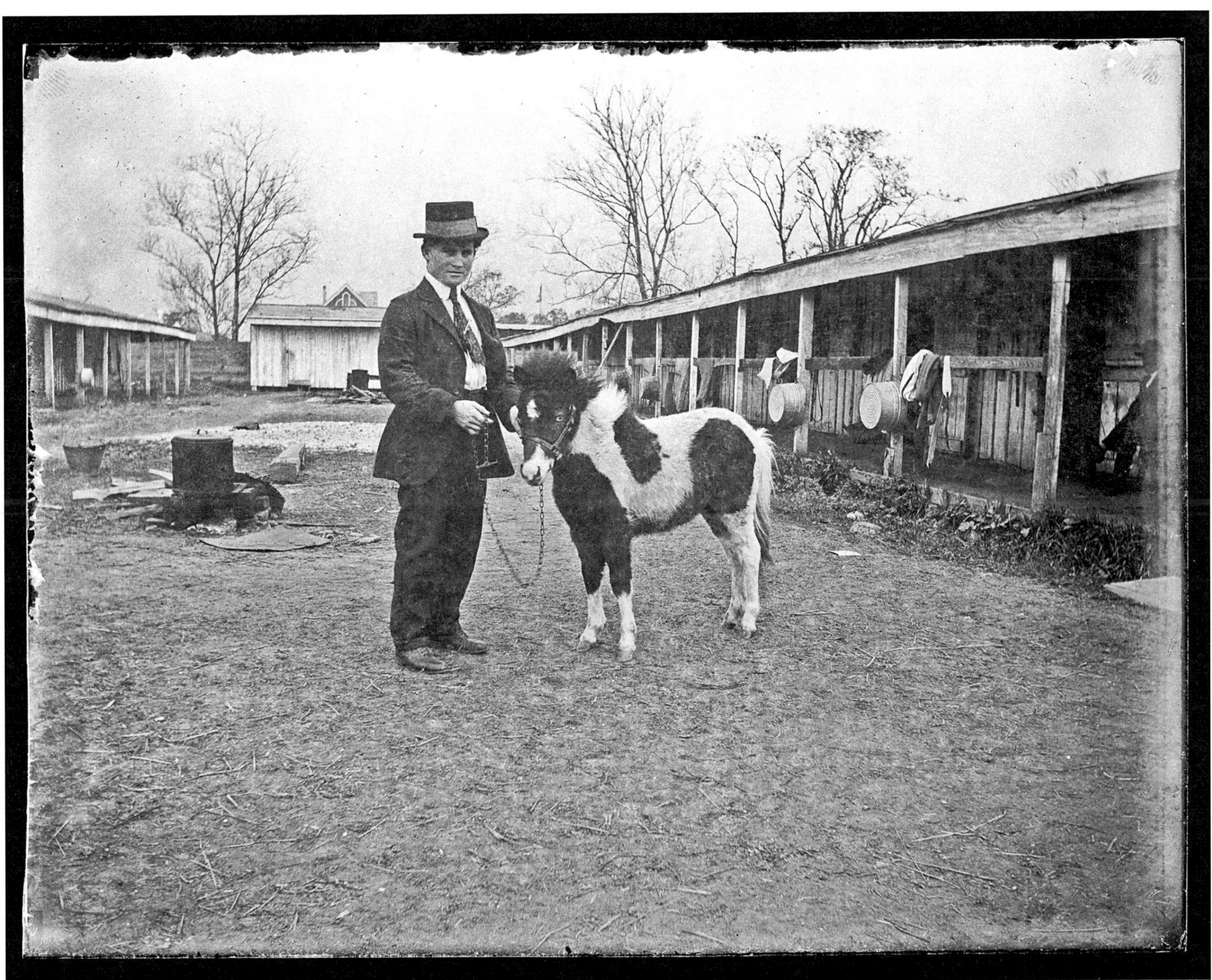

Prince Iko.

2003.182.56
November 11, 1916

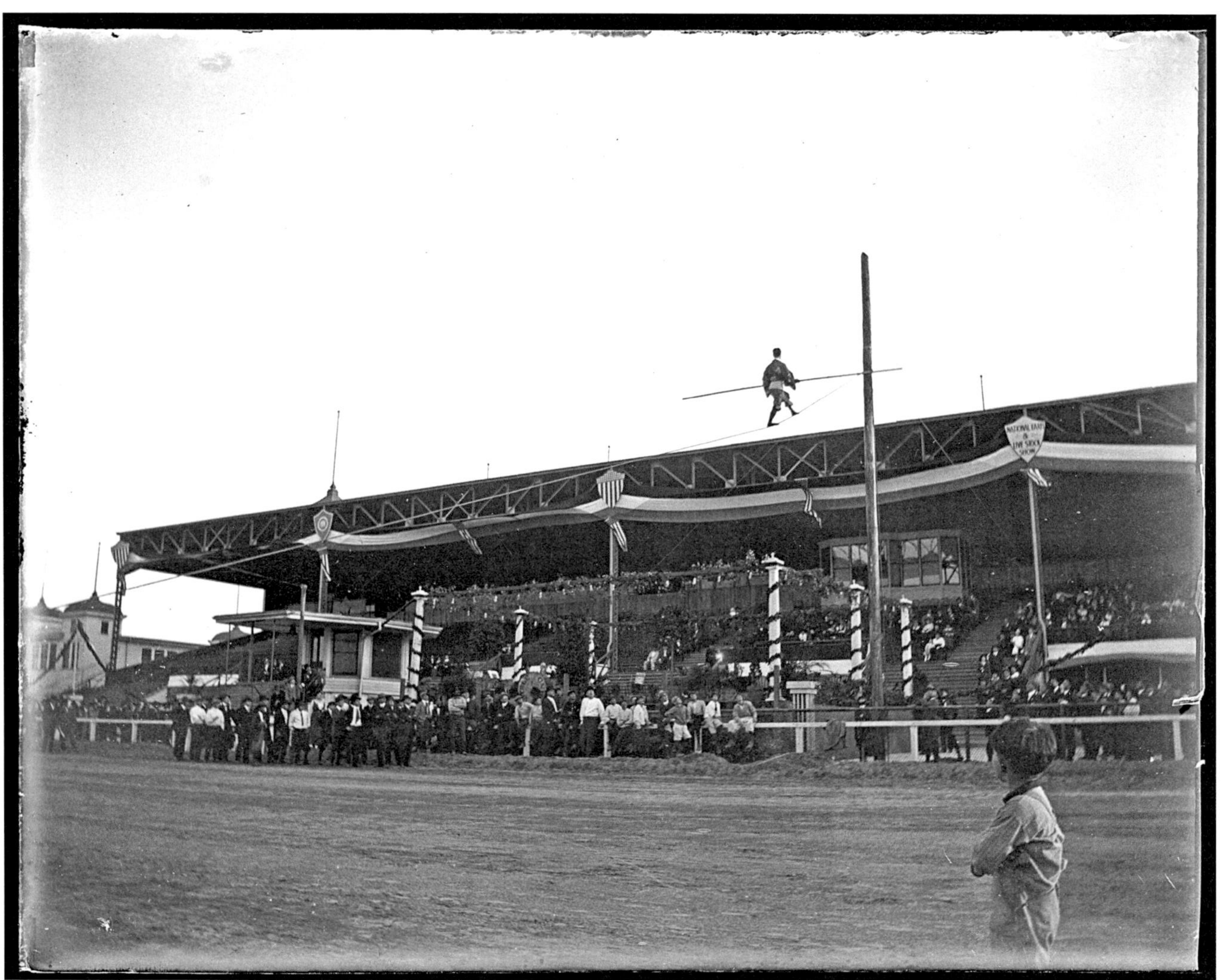

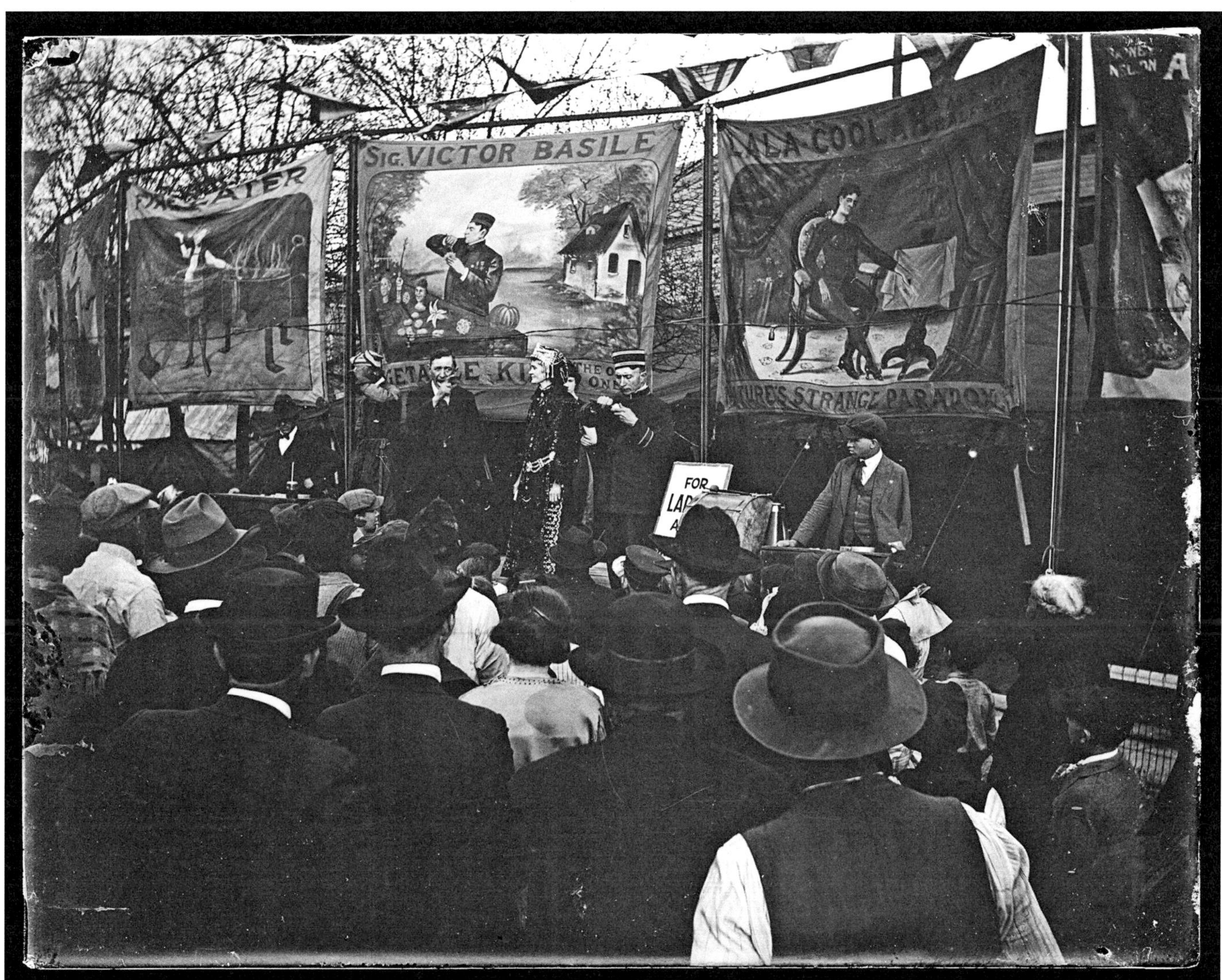

[Uncaptioned]

2003.182.274
February 21, 1920

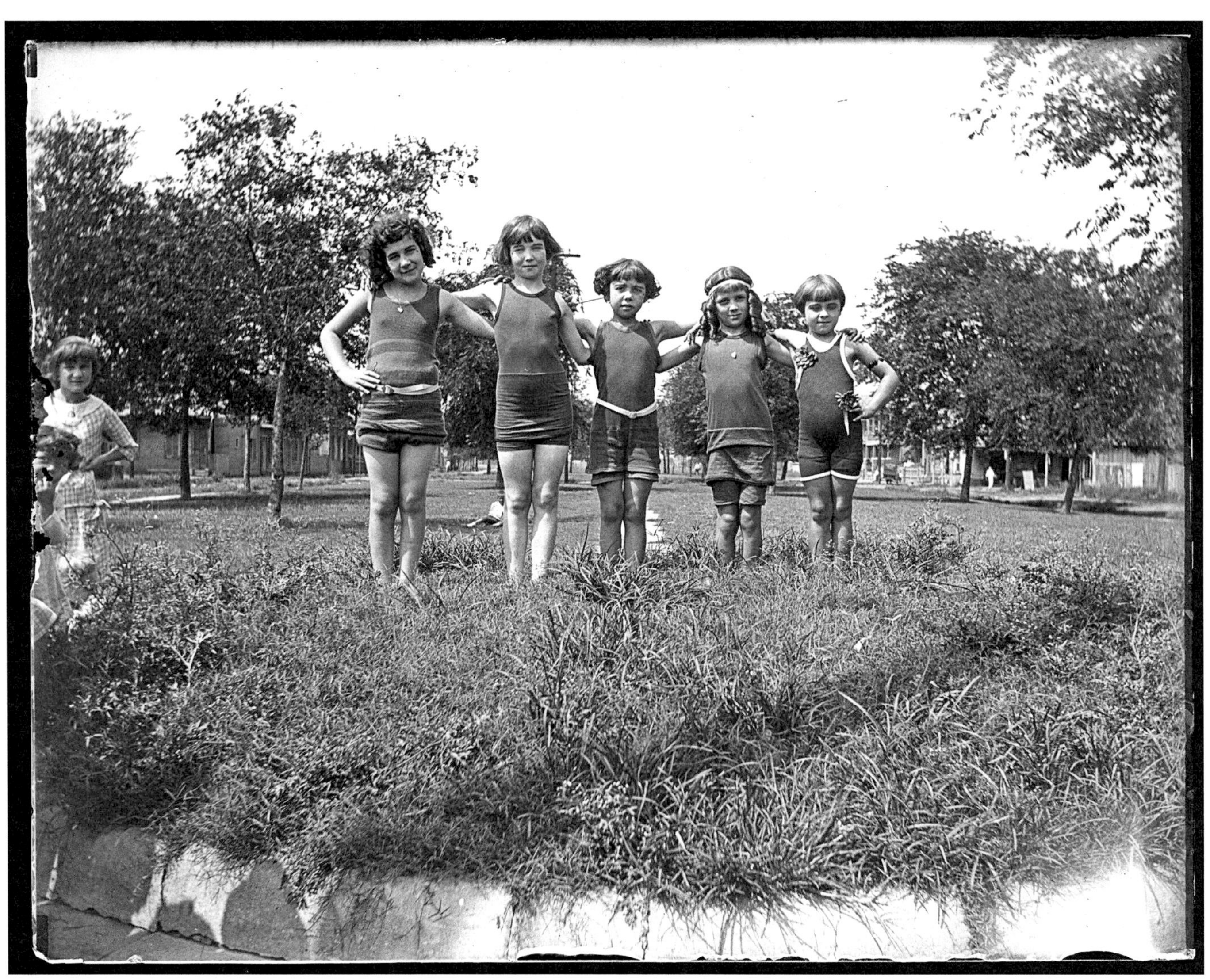

5 girls in swimming suits standing in grass facing camera

2003.182.313
June 30, 1923

Girls on Truck

2003.182.317
February 24, 1924

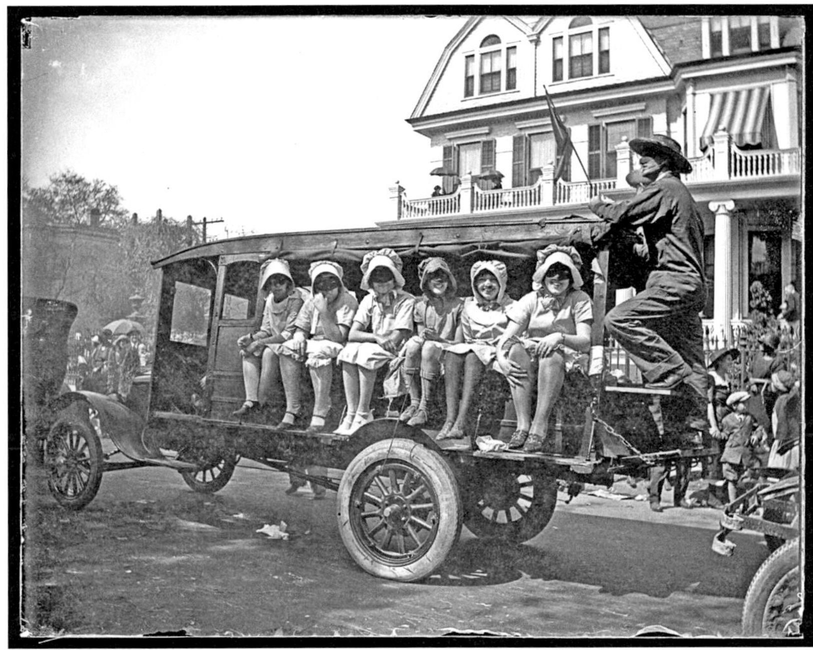

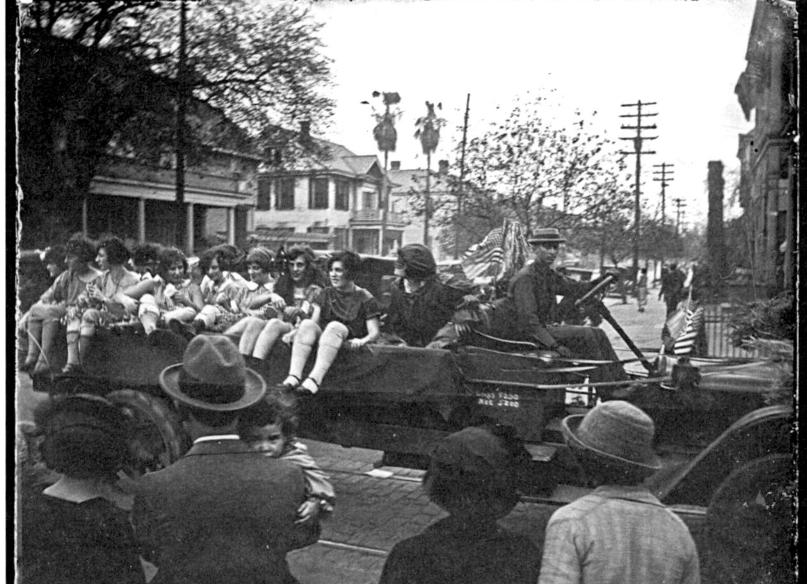

Girl on Float

2003.182.329
March 4, 1924

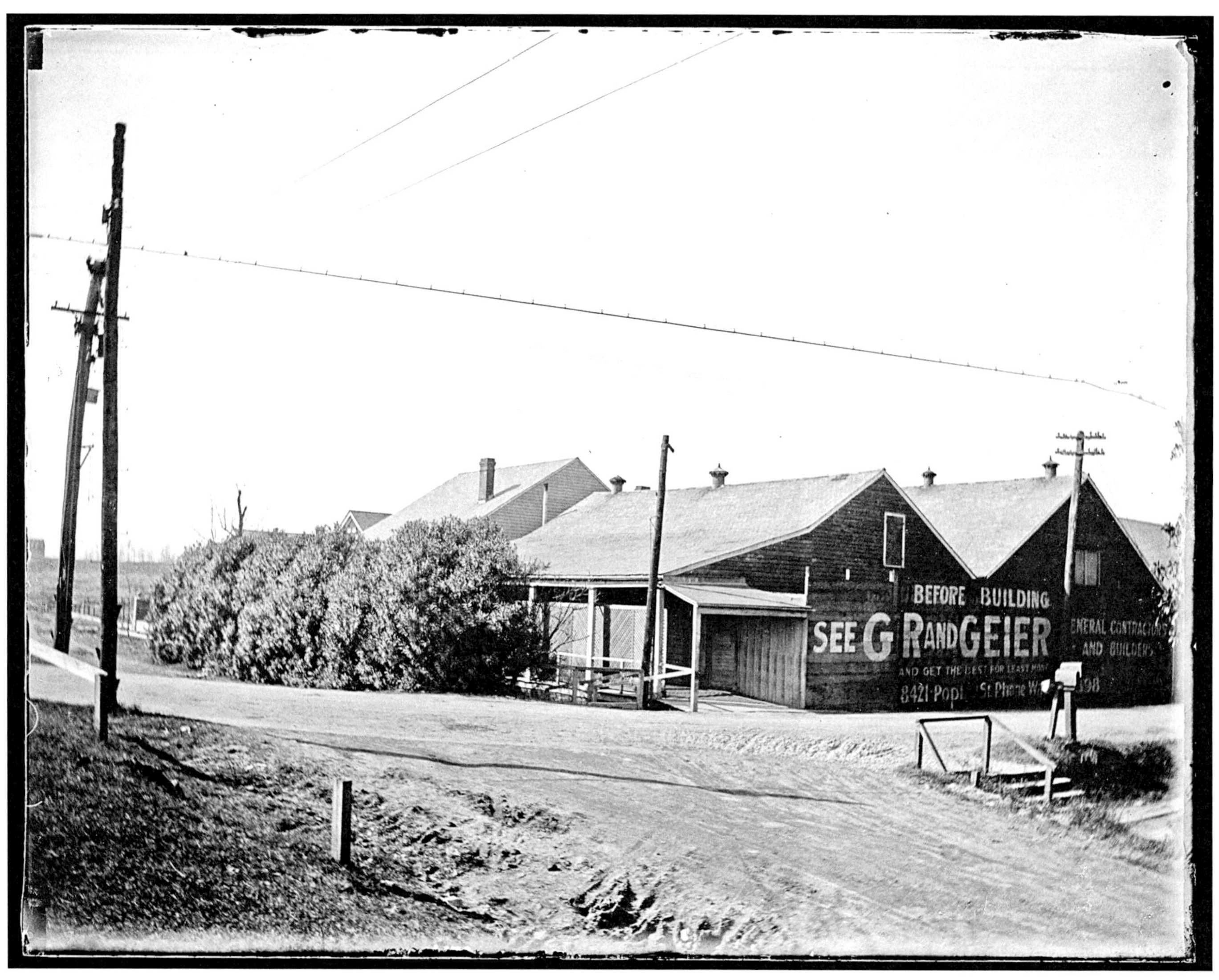

Jefferson Parish

2003.182.239
February 1920

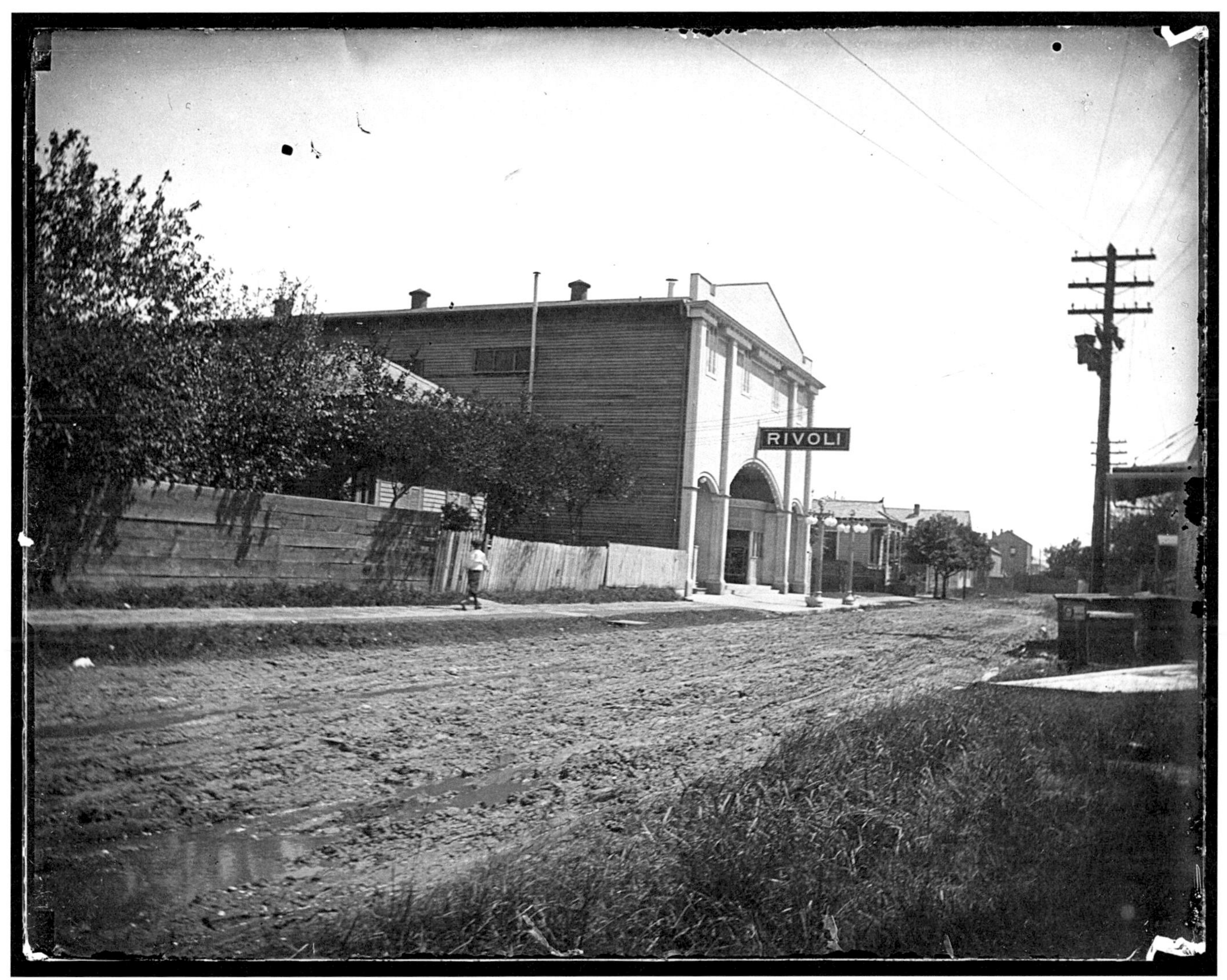

Rivoli

2003.182.291
September 25, 1920

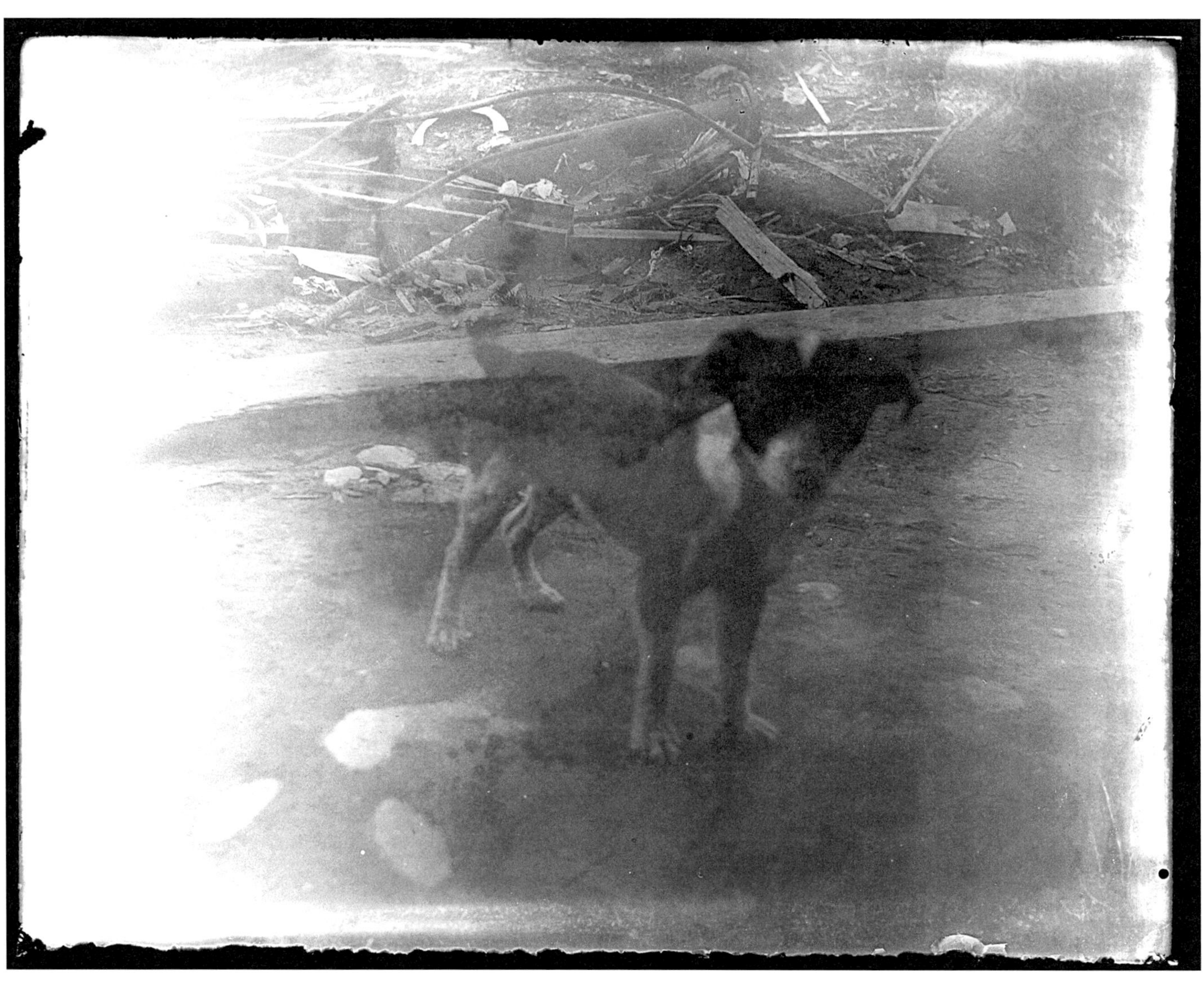

Frisco

2003.182.463
[No date]

When my Mother died in the Hospital, with my arms about her at nearly 82 years of age, August 1st, 1942 I was 54 years of age, and a WPA Watchman. The death of my dear Mother was the hardest, and most cruel blow I had ever felt in my entire life. And I grieved a lot. I had never been away from where my Mother lived for more than two days, and she had only been away from me one week visiting her daughter — my sister.

And while my Mother was in the Hospital, ten years before her death I saw her every day. [...] For 37 years my Mother, and I had sat in the same chairs, at the same table, in the same house, eating Our meals day in, and day out (except when she was sick in bed) facing each other. Now I faced a vacant chair.

-Dogs in My Life, 45

[Uncaptioned]

2003.182.449
[ca. 1921]

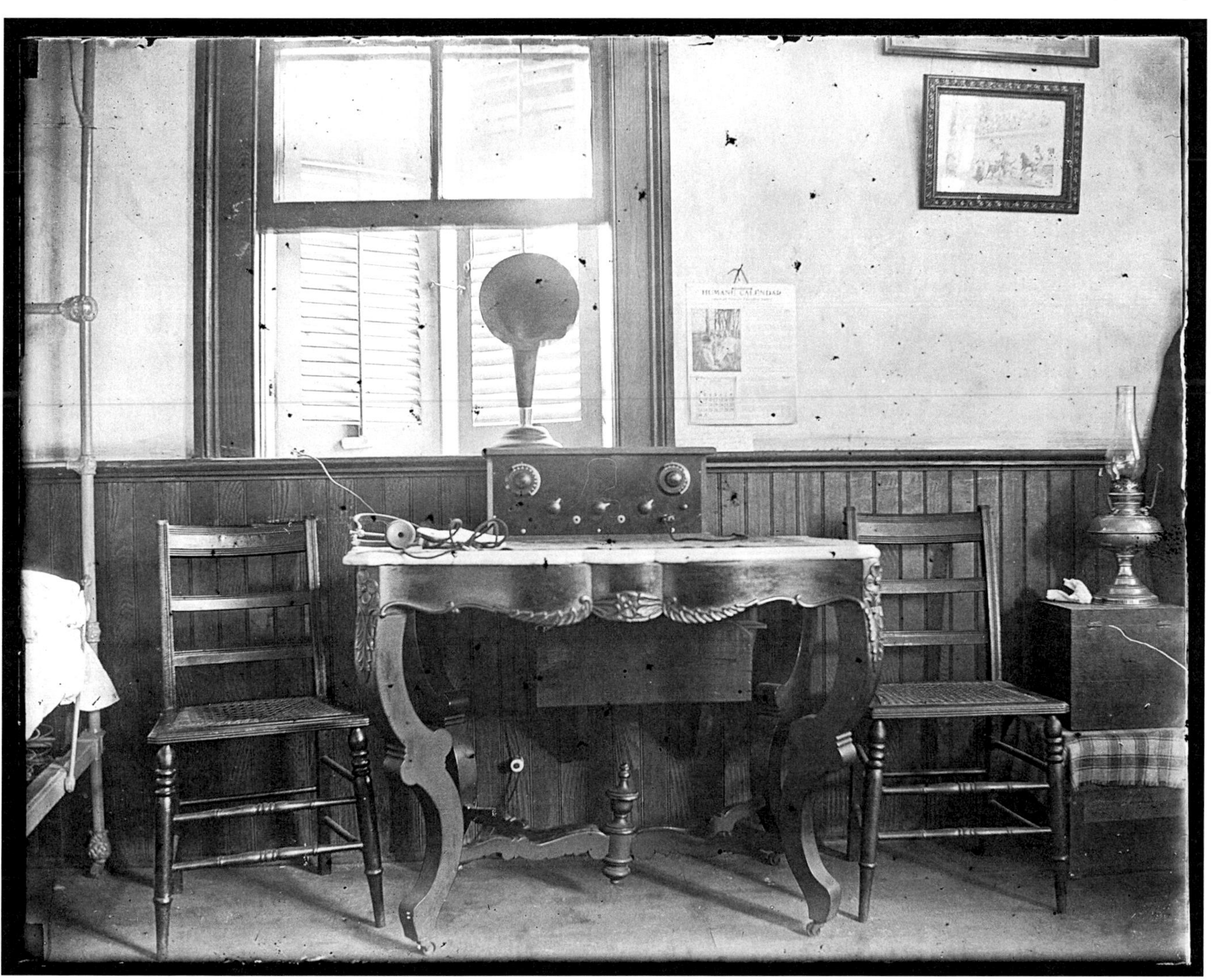

Jockey Club
[Luling Mansion, 1438 Leda Street, 1865]

2003.182.33
1916

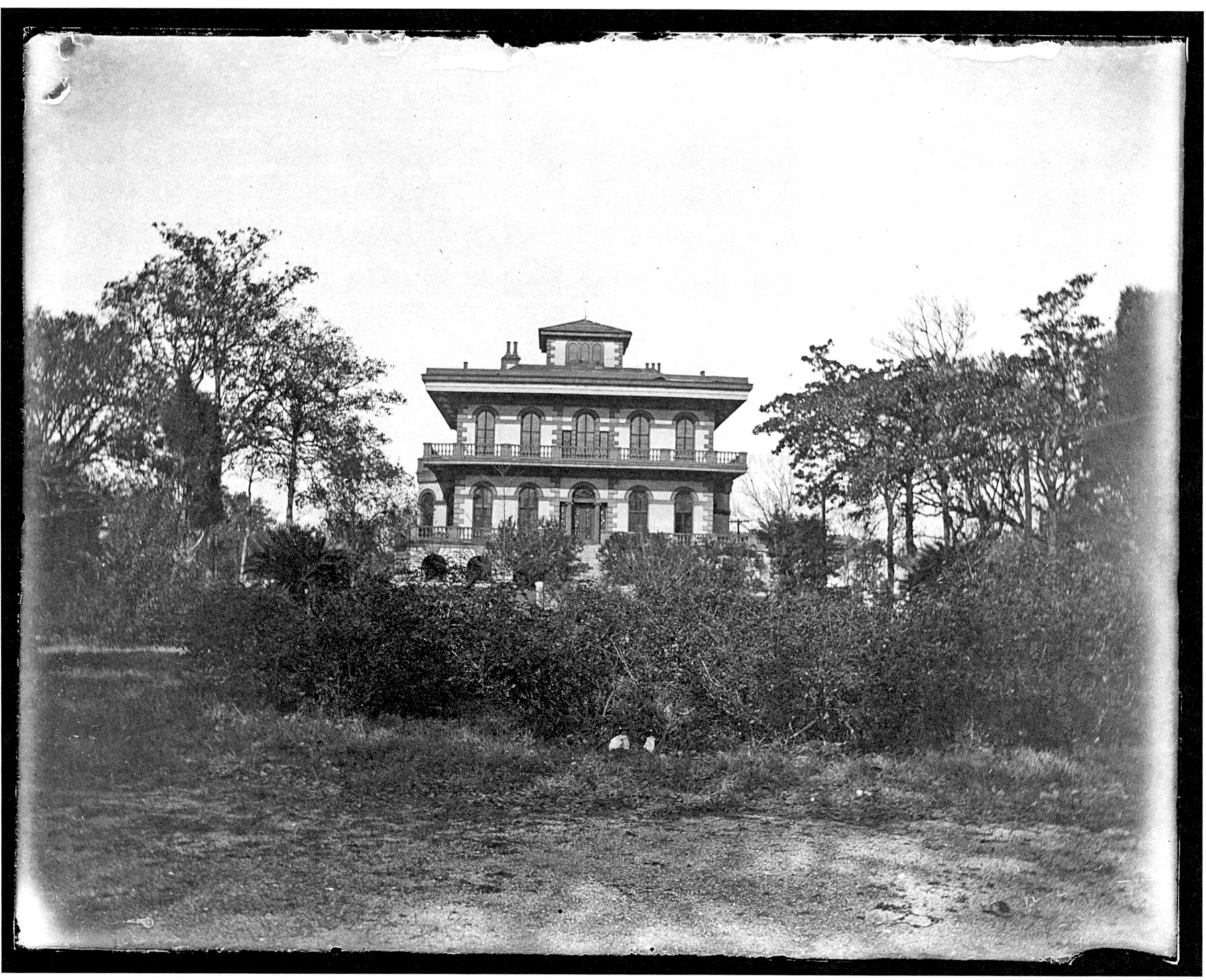

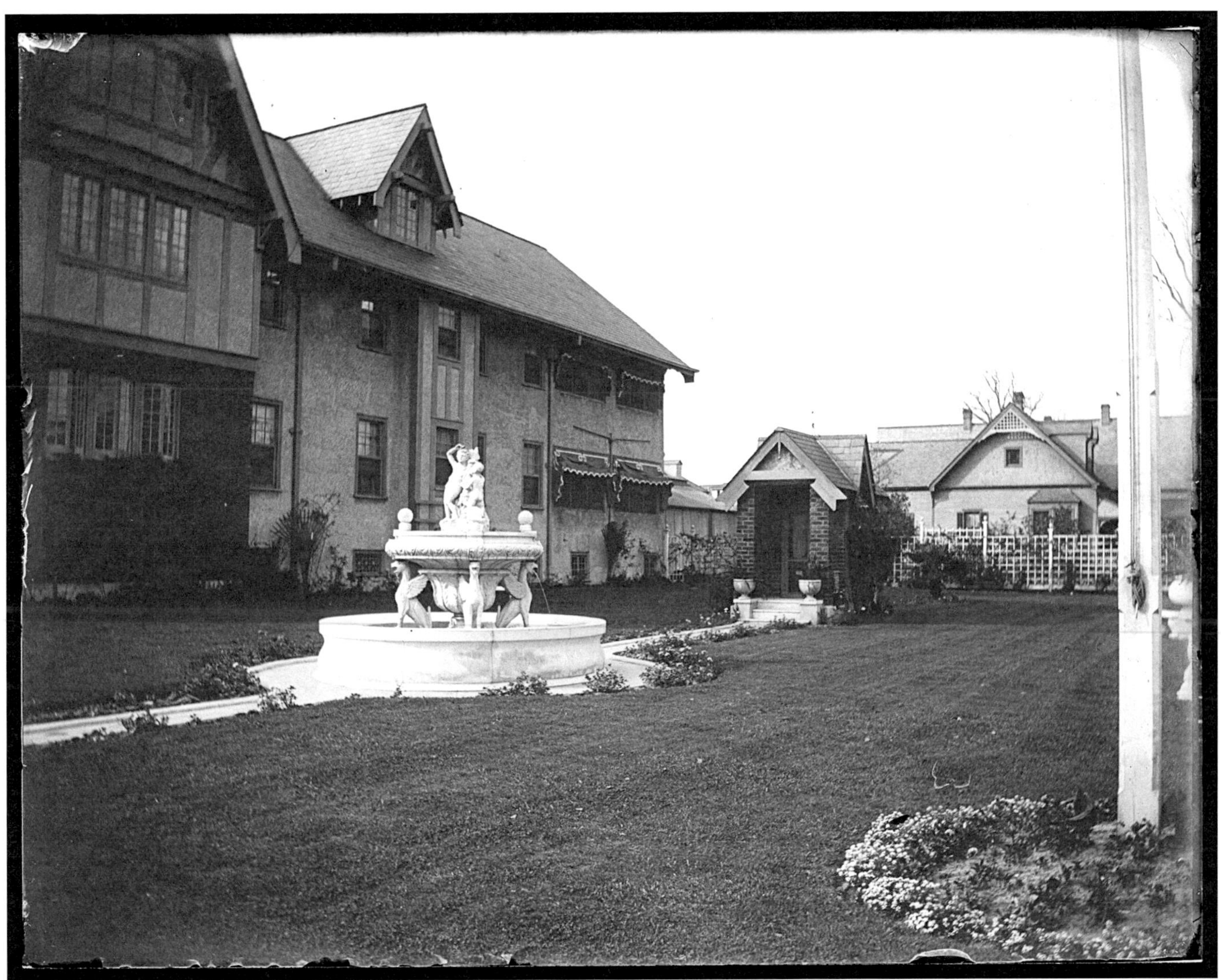

Childs play house
St. Charles and B.Way

2003.182.277
April 1920

One-two-three
Mary Pickford

2003.182.68
1917

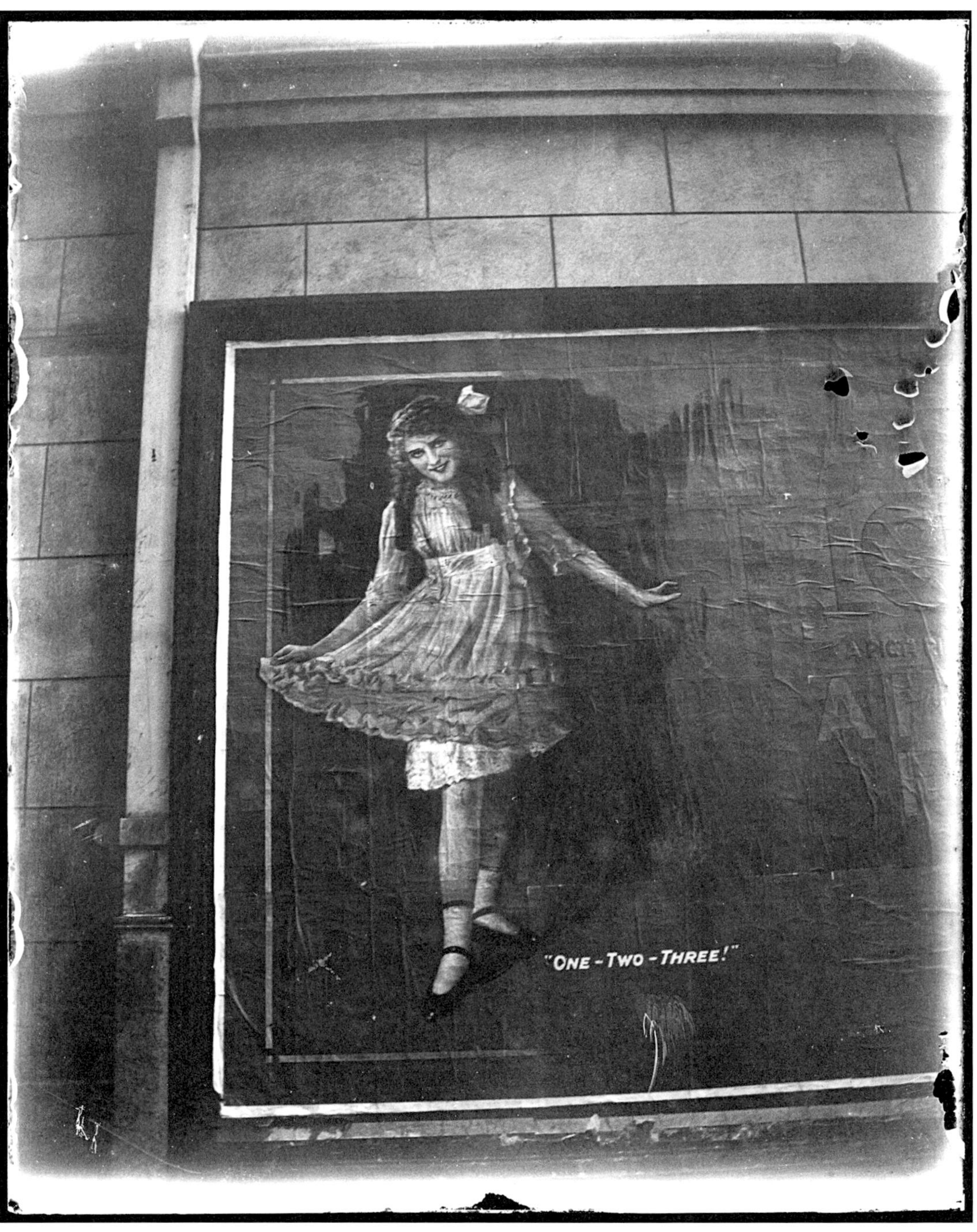

[Uncaptioned. Pearce's Tudor Theatre, Mary Pickford]

2003.182.495
March 1917

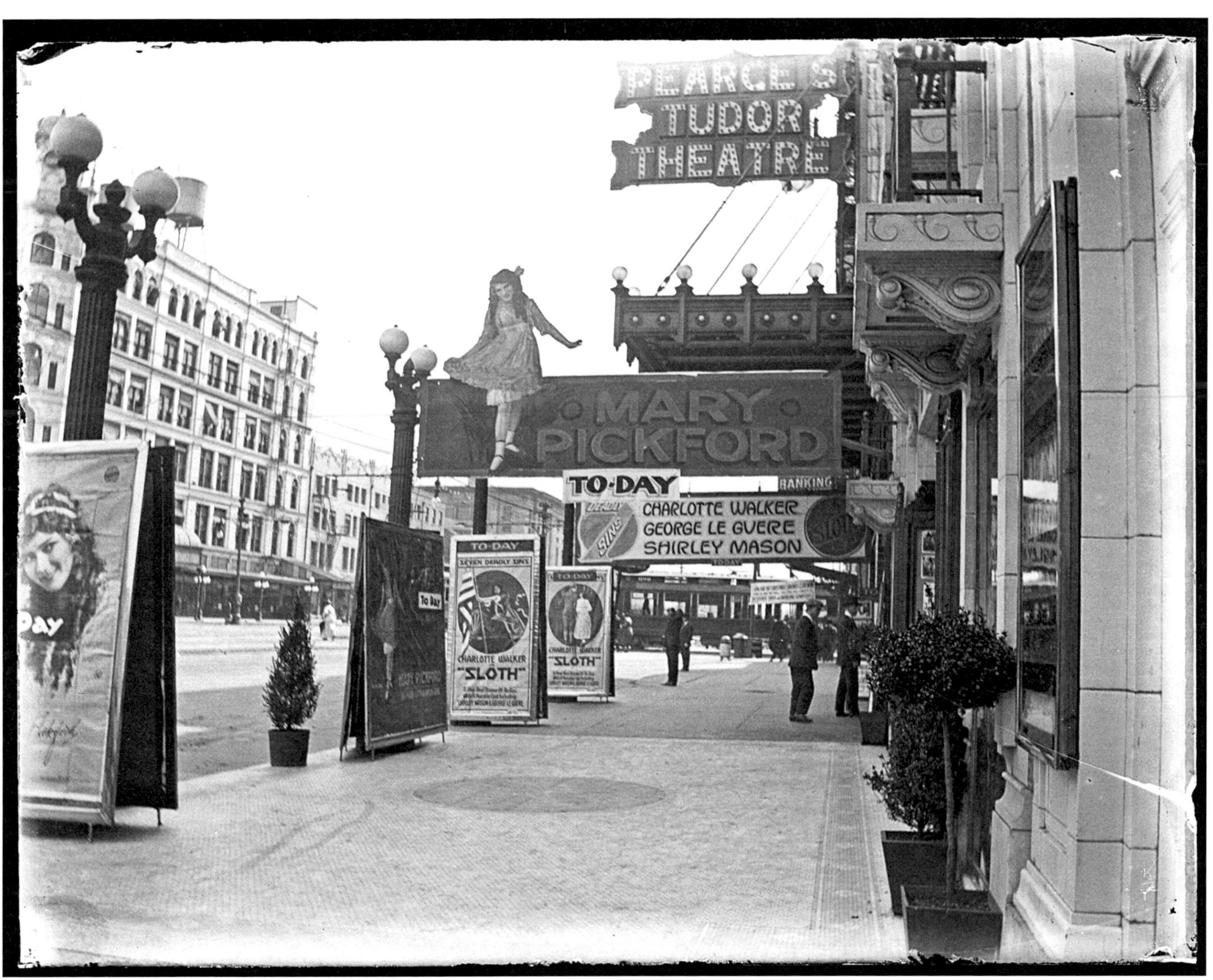

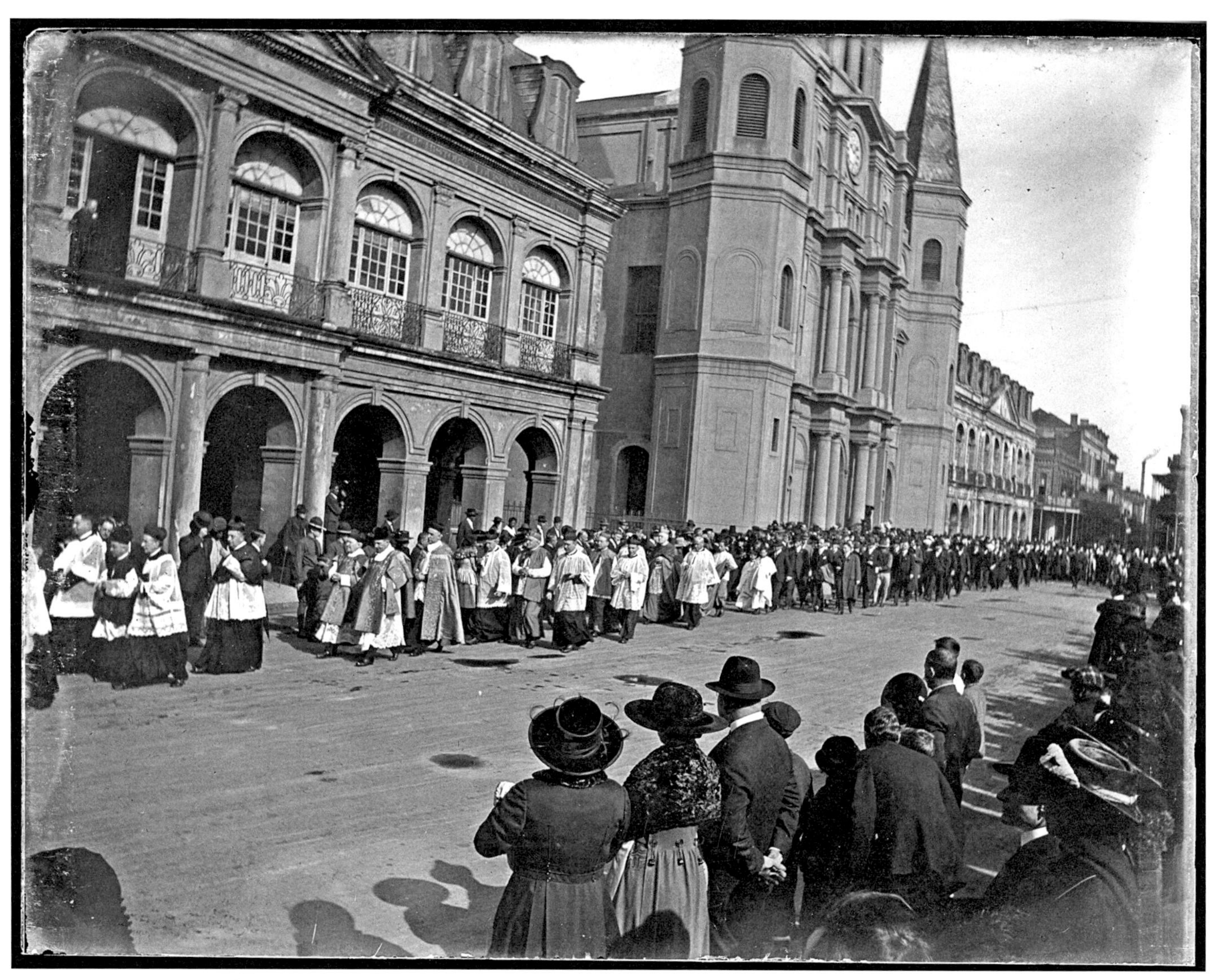

Priests in Parade. (Archbishop Shaw seen) Victory Mass Day

2003.182.147
[November 17, 1918]

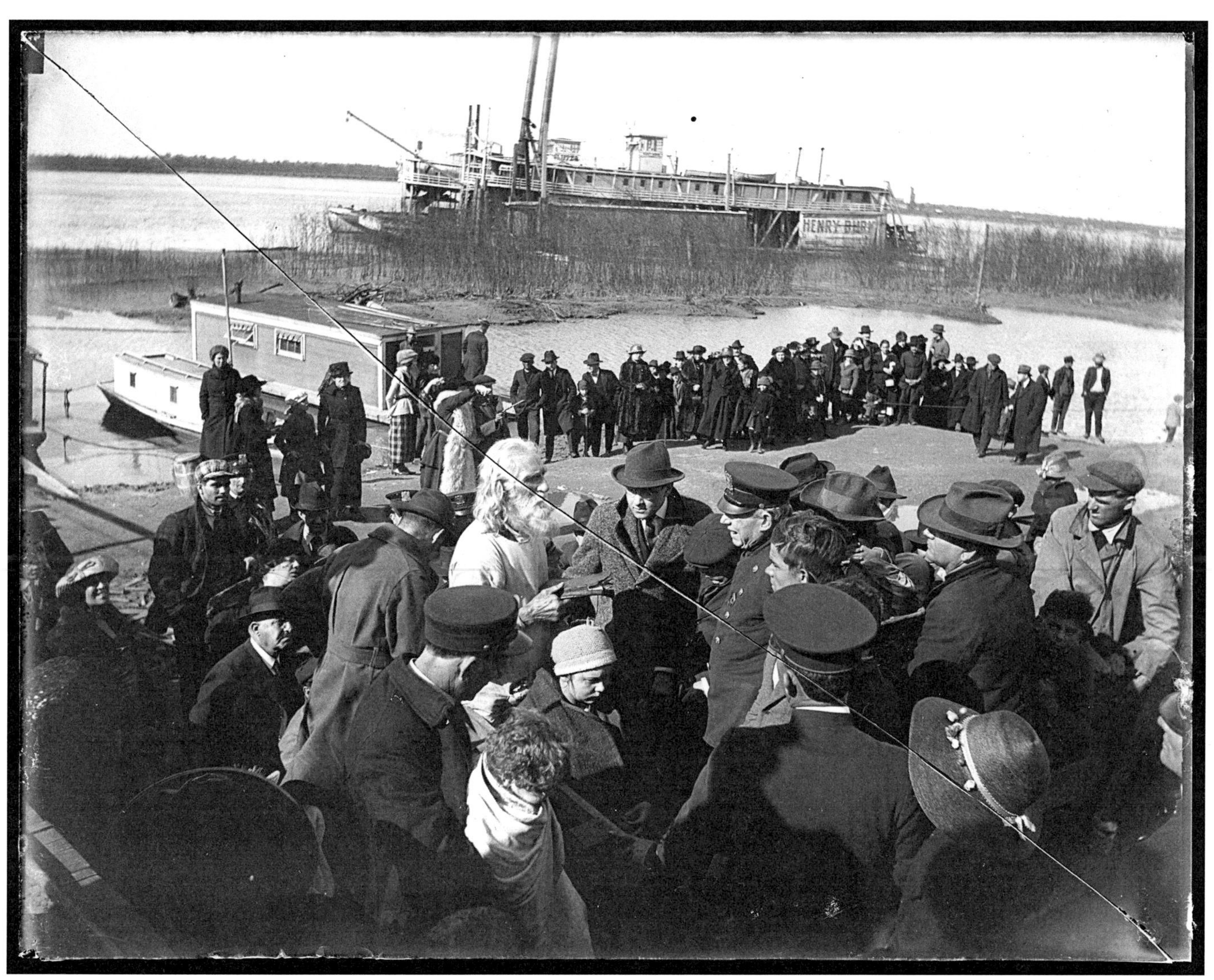

John Cudney known as "Brother Isaiah" speaking to a great crowd while attempting a cure

2003.182.254
March 13, 1920

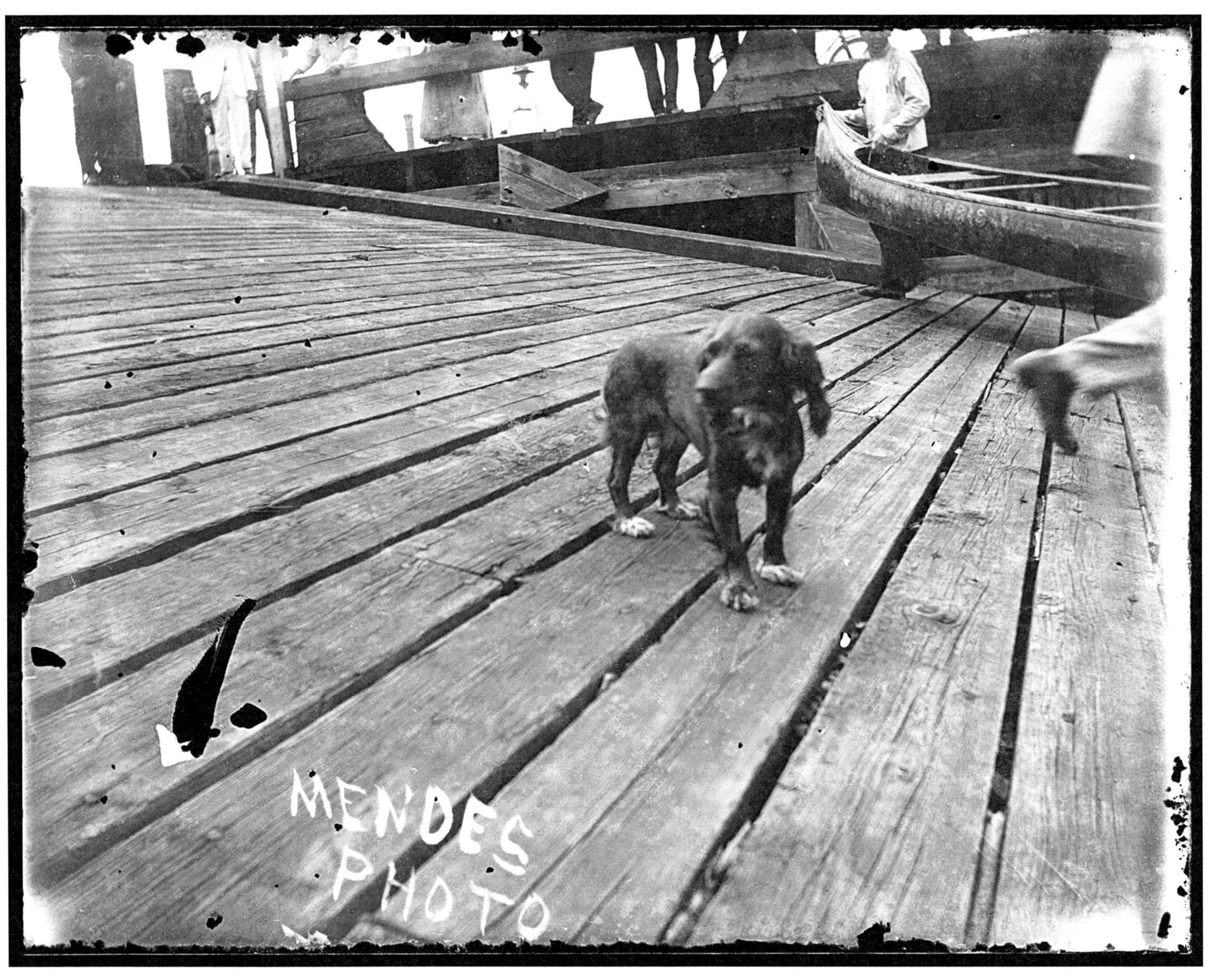

Patsie May

2003.182.143
July 28, 1916

A young mother, and her talking, and walking daughter, a first child came to Our home one day. The child without consulting her mother, or grandmother, stood in the middle of my bed room, and flooded the floor! Think of that! No dog my Mother or I ever had did such a thing — once trained. The entire blame for what that child did was not her's but her lazy own mother. The child was old enough to have been trained, or at least able to inform her mother of her wants, but she did not.

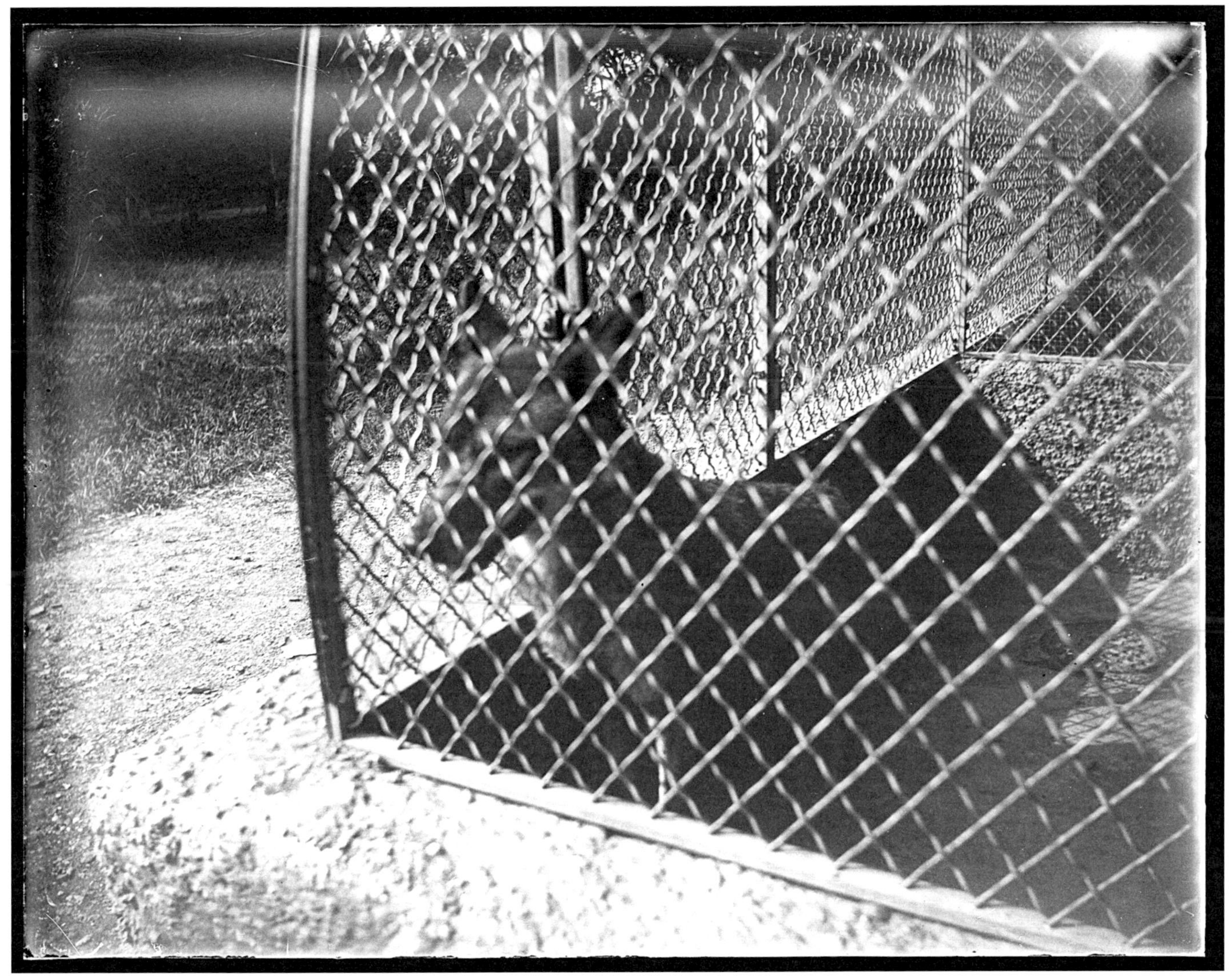

[Uncaptioned. Fox, Audubon Zoo.]

2003.182.508
[ca. 1921]

To train a dog to be clean, you must have patience, understanding, and consideration at all times, and never scold or hit your dog. To be "hard" or cruel is unfair because no young dog can reason like you do. But the time, and trouble you take will be well rewarded by having a clean dog in your home for the rest of the dog's life.
- *Dogs in My Life*, 68-69

[Uncaptioned]

2003.182.466
[ca. 1921]

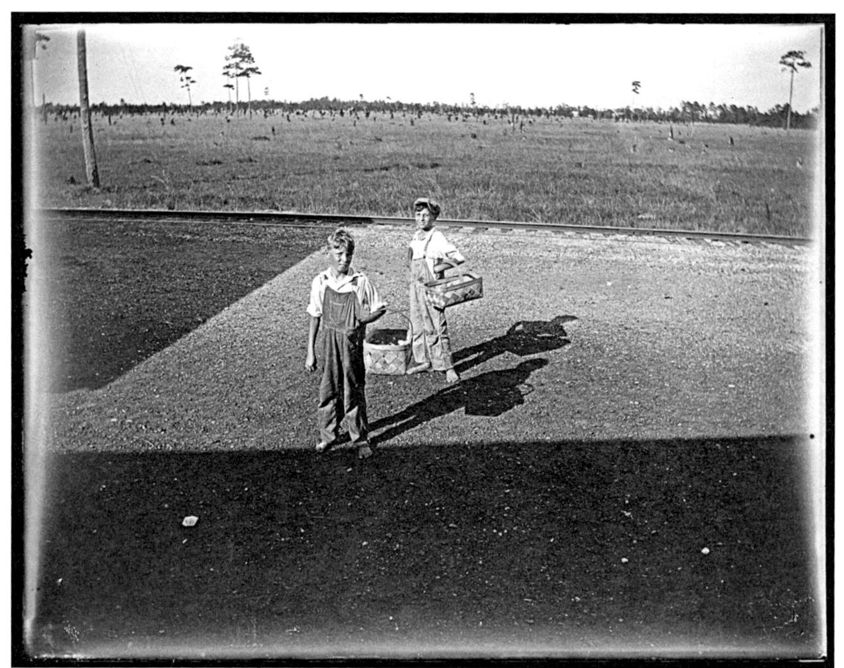

Answer the call.
Taylor.

2003.182.95
May 13, 1917

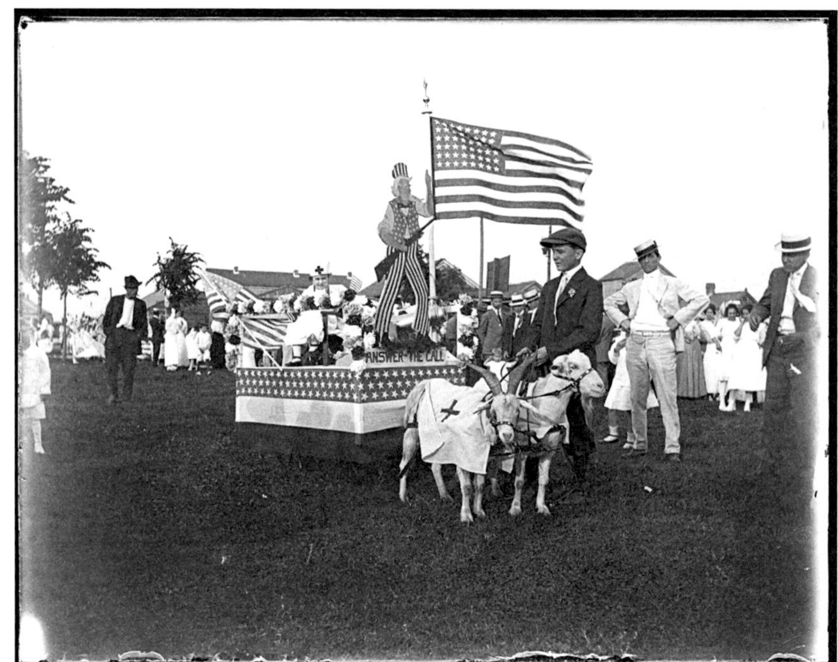

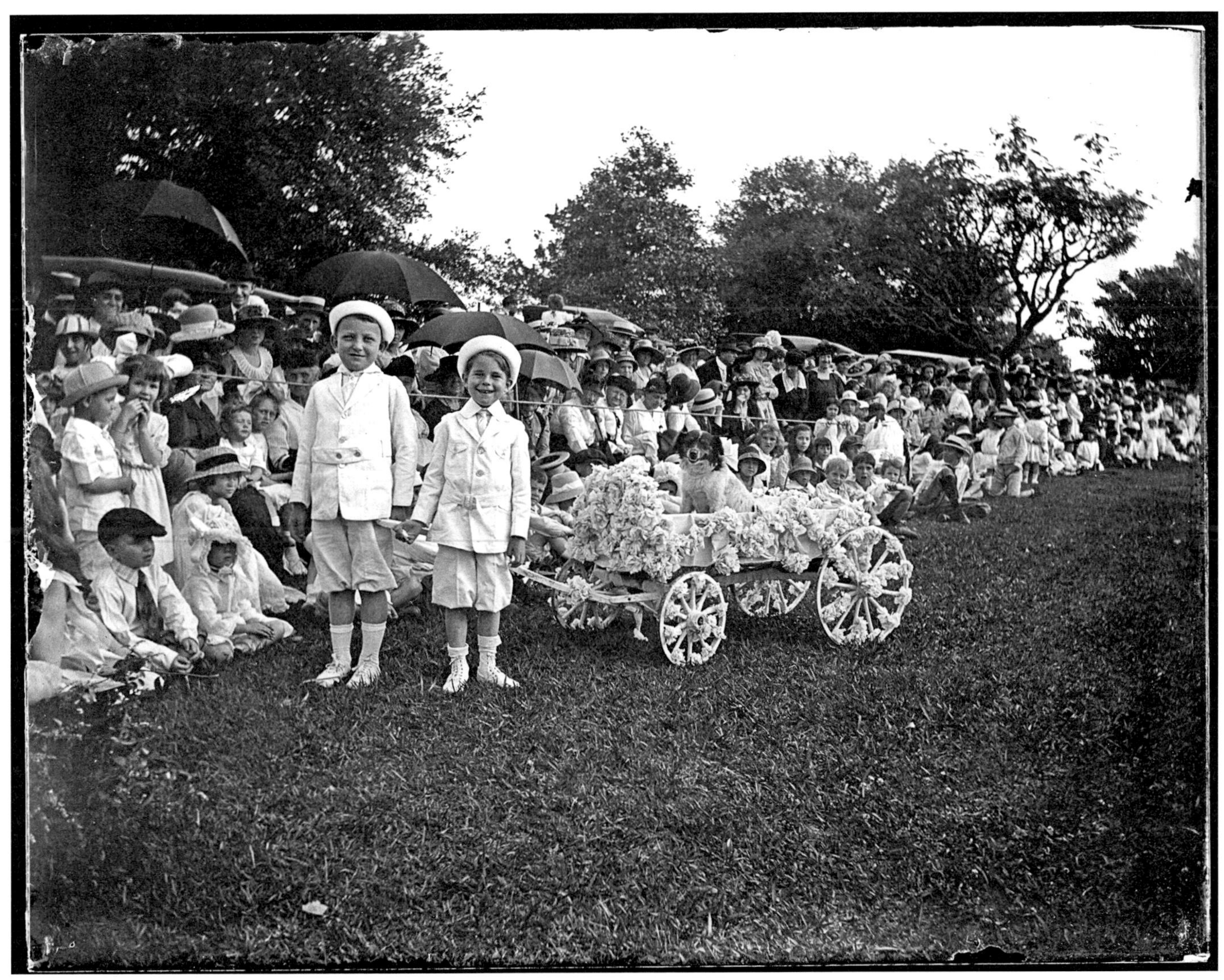

Dog in flower cart drawn by 2 boys. Audubon Festival. Special pose.

2003.182.197
May 2, 1919

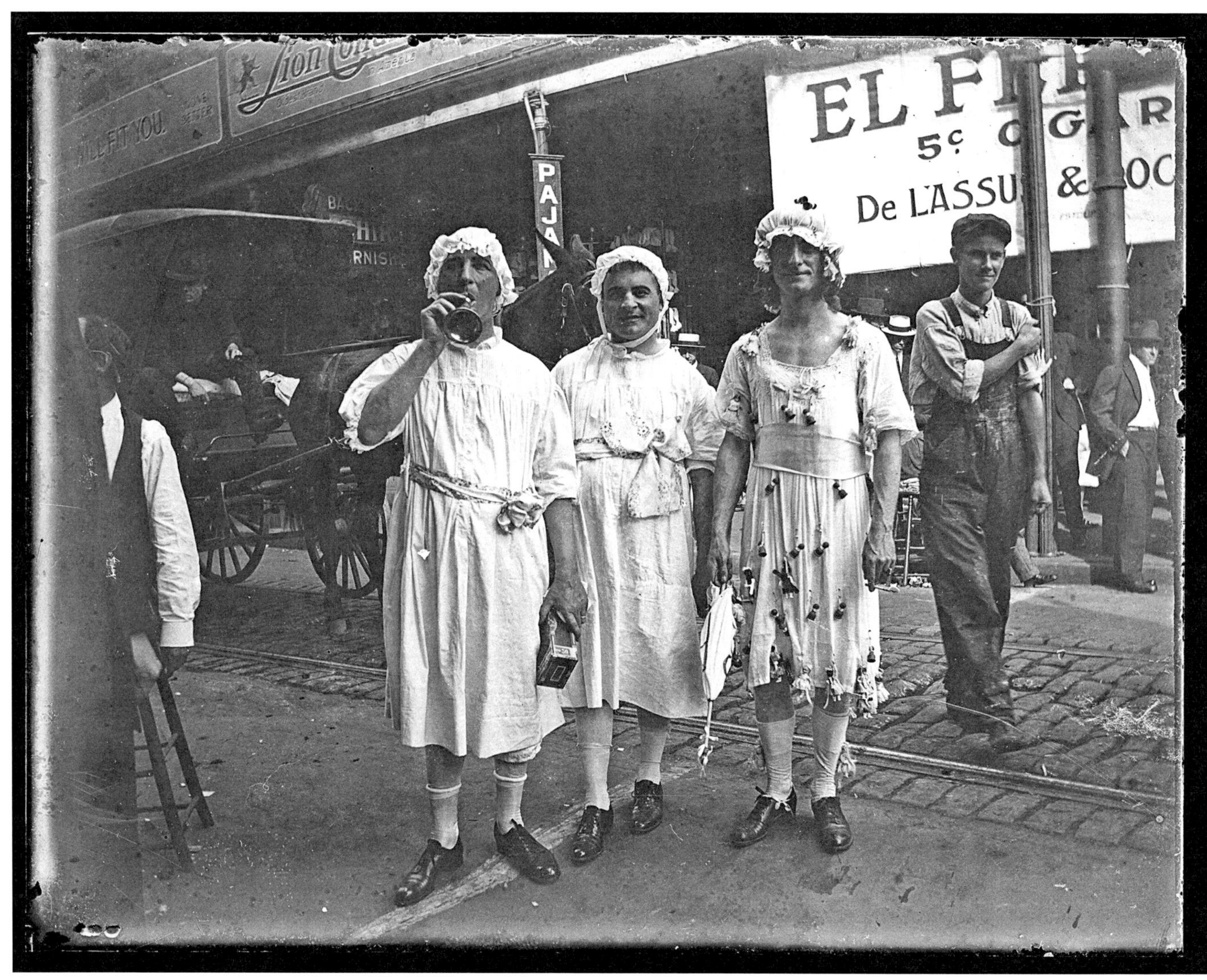

3 Baby Elks

2003.182.20
May 20, 1916

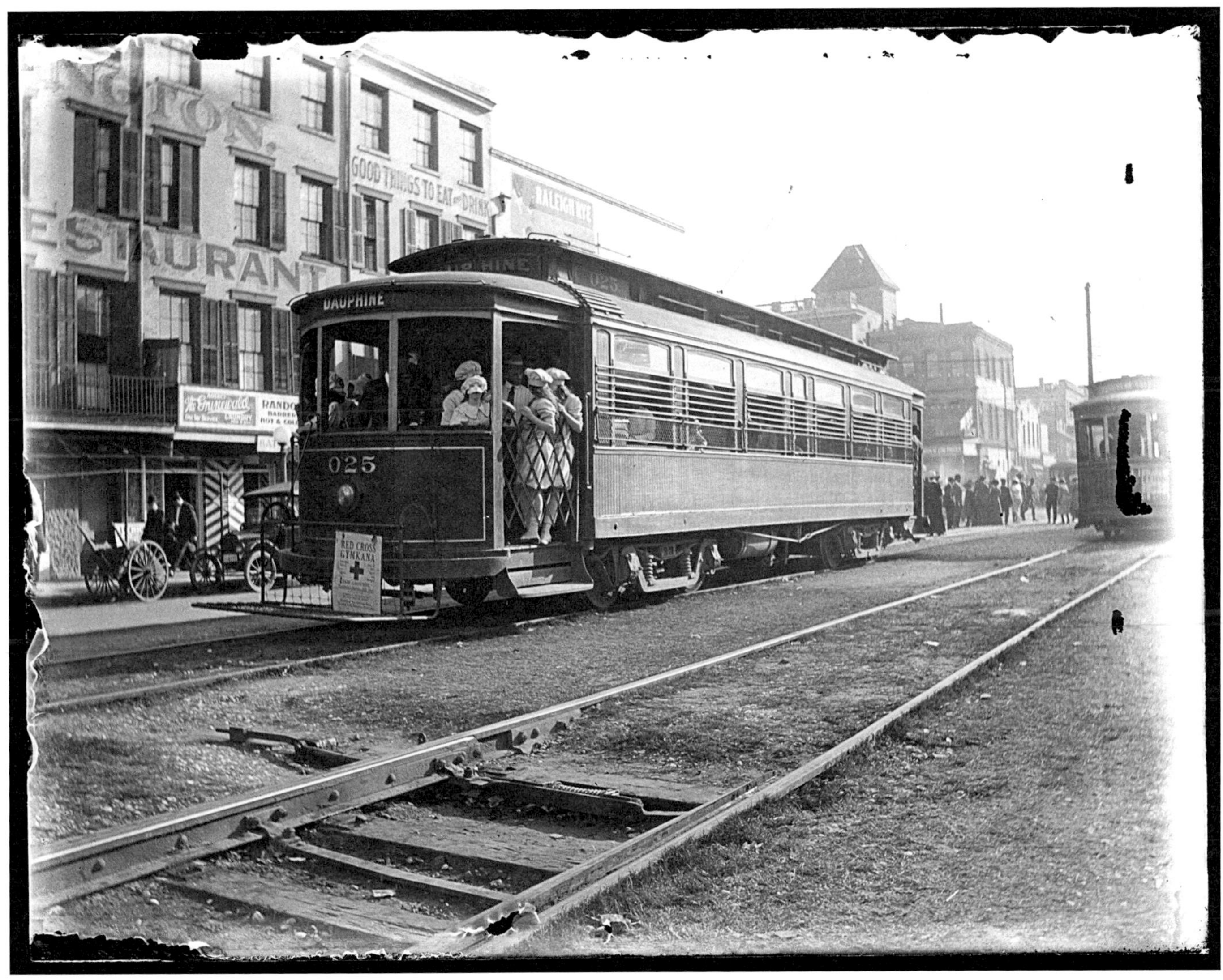

[Uncaptioned. 100 block of N. Rampart Street, Mardi Gras Day]

2003.182.493
[ca. 1918]

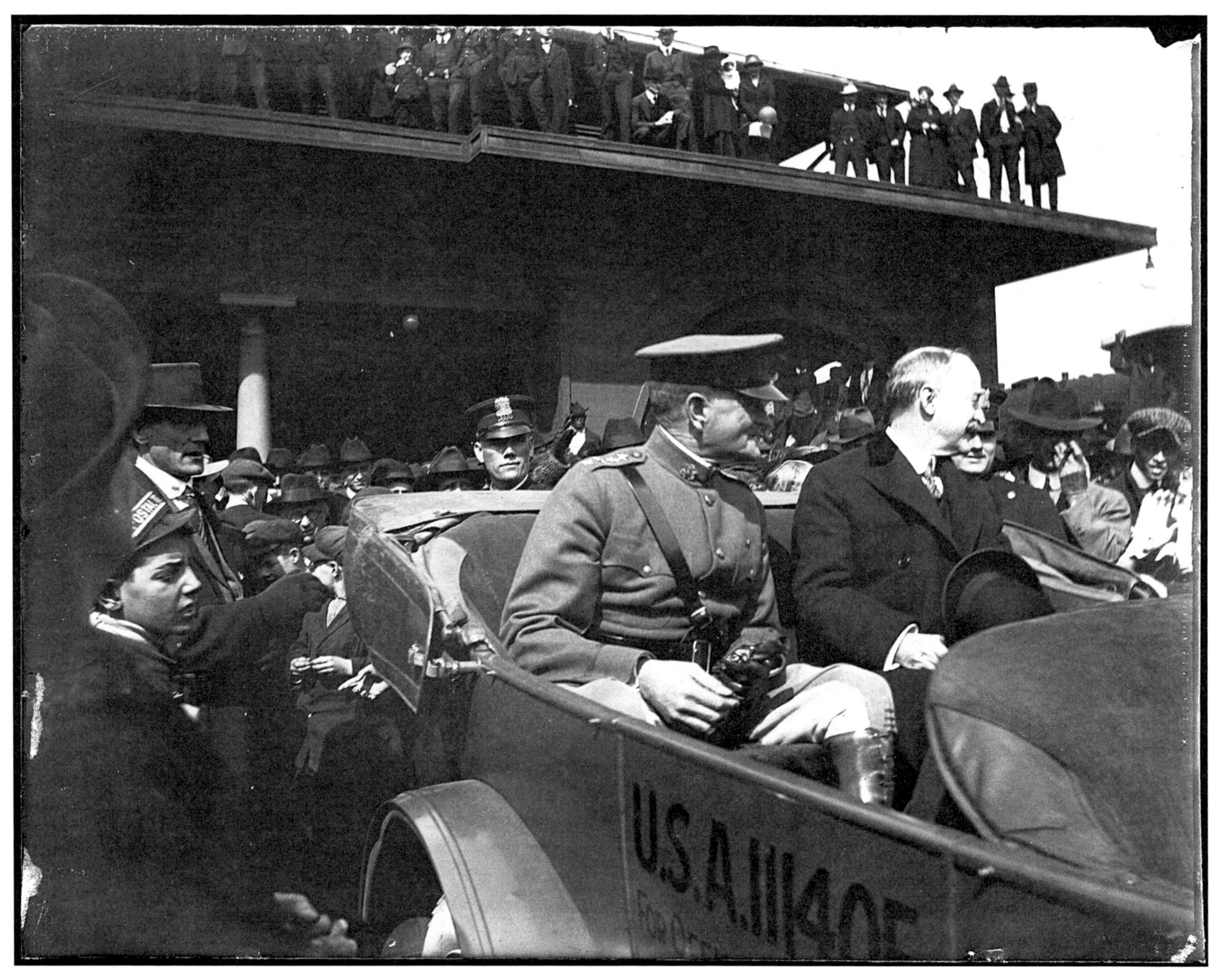

General Pershing in auto with F.B. Hayne. Close up

2003.182.233
February 16, 1920

Smoke hiding an attack with hand grenades

2003.182.249
February 25, 1920

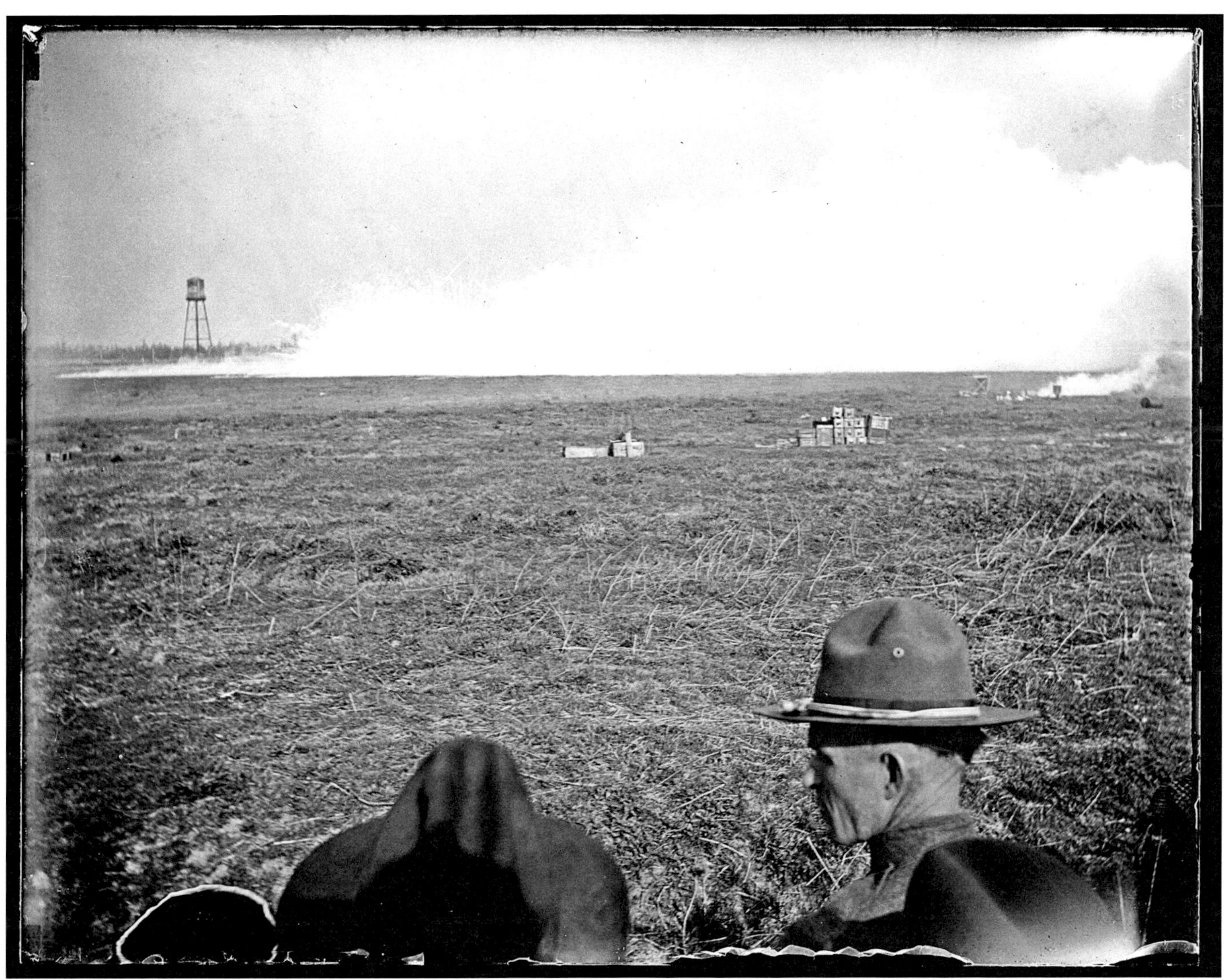

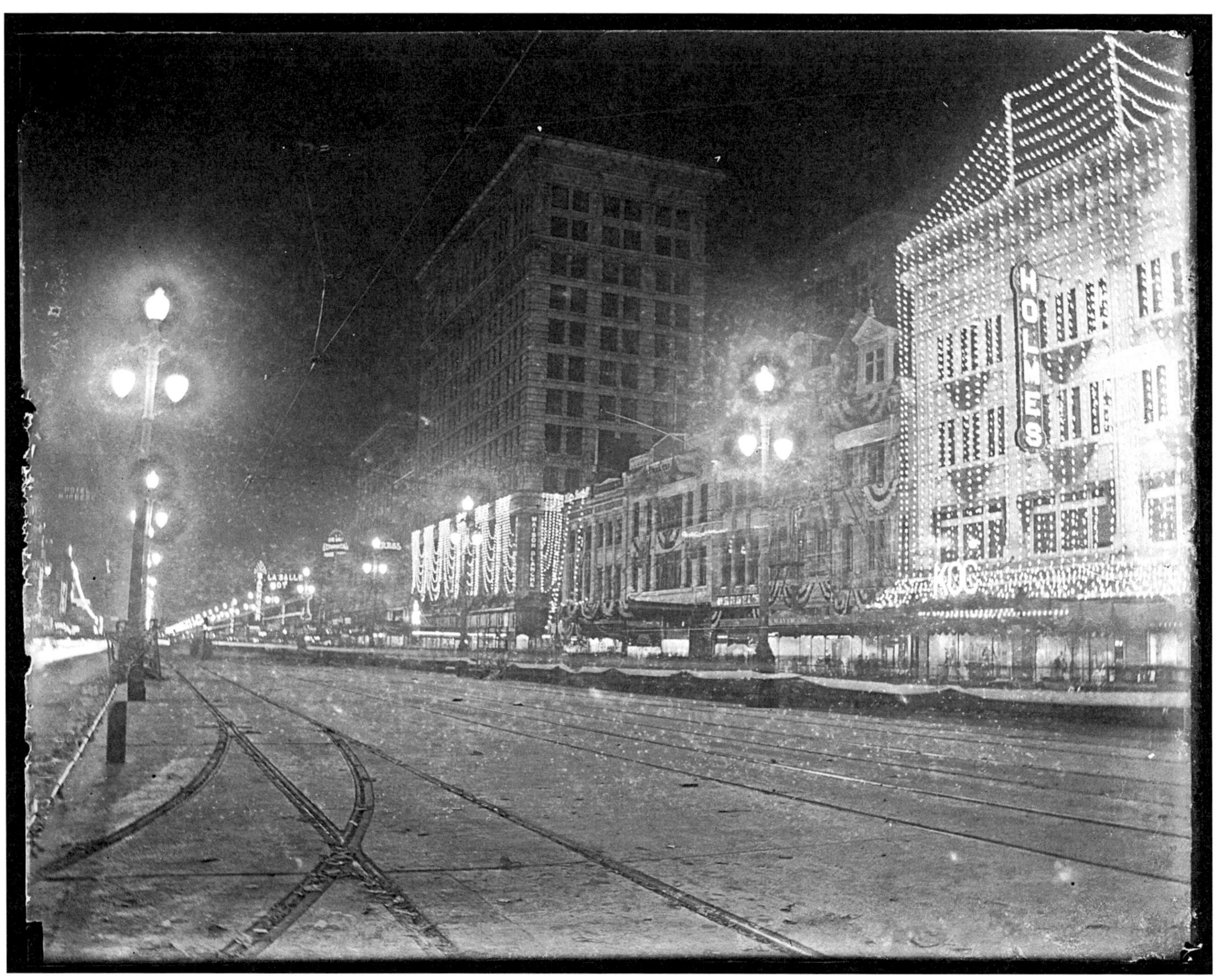

[Uncaptioned. Canal Street at night showing newly established electrical service.]

2003.182.486
[ca. 1930]

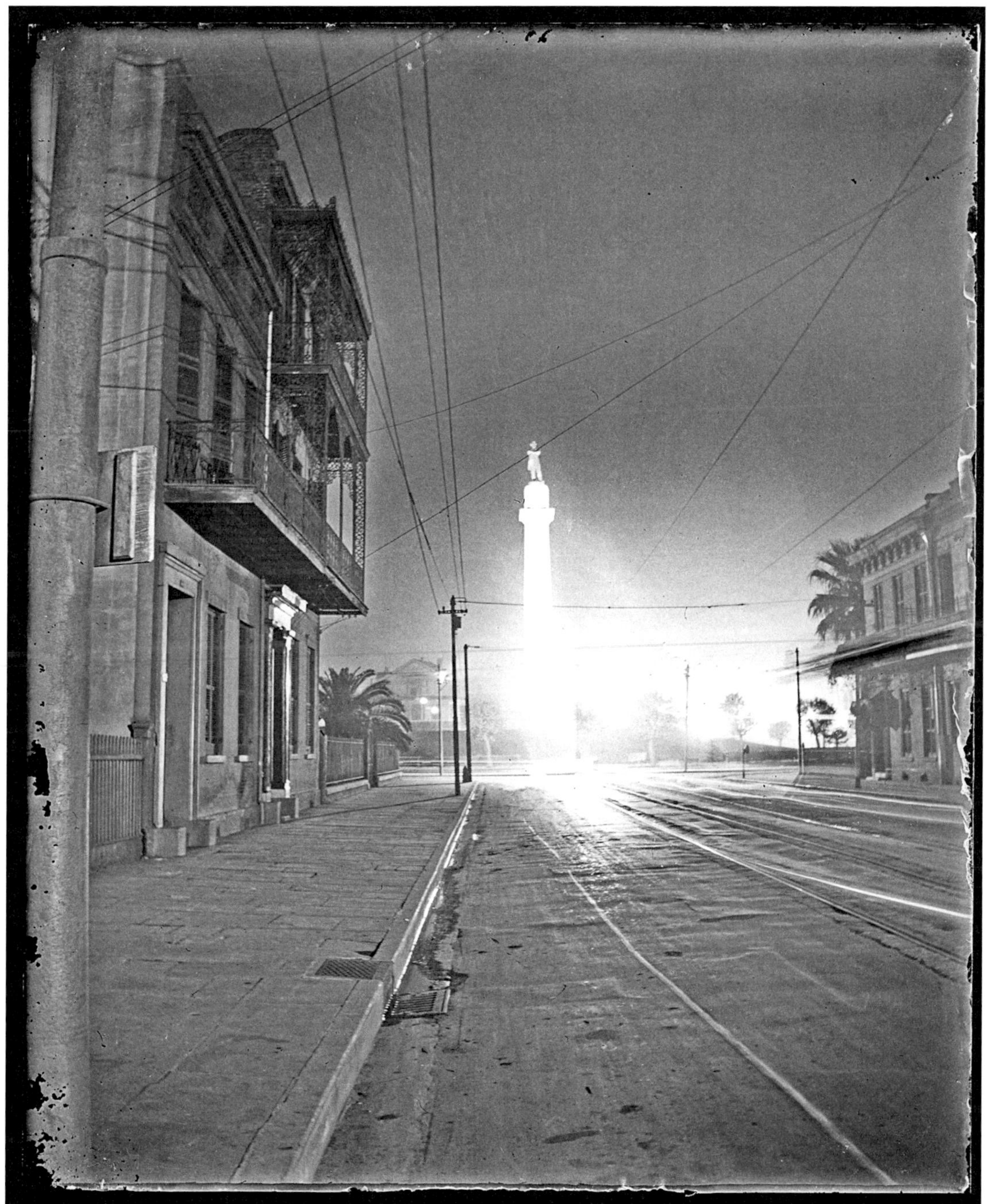

[Uncaptioned. Robert E. Lee Monument at night.]

2003.182.520
[ca. 1925]

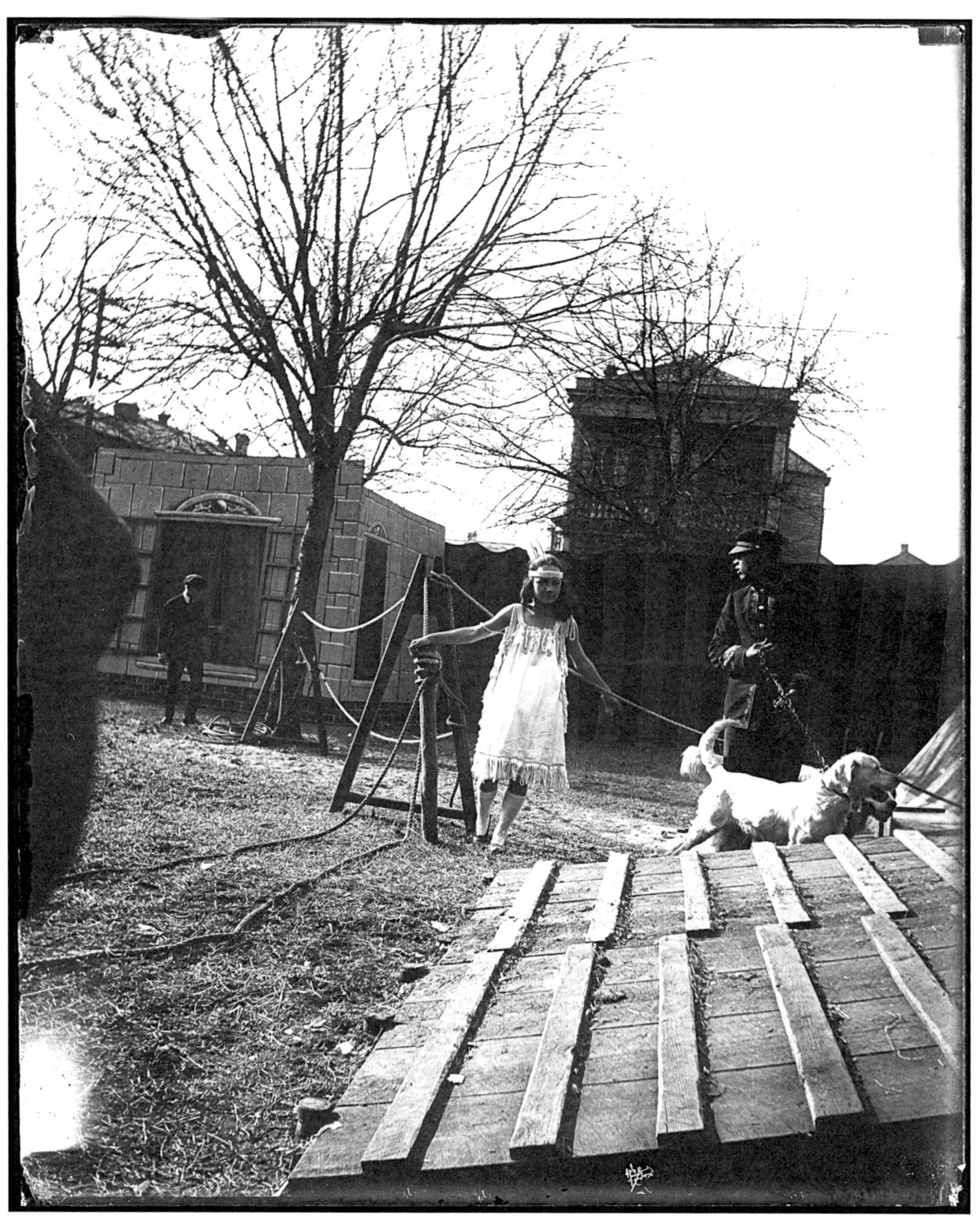

Well meaning people had suggested that I have Sunday dinner with them. But to me the rub was this: I could go, and see a happy family group, and then return to my lonely home — how silent, and empty! Having a vivid imagination I would then compare my situation with the apparently happy family. The same result would be going to the movies, and seeing the ever present "happy ending."

- *Dogs in My Life*, 73

Little girl who poses with trained horse and dogs
S. Claiborne St.

2003.182.238
February 22, 1920

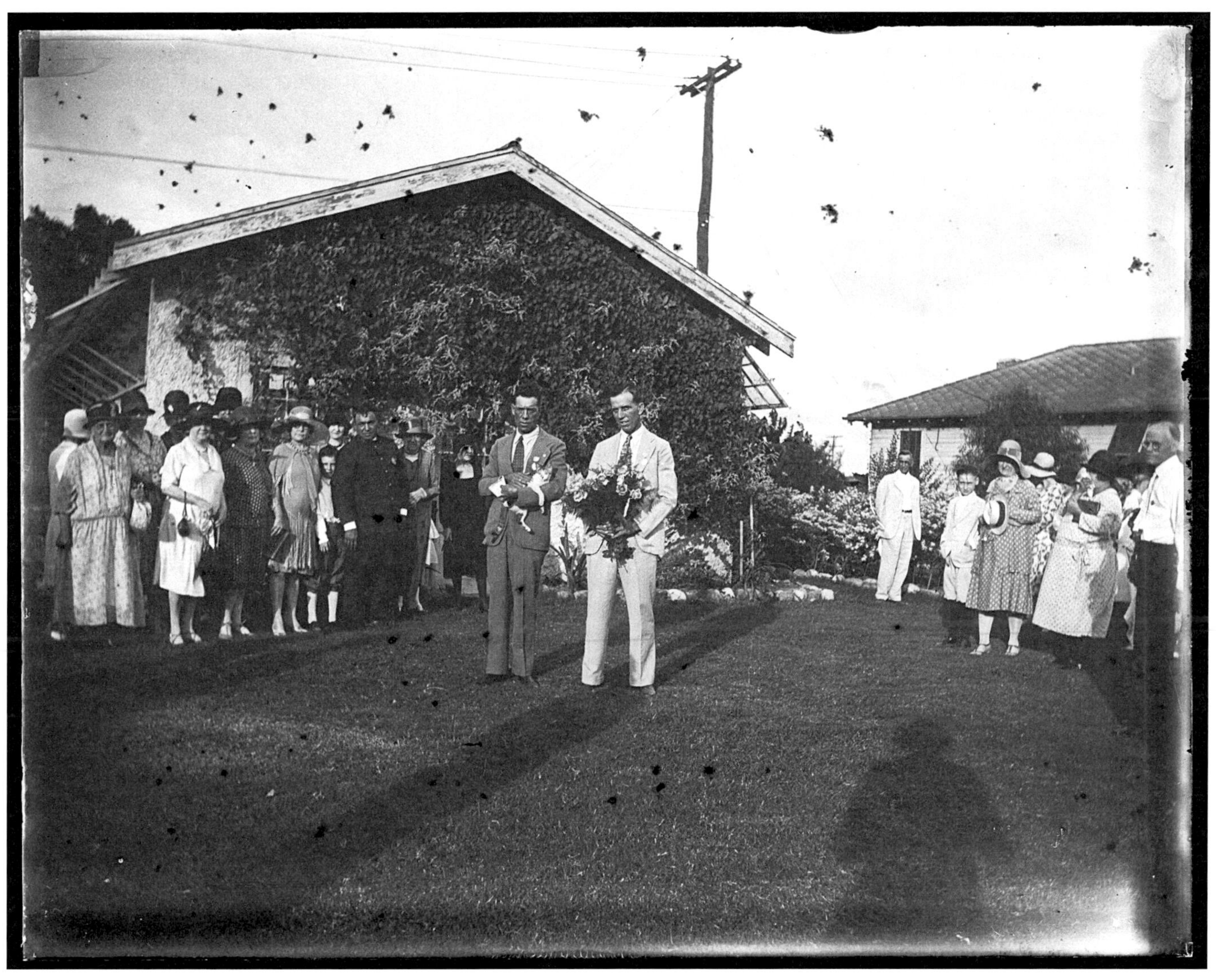

[Uncaptioned]

2003.182.411
[ca. 1930]

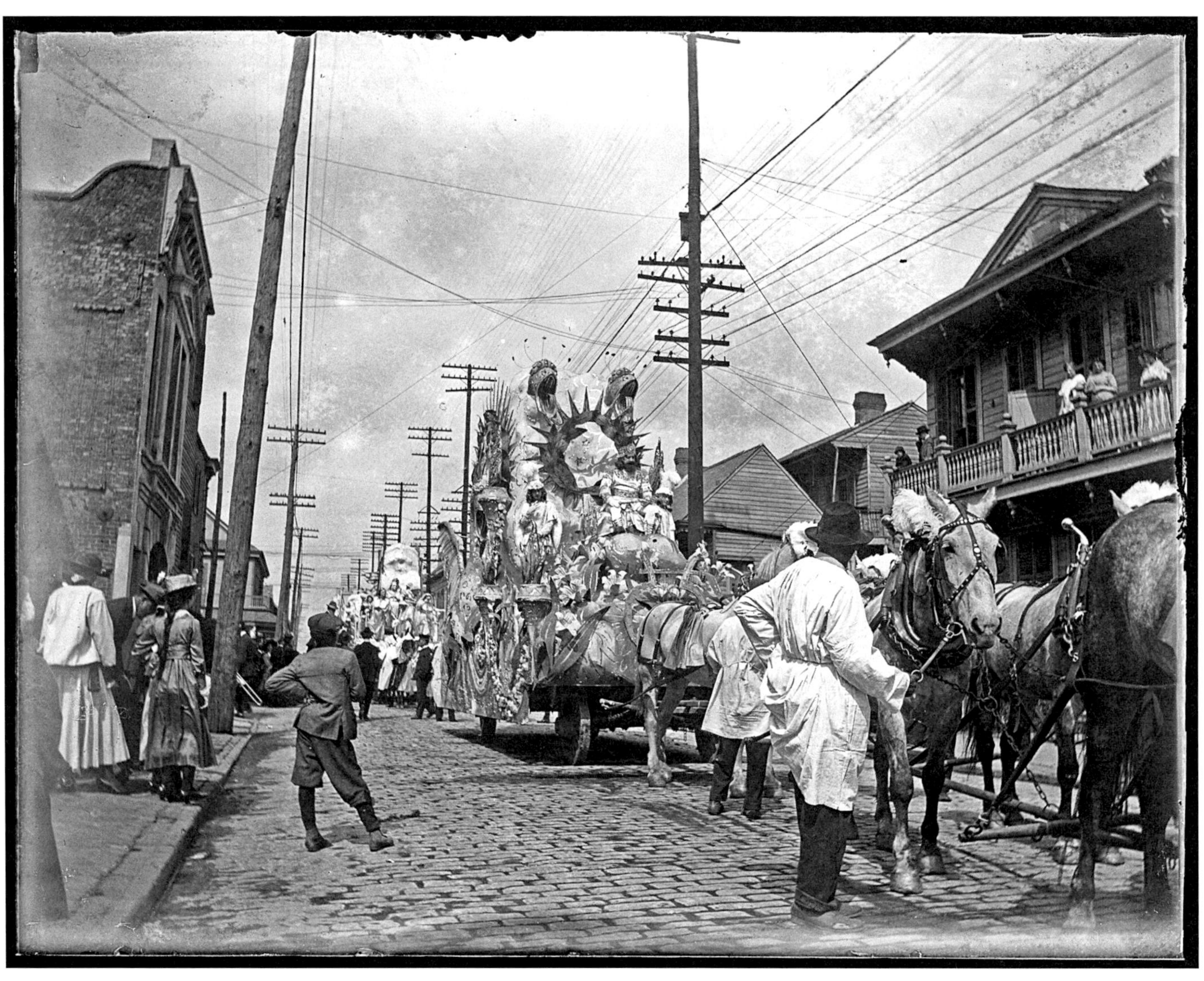

King on float on Calliope St.

2003.182.61
March 7, 1916

Float, Rex Parade

2003.182.396
March 7, 1916

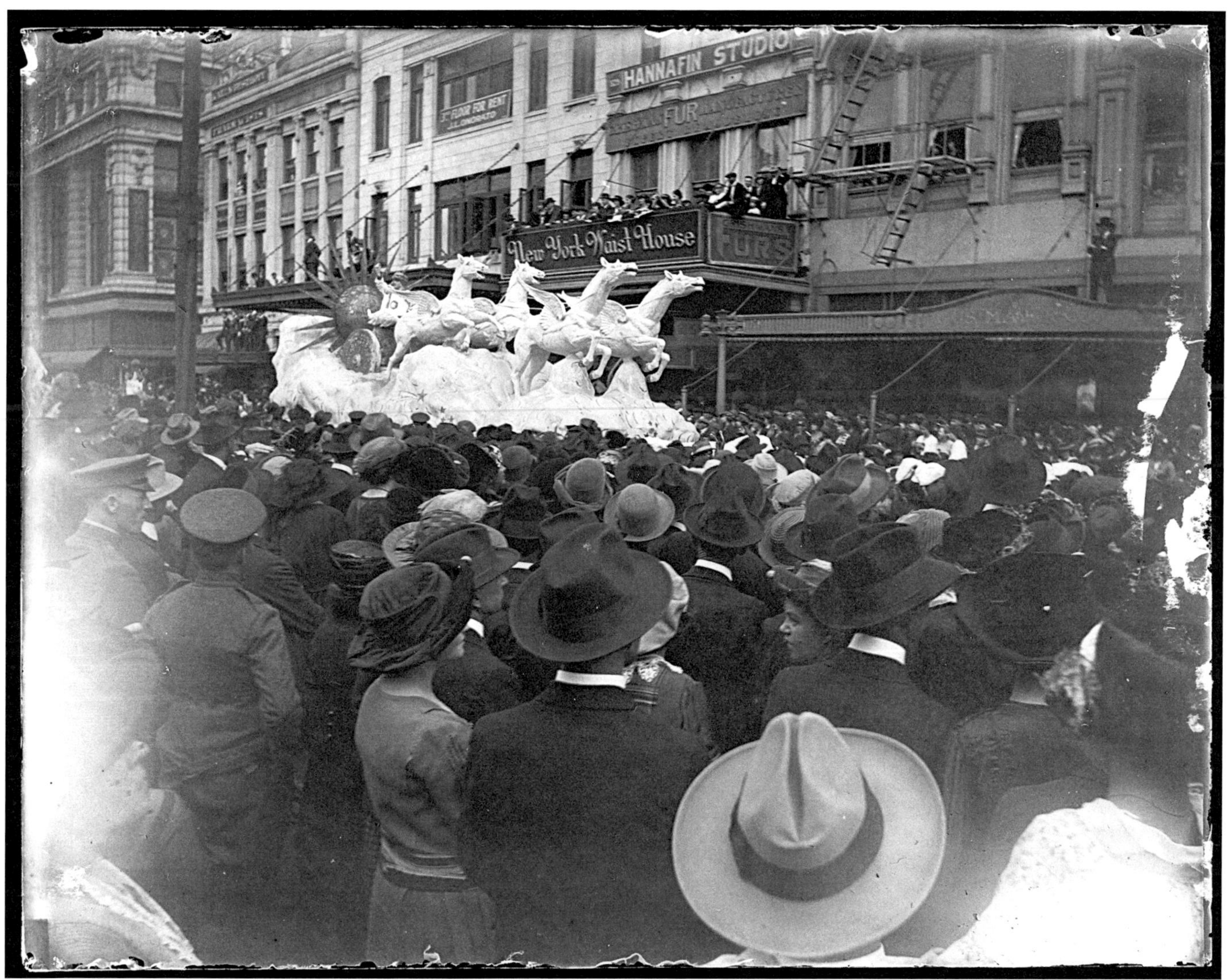

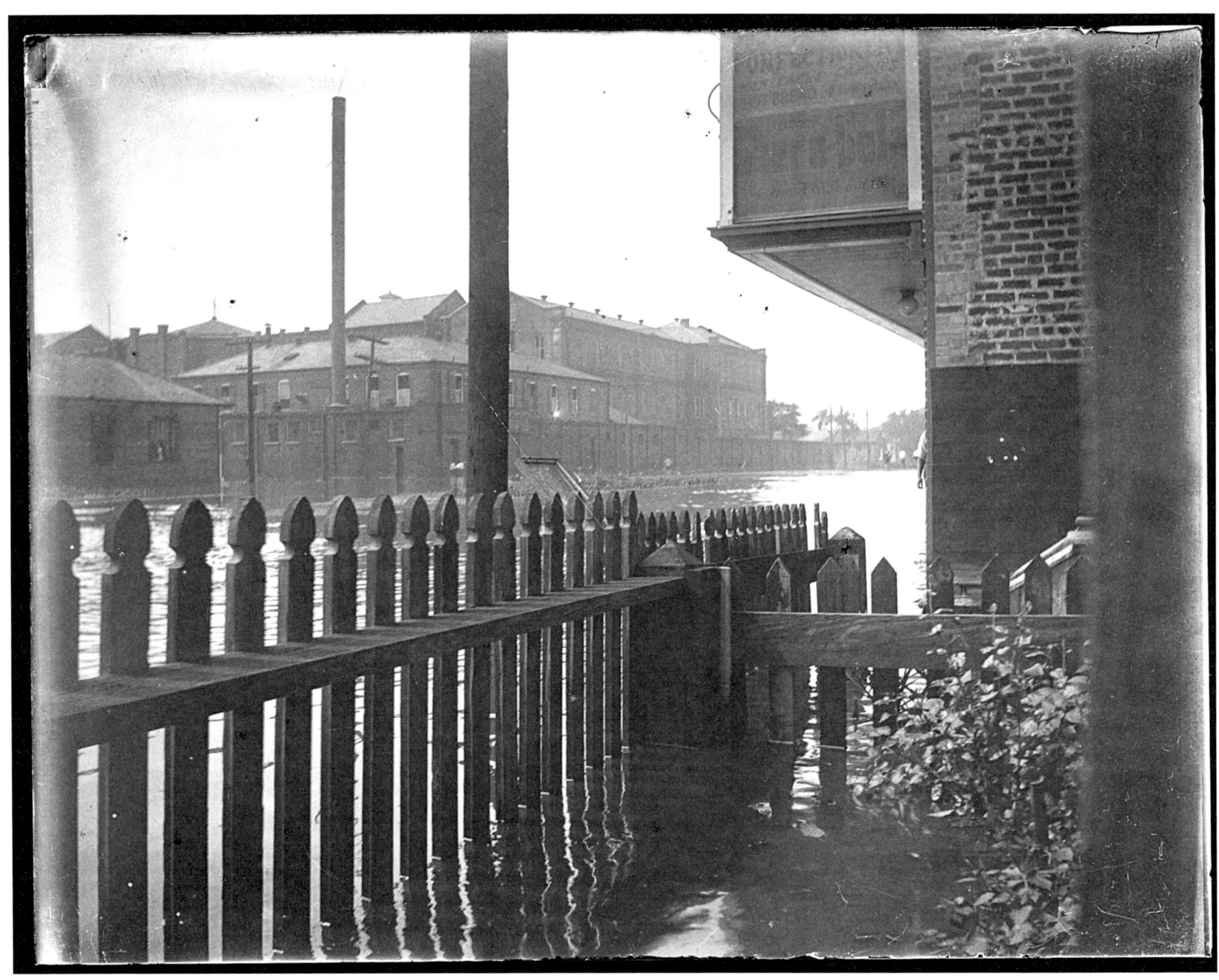

[Uncaptioned. Flood, 400 block of N. Broad St.]

2003.182.447
[ca. 1927]

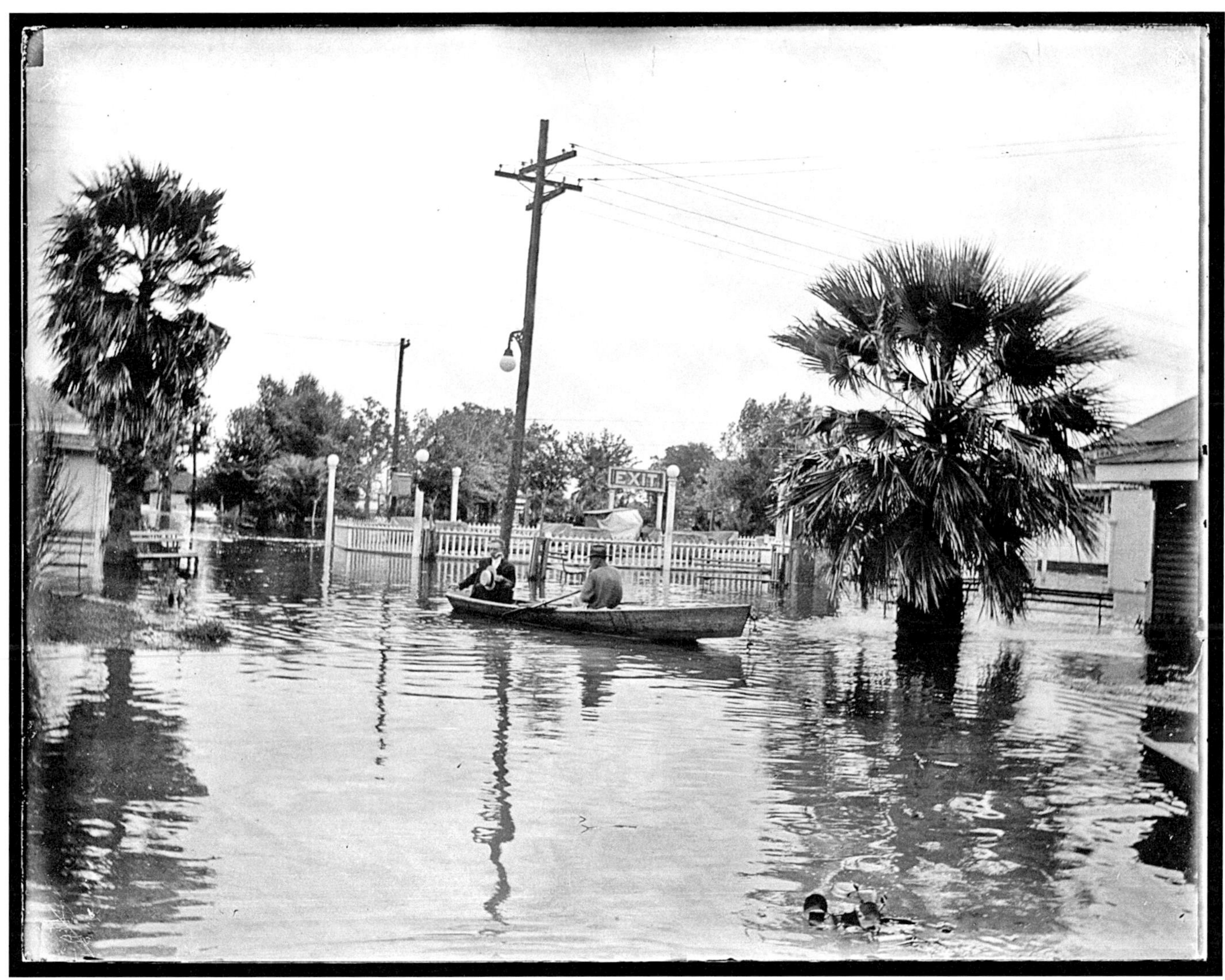

Spanish Fort à la Venice (Due to overflow of Lake)

2003.182.229
[September 14-15,] 1919

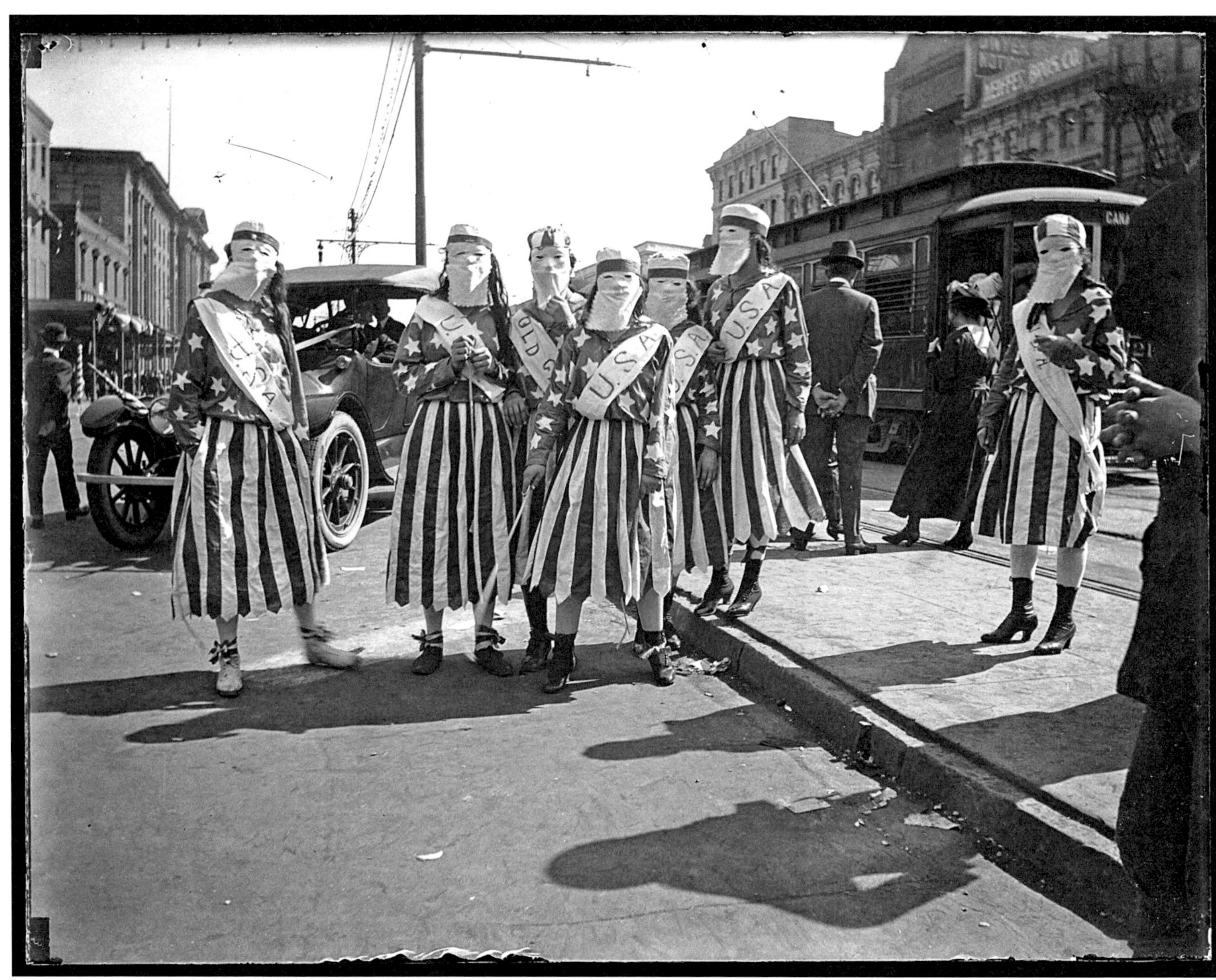

USA Maskers

2003.182.91
1917

Female impersonator

2003.182.159
March 4, 1919

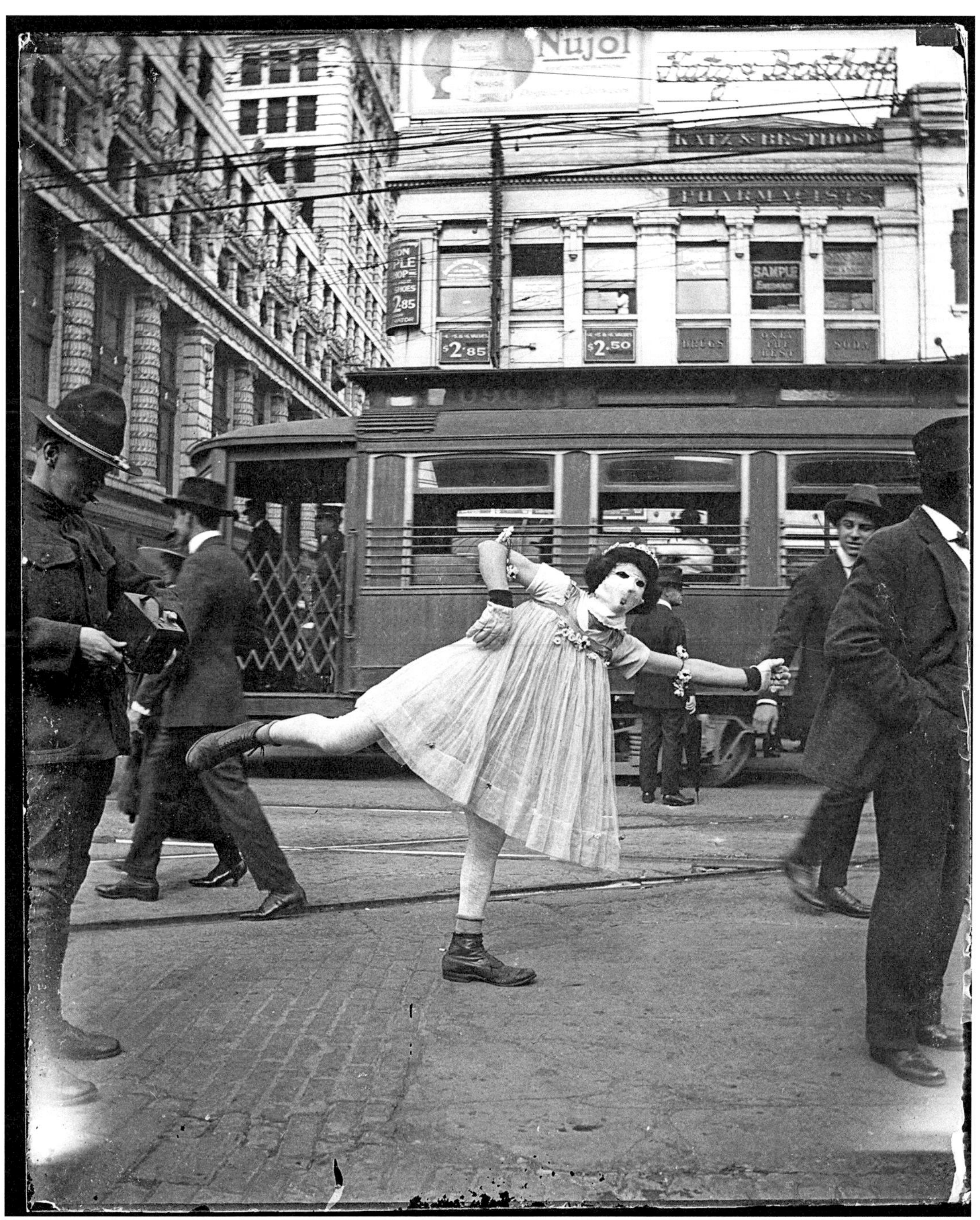

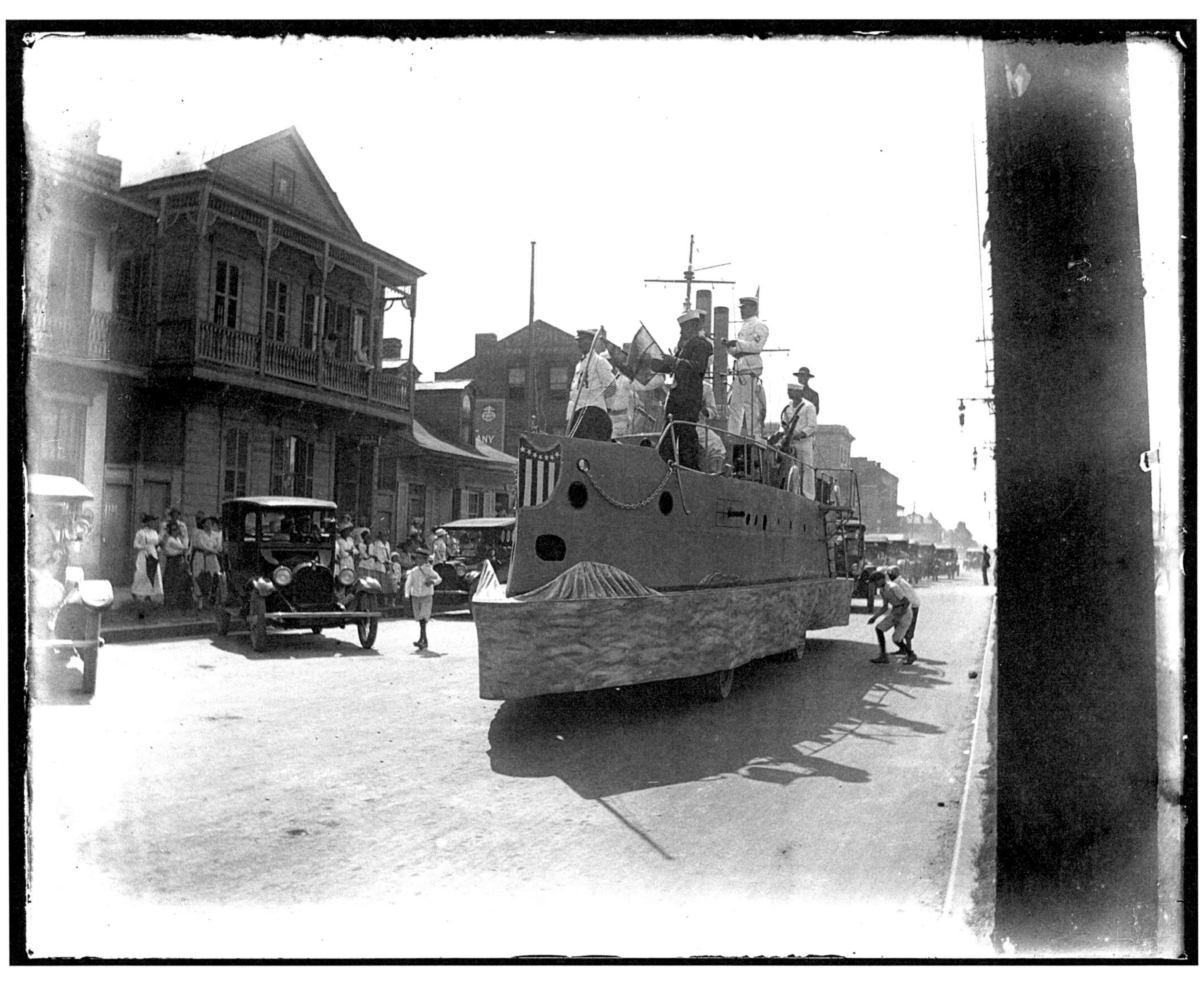

Model of Olympia. Elk Biff Bang Parade

2003.182.120
July [3-4,] 1918

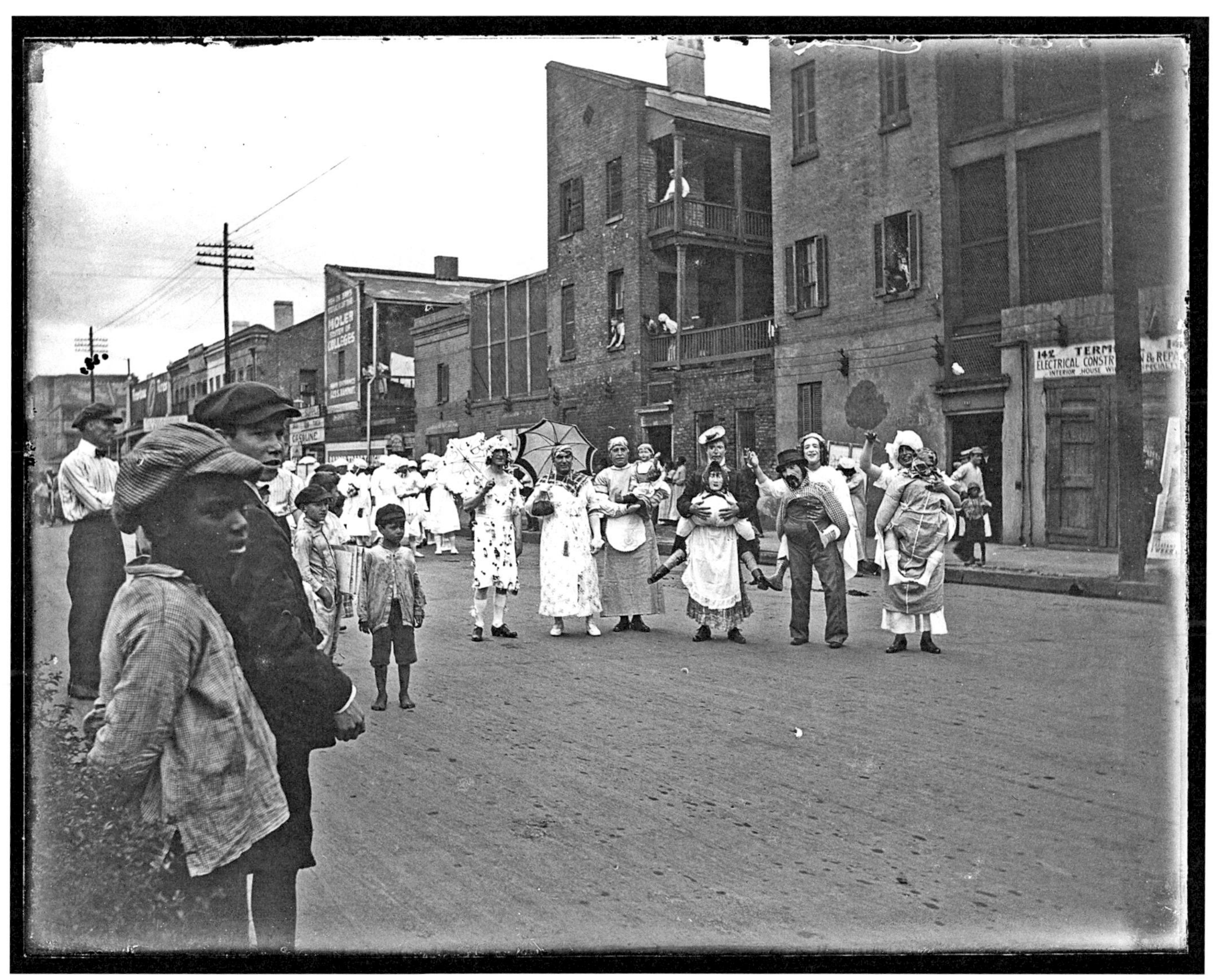

Elk babies

2003.182.28
1916

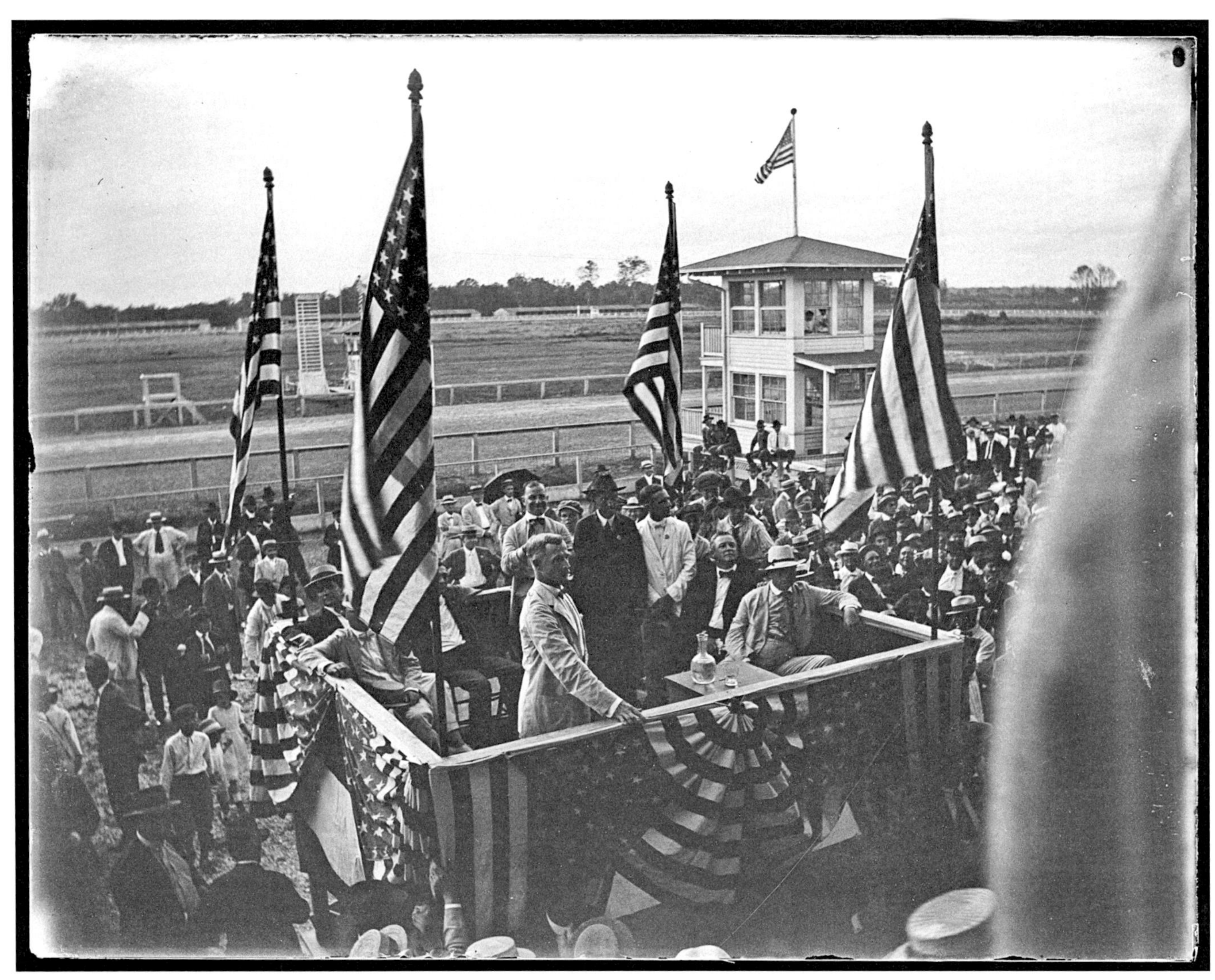

John M. Parker at Jefferson Race Track speaking in the State Campaign

2003.182.405
[No date]

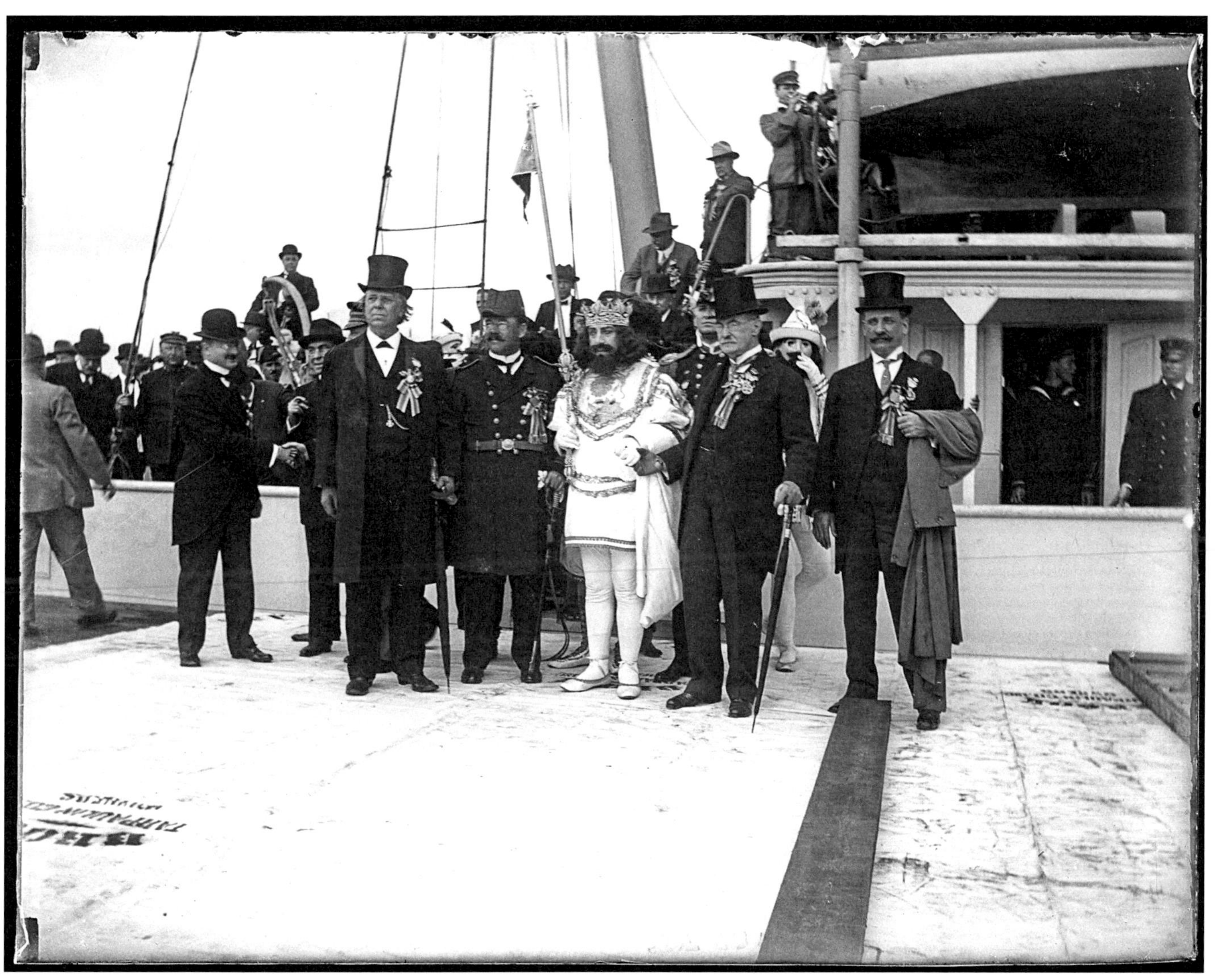

The King and Party

2003.182.84
1917

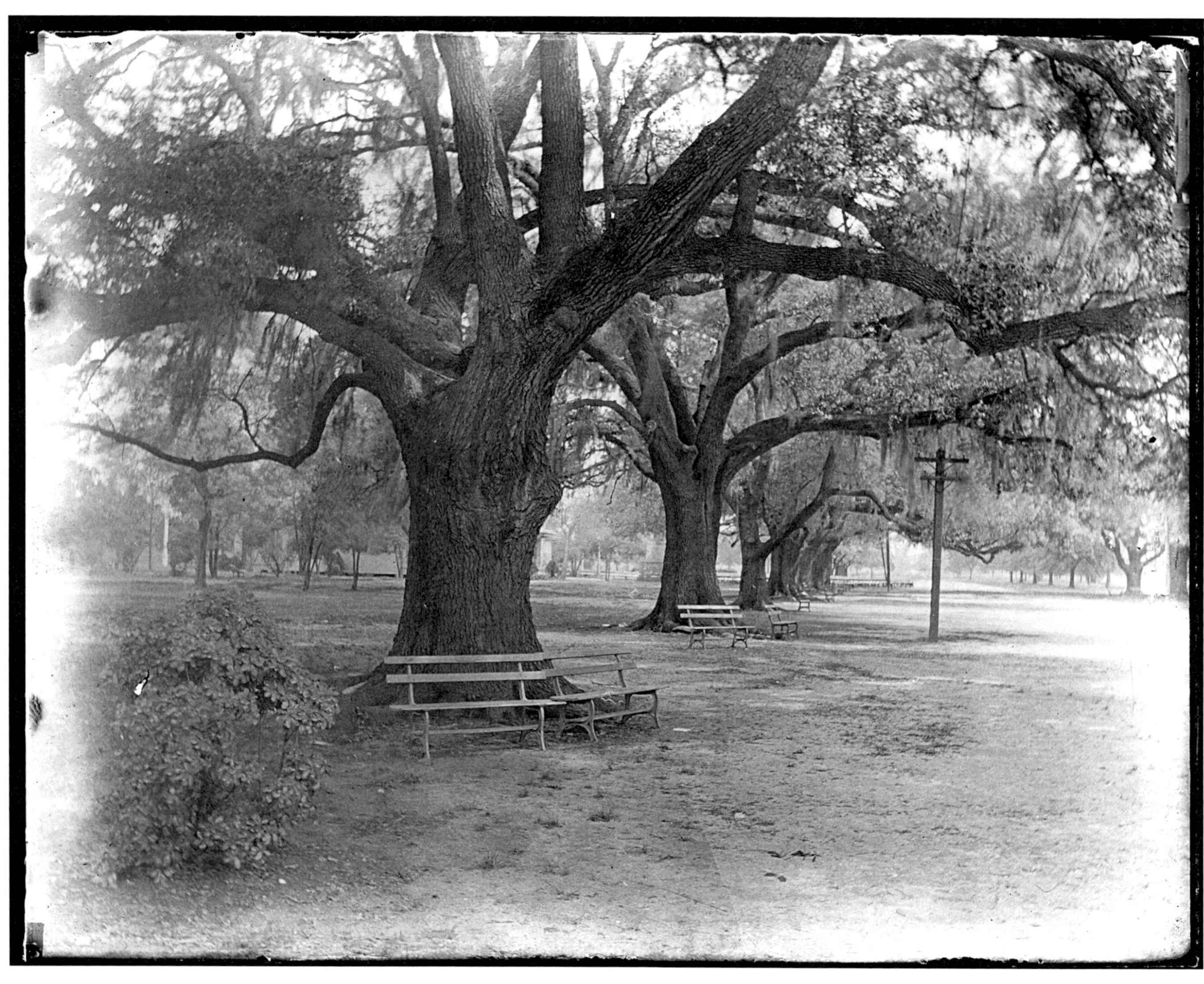

Under the Oaks (looking towards the lake)

2003.182.188
1919

Most any mother of several small children, could if she was frank enough to admit it out match the list I have made of some of the things Don put in his mouth, and I took away from him, like:— Clam shell, piece of Lifebuoy soap, tin can covers (rusty), bit of china, small stone, china tree berries, piece of flat glass, old razor blade. Any large city hospital can give you a list, and might show you things that have been removed from the stomachs of small children that will be more incredible than the things Don might have swallowed had I not been vigilant. Some people who claim to know all about dogs will likely tell you that when dogs, especially young ones, put foreign things in their mouth it is a sign of worms or indigestion. But I assert those claims are 99 out 100 all wrong. The many long years experience I have had with dogs living right inside the rooms of Our homes — I should have the answer.

- *Dogs in My Life*, 81

[Uncaptioned]

2003.182.586
[ca. 1921]

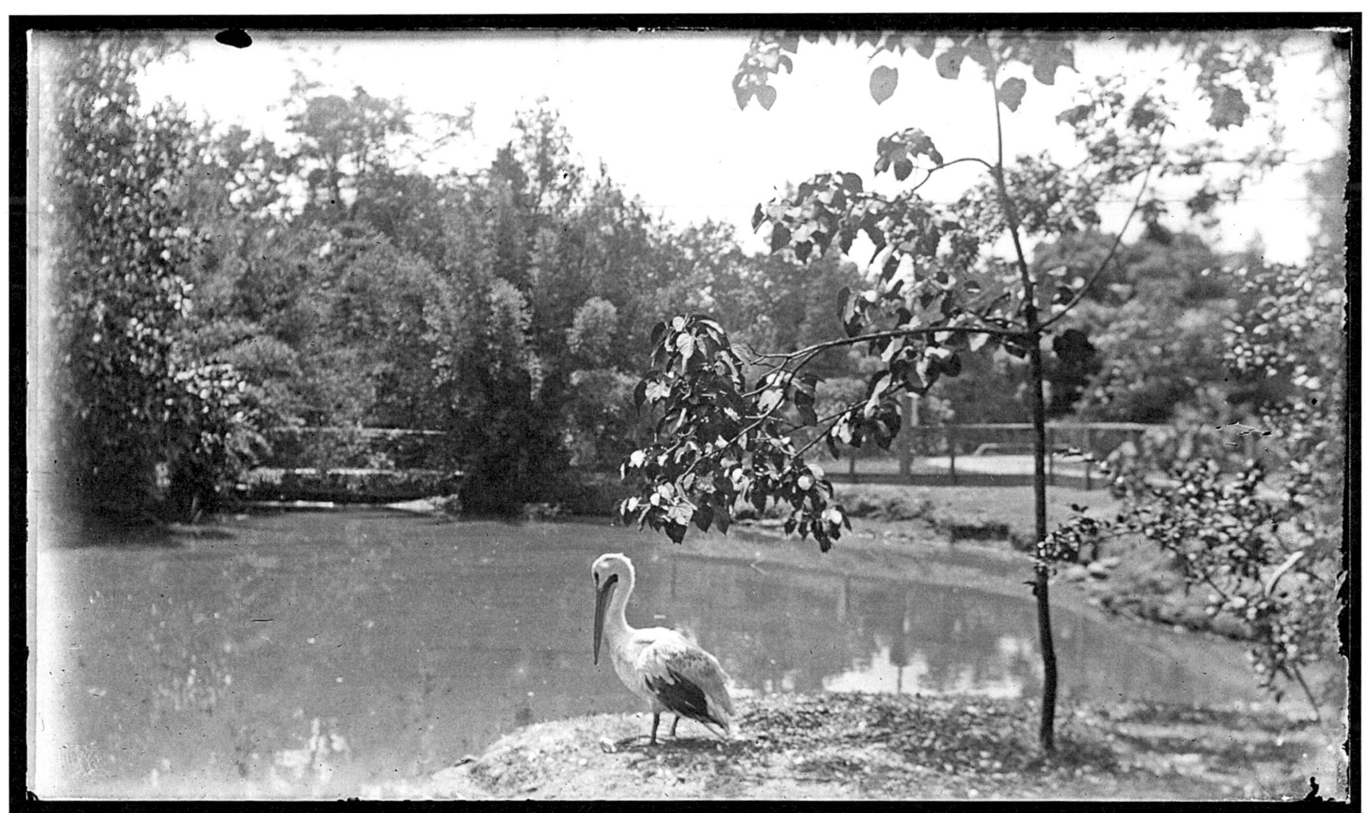

Spot
Copy made from a photo
Photo of enlargement
showing dog only

2003.182.553
April 18, 1919

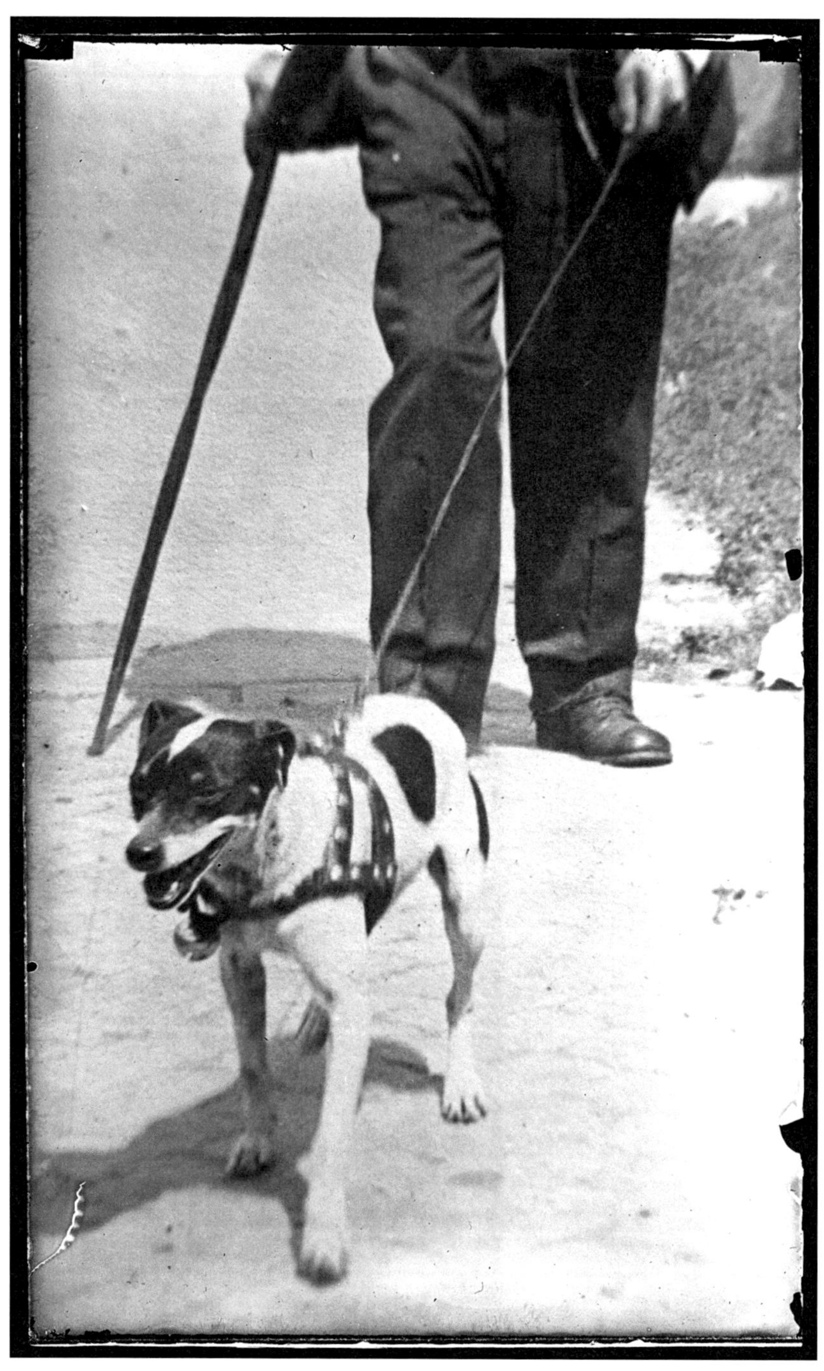

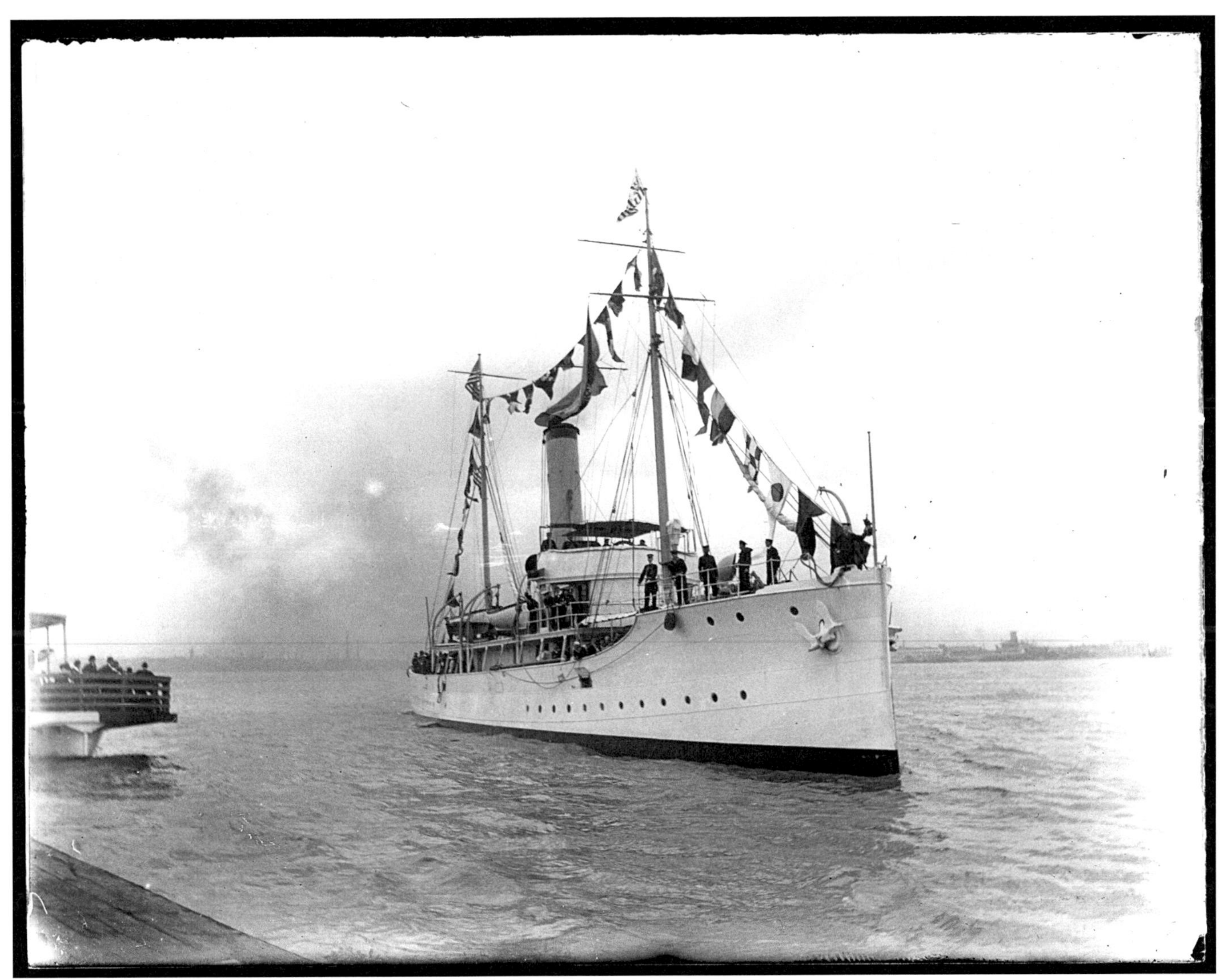

The Royal Yacht nears landing

2003.182.83
1917

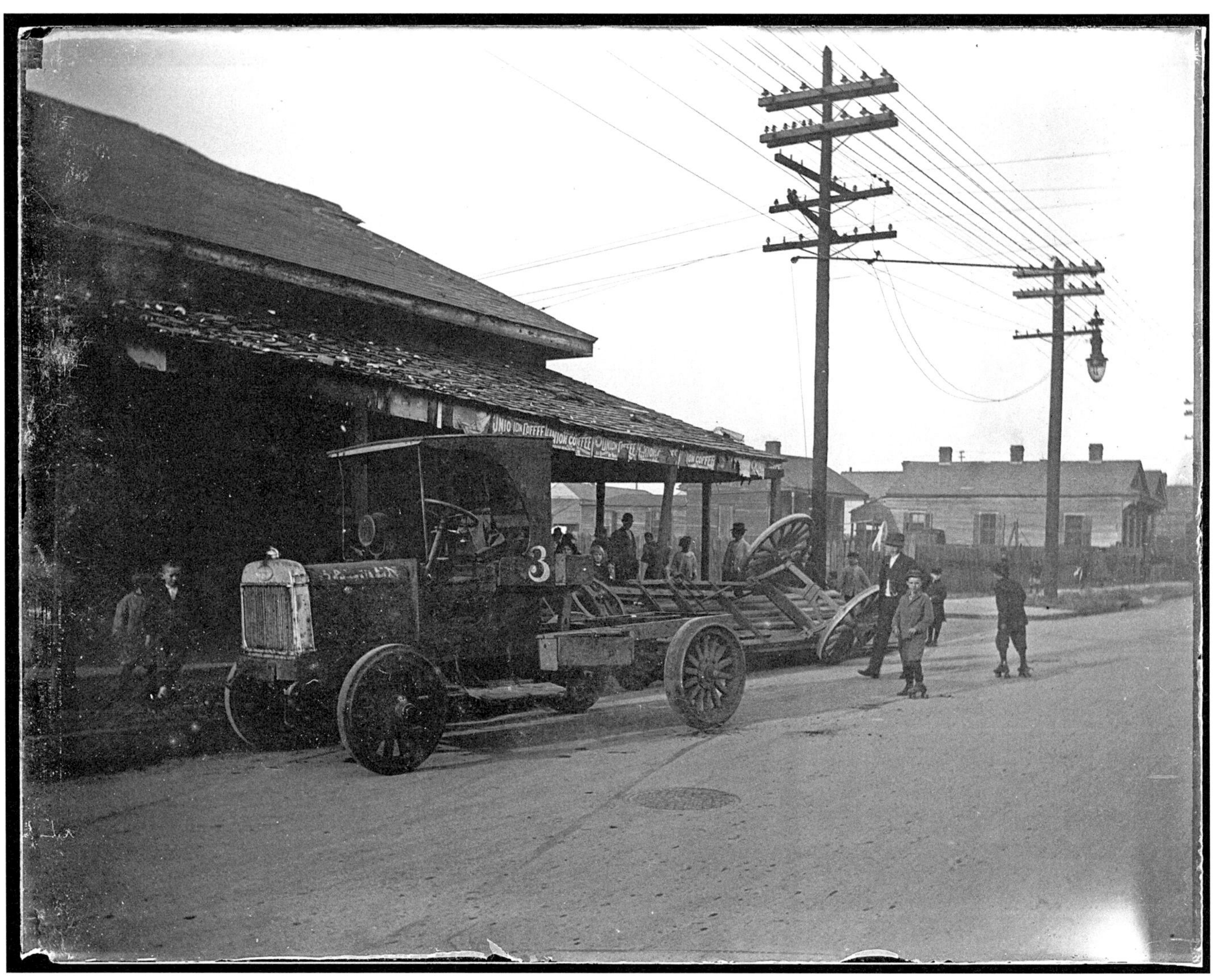

Overturned lumber trailer

2003.182.139
January 11, 1919

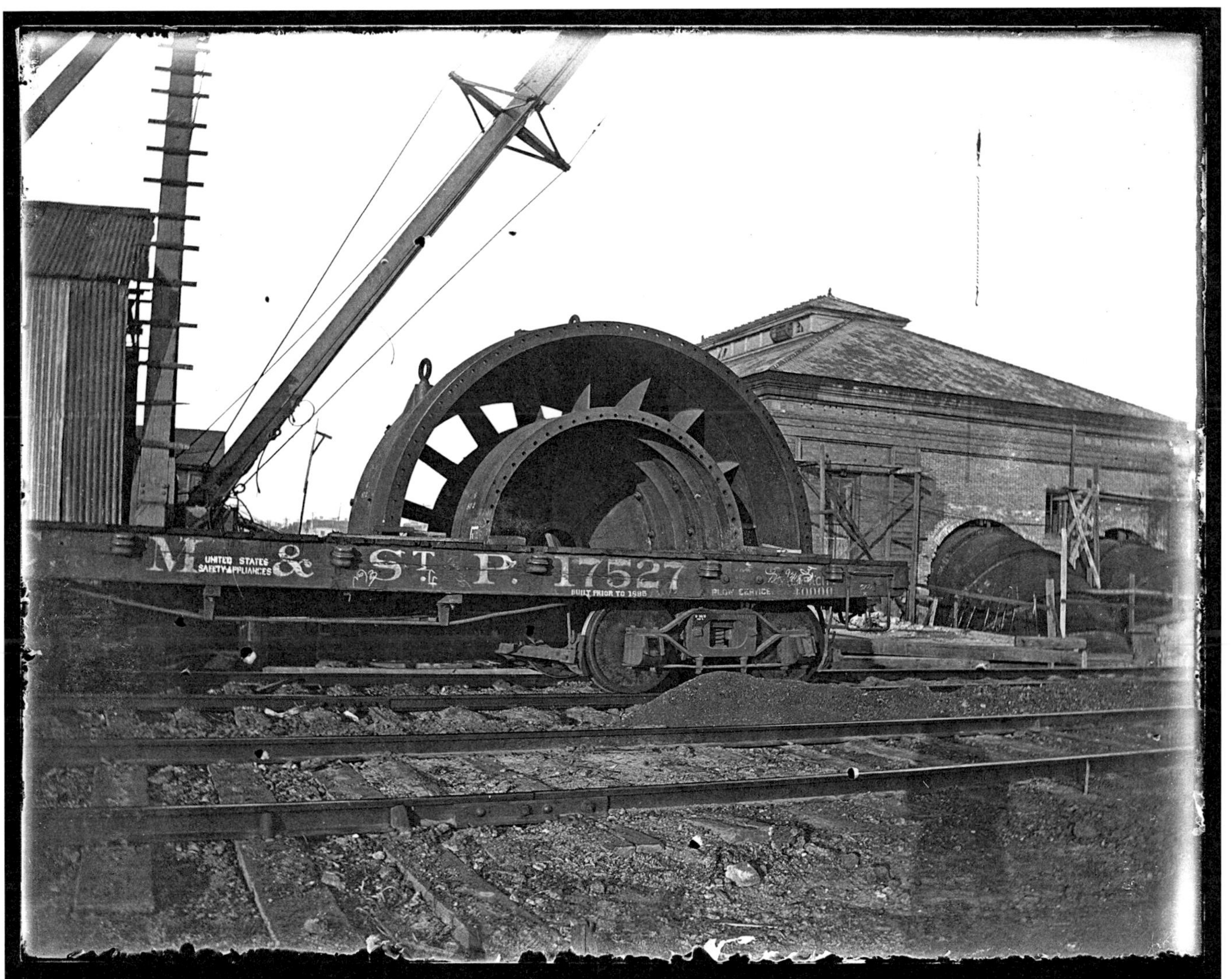

Part of Big Pump [St. Louis Pumping Station, 444 N. Broad St.]

2003.182.32
May 1916

Little Girl
Hoop Skirt

2003.182.352
February 24, 1925

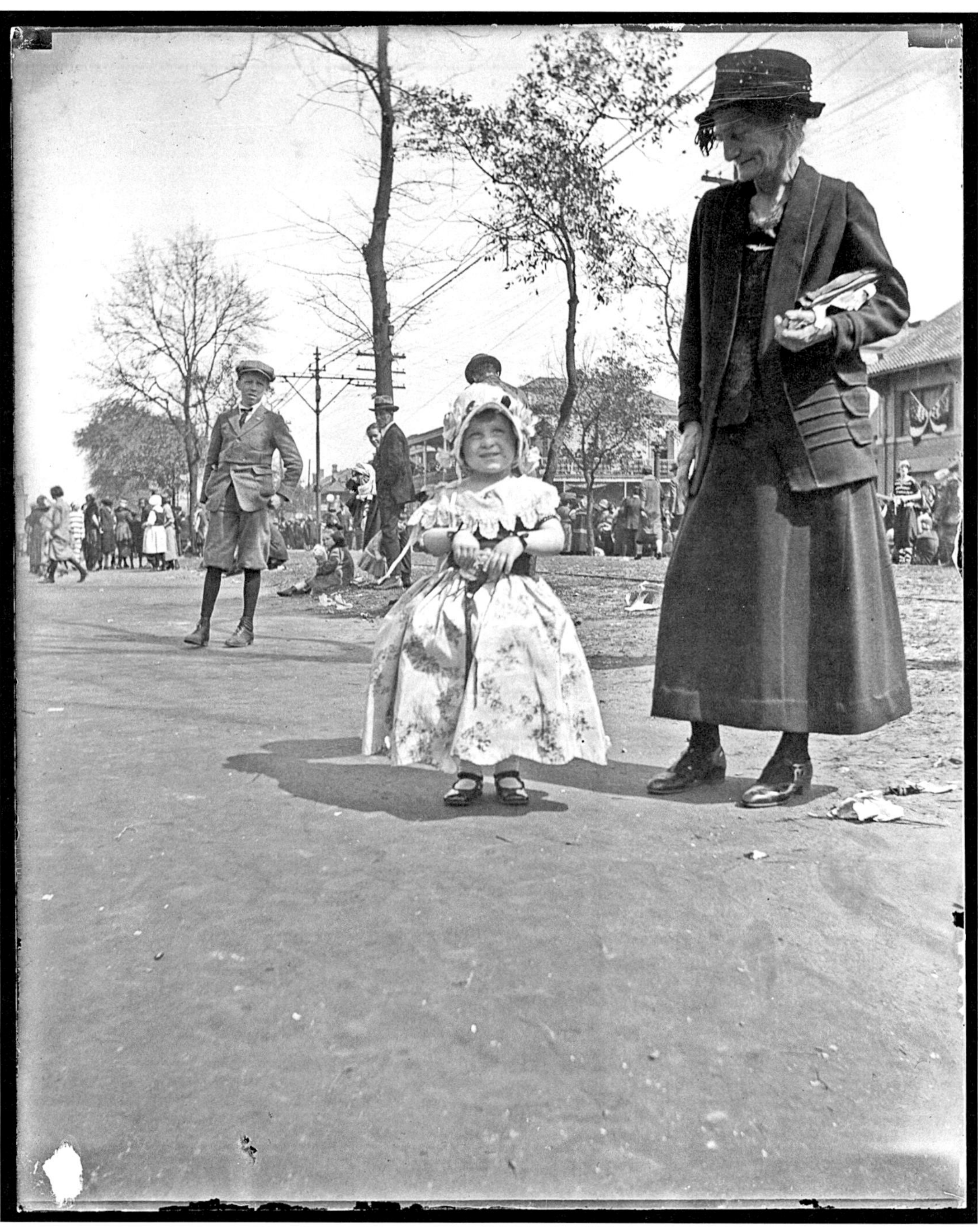

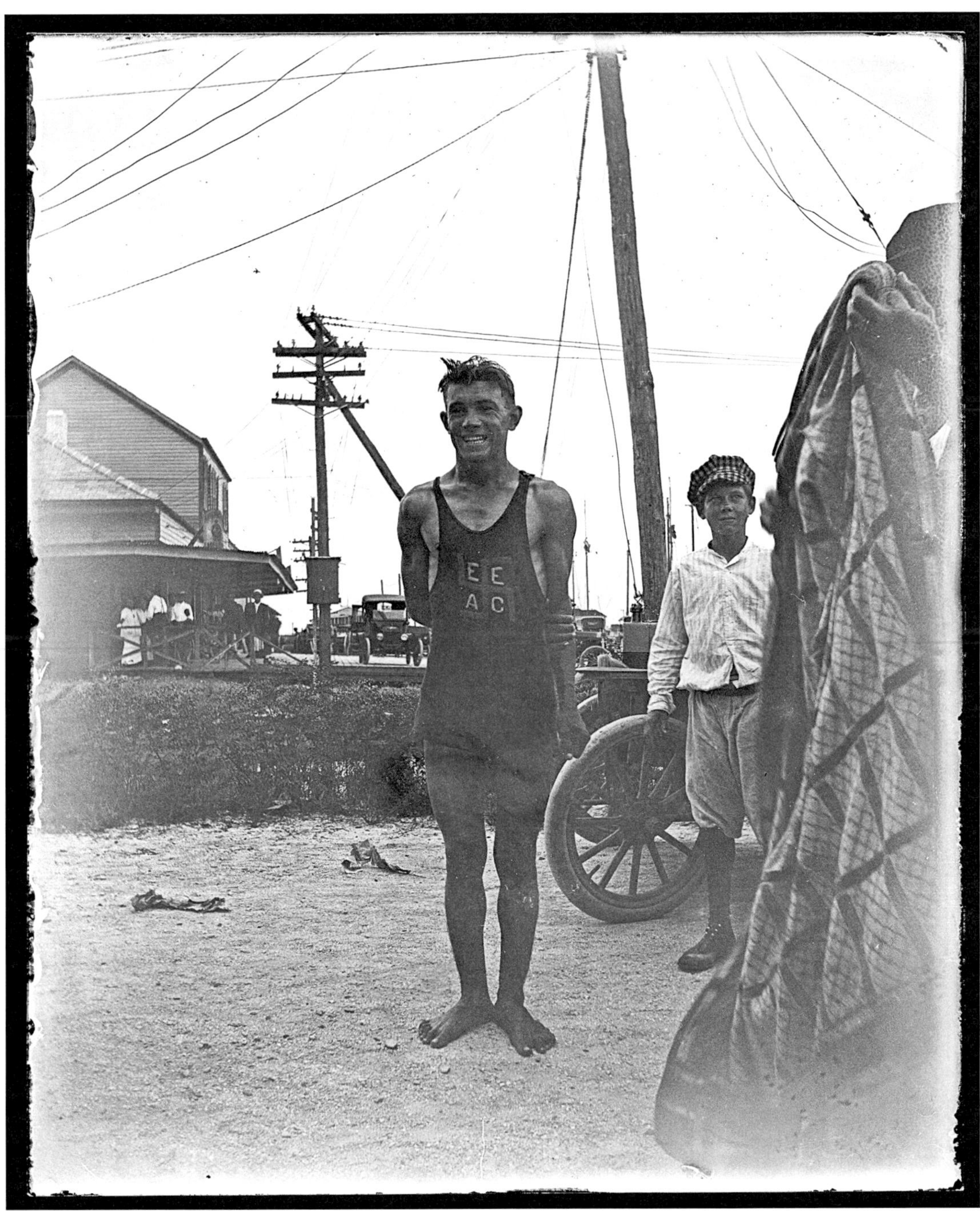

Charles Fereday

2003.182.43
September 9, 1916

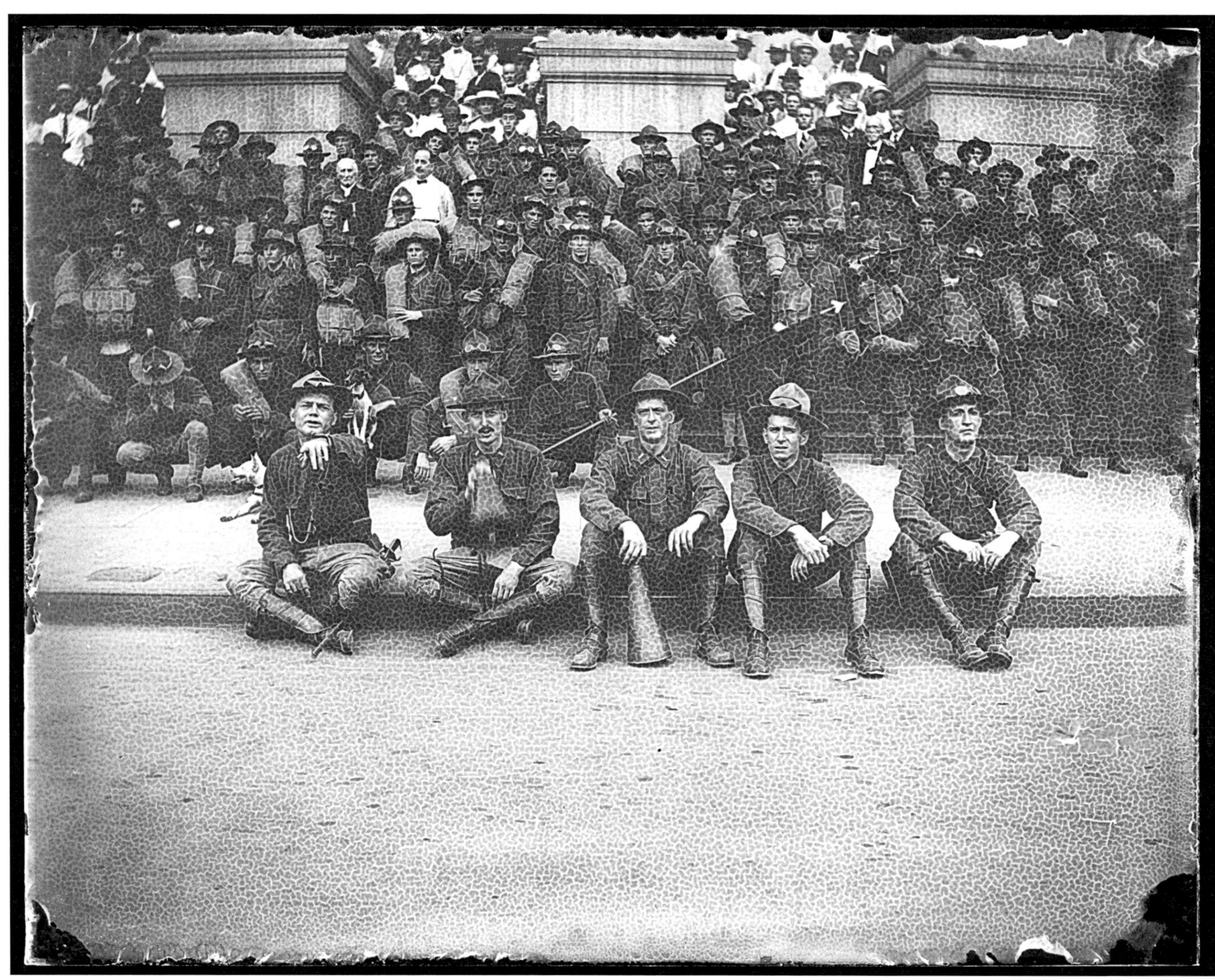

Washington Artillery Officers
Recticulation

2003.182.406
[No date]

“Rags” Man
Masker

2003.182.163
March 4, 1919

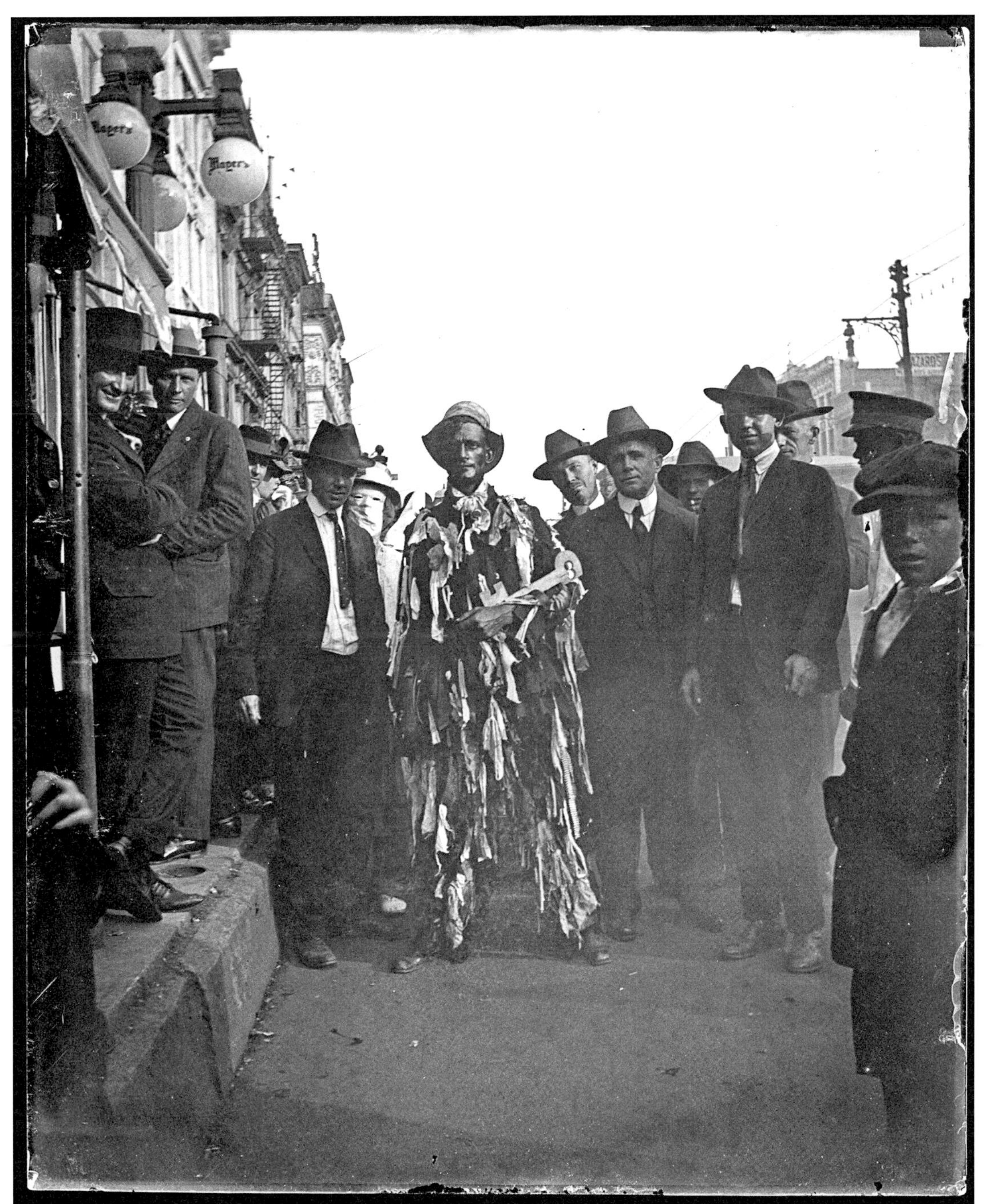

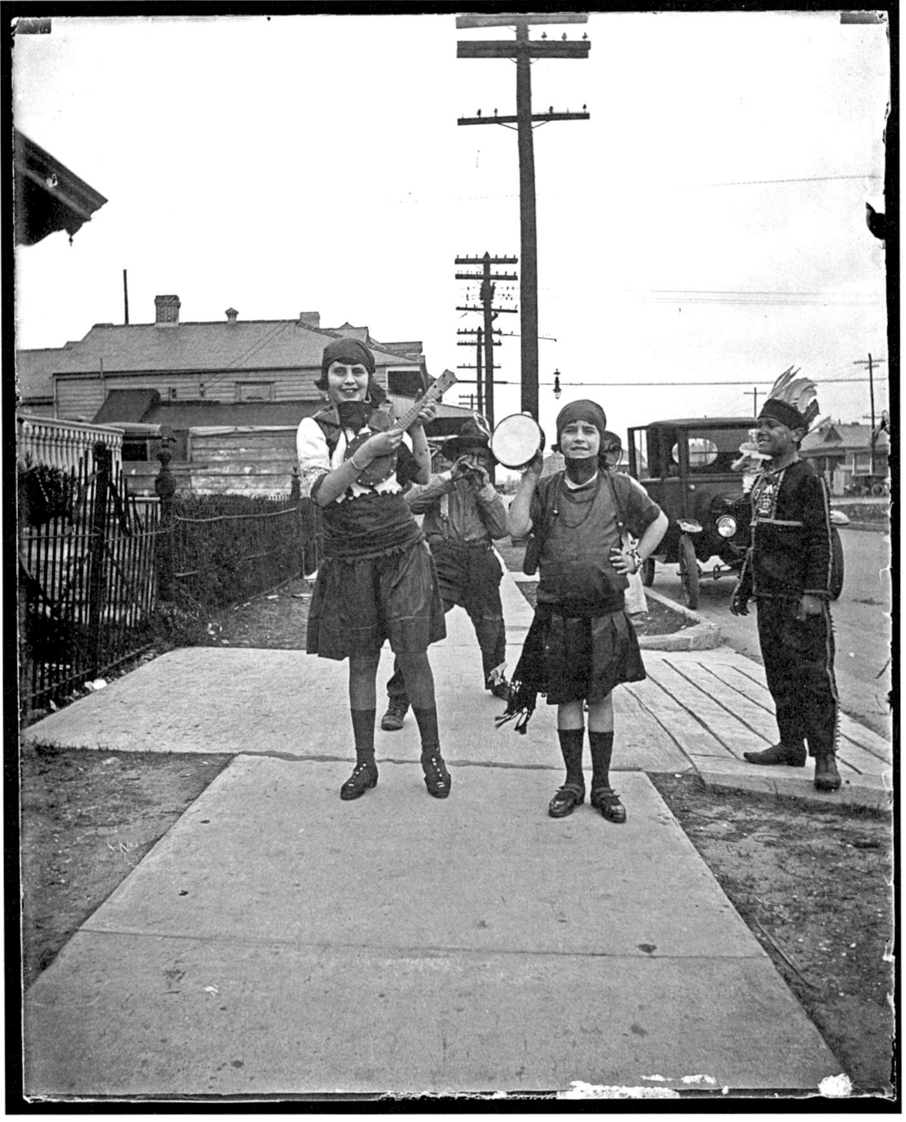

Two Girls
Small Girl Bertha
314 Hagan Ave.

2003.182.332
March 4, 1924

An earlier "ad" in The Times-Picayune got me a free writeup from the "ad reporter."

"CALLING ALL DOG LOVERS

JOHN TIBULE MENDES is a name well known to dog lovers of New Orleans, and to readers of "Letters To The Editor" column of The Times Picayune. In the past 30 years Mr. Mendes claims he has succeeded in having more than 150 letters published on the Times Picayune editorial page — probably a record. Practically all of the letters were about dogs. A tall graying, mild mannered individual Mr. Mendes appeared at the "Want Ad" counter yesterday with a letter (no, not for the editor) "Dear Up and Down the Street," it said, "After 38 years on North Broad avenue I am forced to leave at once as the owner wants to tear the house down. My problem as a bachelor, is to find a place not only for myself but my dearly loved dog. The dog is a kiyoodle" — (Note: I positively did not write that word, and I may add that never in my entire lifetime have I ever referred to a stray dog like that — the writer took upon herself undue liberty).

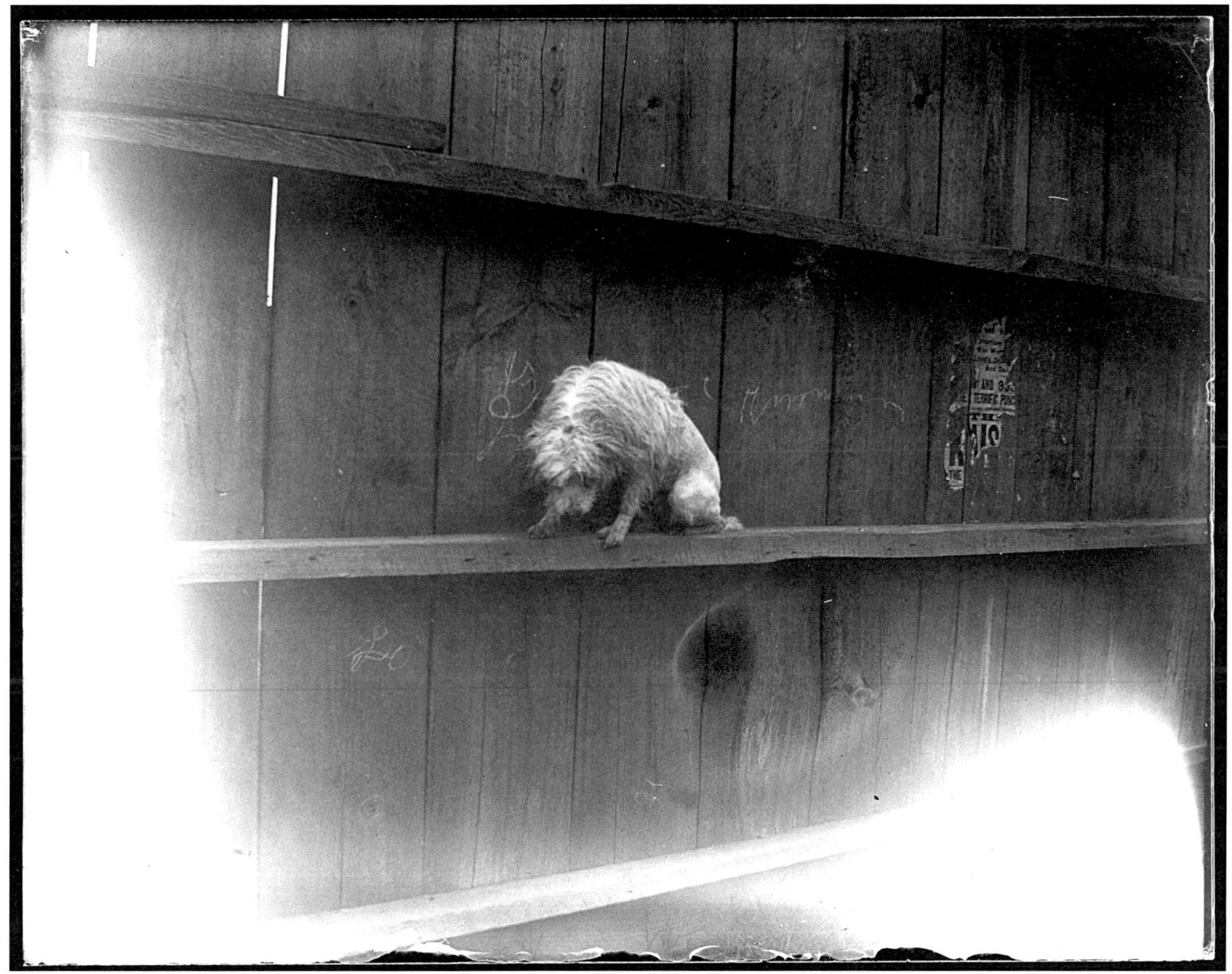

Gentry Bros. Shows. Small dog.

2003.182.190
Monday, April 21, 1919

Now to continue the write up: "I picked up as a stray on the streets seven months ago, and I won't give him up! I have my own furniture. I am advertising for an unfurnished residence, and I hope some dog lover will rent to us." I gave a friend's telephone number for a call for me. That fine write up, and my "ads" failed to get me a suitable home.

- *Dogs in My Life*, 86-87

The great swimmer

2003.182.220
June 1, 1919

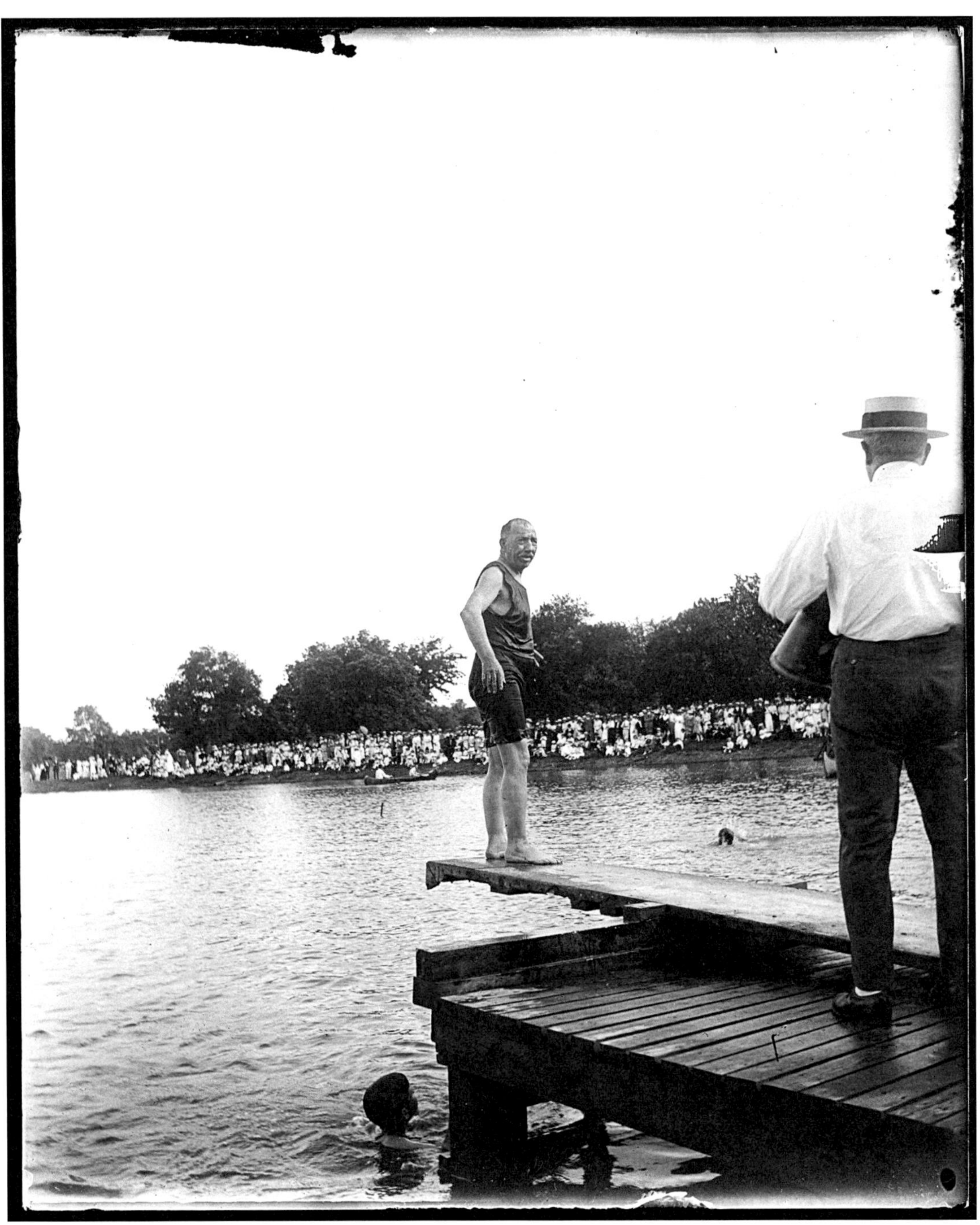

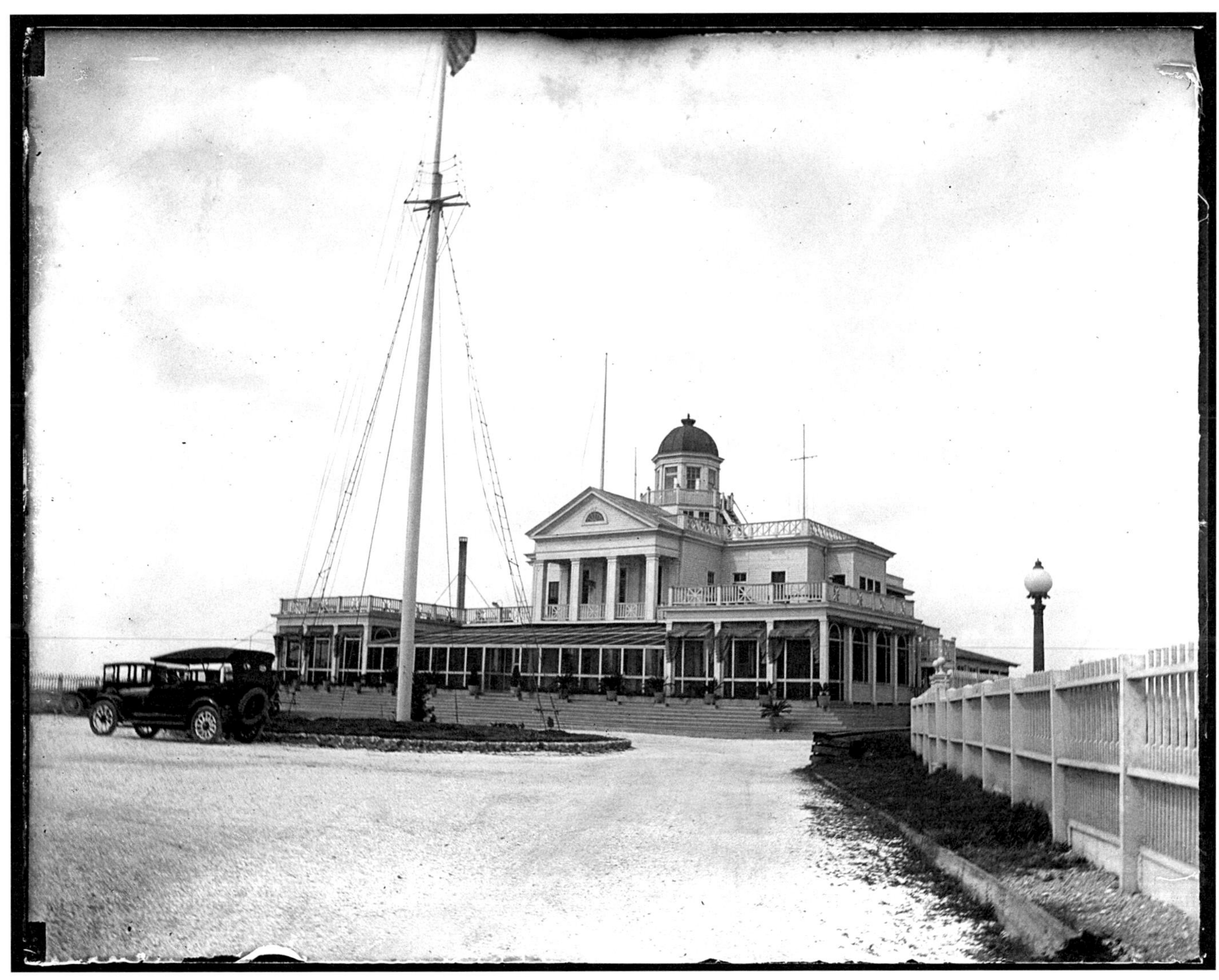

Near view of Southern Yacht Club at West End

2003.182.170
March 16, 1919

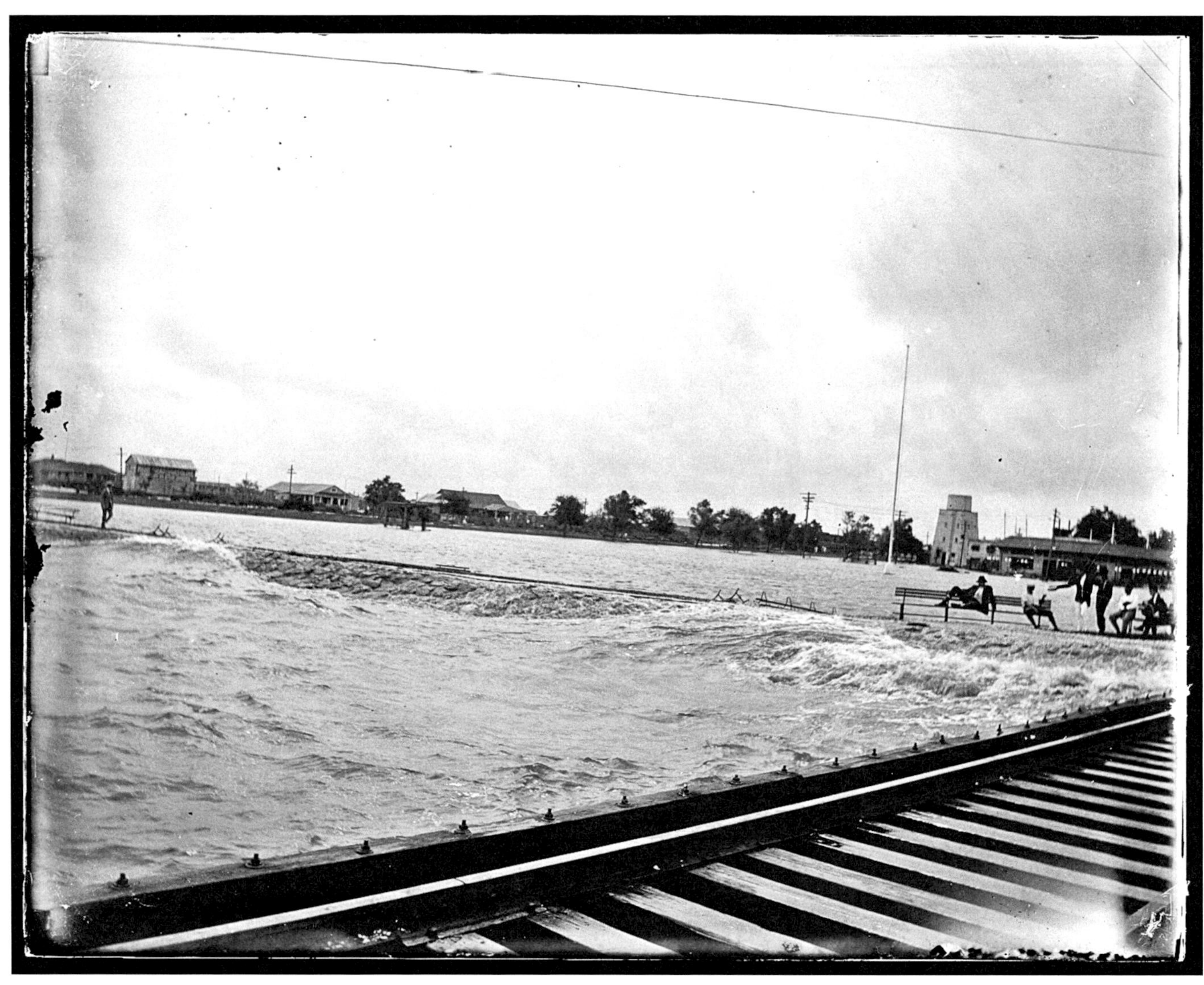

Water covering the entire Spanish Fort resort.

2003.182.227
[September 14-15,] 1919

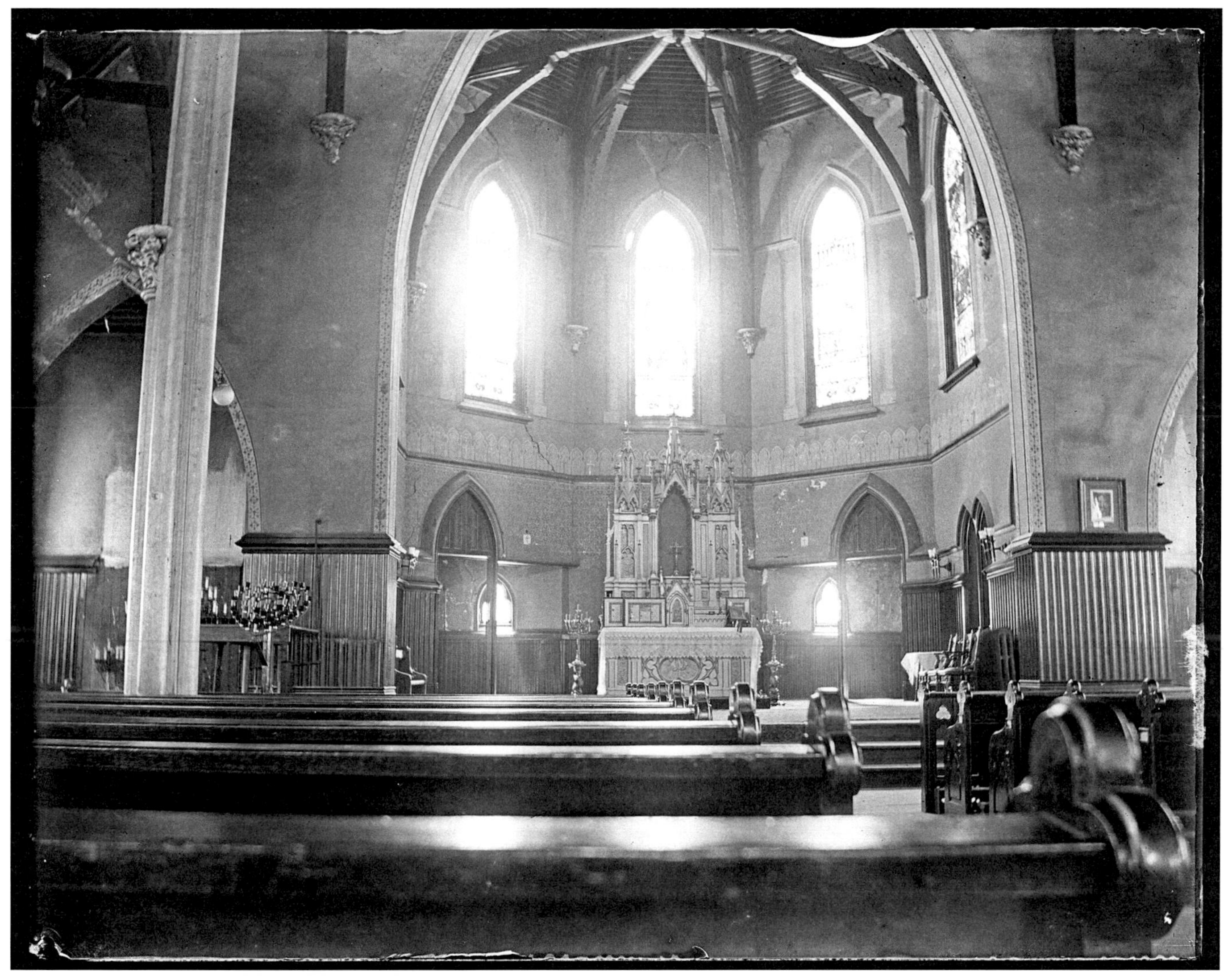

Interior of Old Sacred Heart Church. Old benches,
St. Josephs altar in center

2003.182.321
March 2, 1924

My Mother and I never let any dog we ever owned run the streets freely, and when one of those free running dogs would want to fight Don I had a notion that they did so because they realized that he — Don — was taken well care of, and loved, and they did not like that. During all of my retirement I never went to a place of amusement, and stayed home with Don, and we both liked it that way.

- *Dogs in My Life*, 100

[Uncaptioned]

2003.182.381
[ca. 1916]

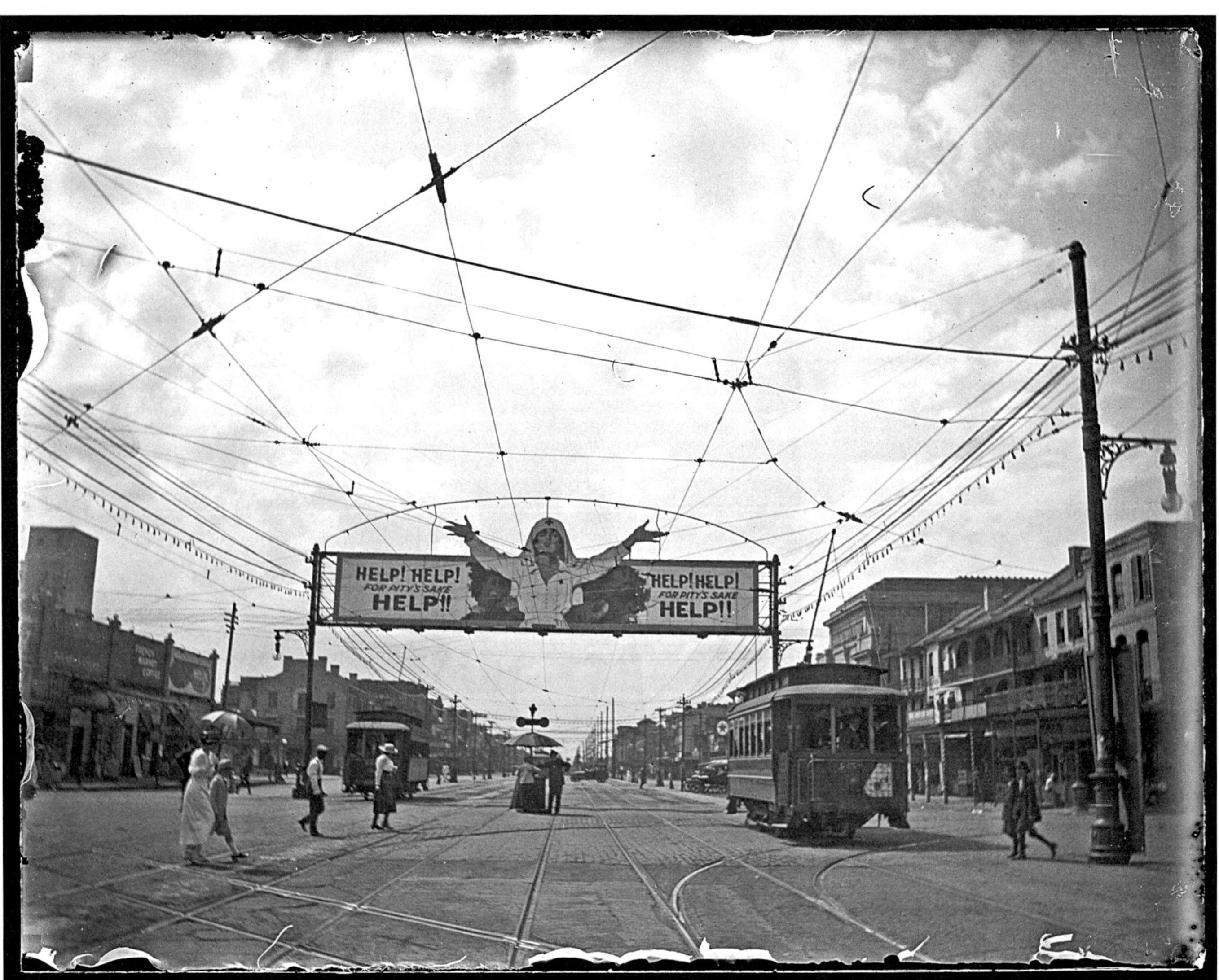

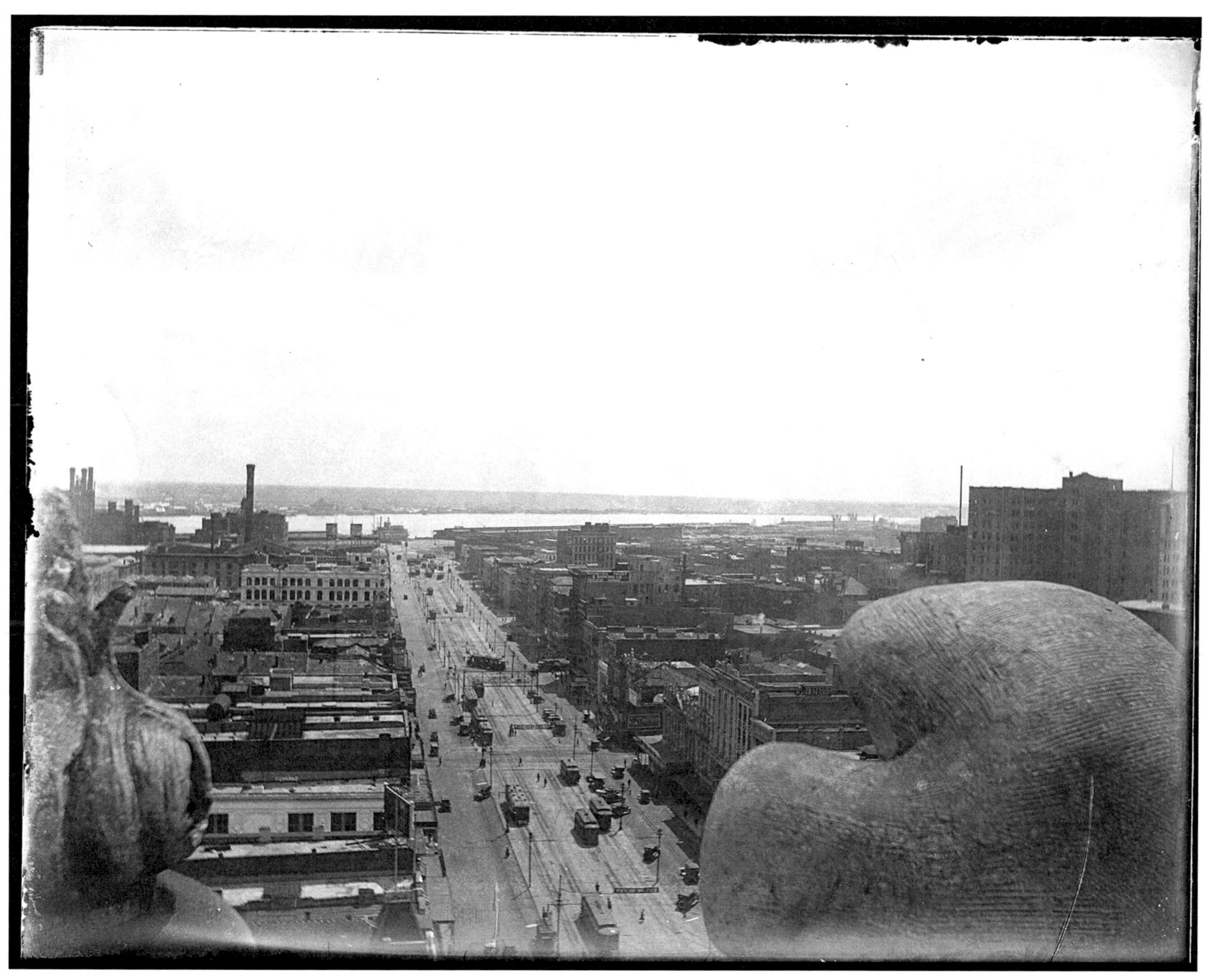

Looking out Canal St. to the River

2003.182.9
1916

I am ending this book writing these words, seated in the very same chair that Don, and Our other dogs liked to rest, and sleep in. It may be a bit of comfort to me to know that the age that Don died, compared to that of a human being, was at least 115 years, and that all of Our dogs (with the possible exception of one only) and my own beloved Mother had someone beside them, some one that loved them, and they did not depart this life on earth alone, and unloved — something when I die I will not have. [...]

[Uncaptioned]

2003.182.471
[ca. 1925]

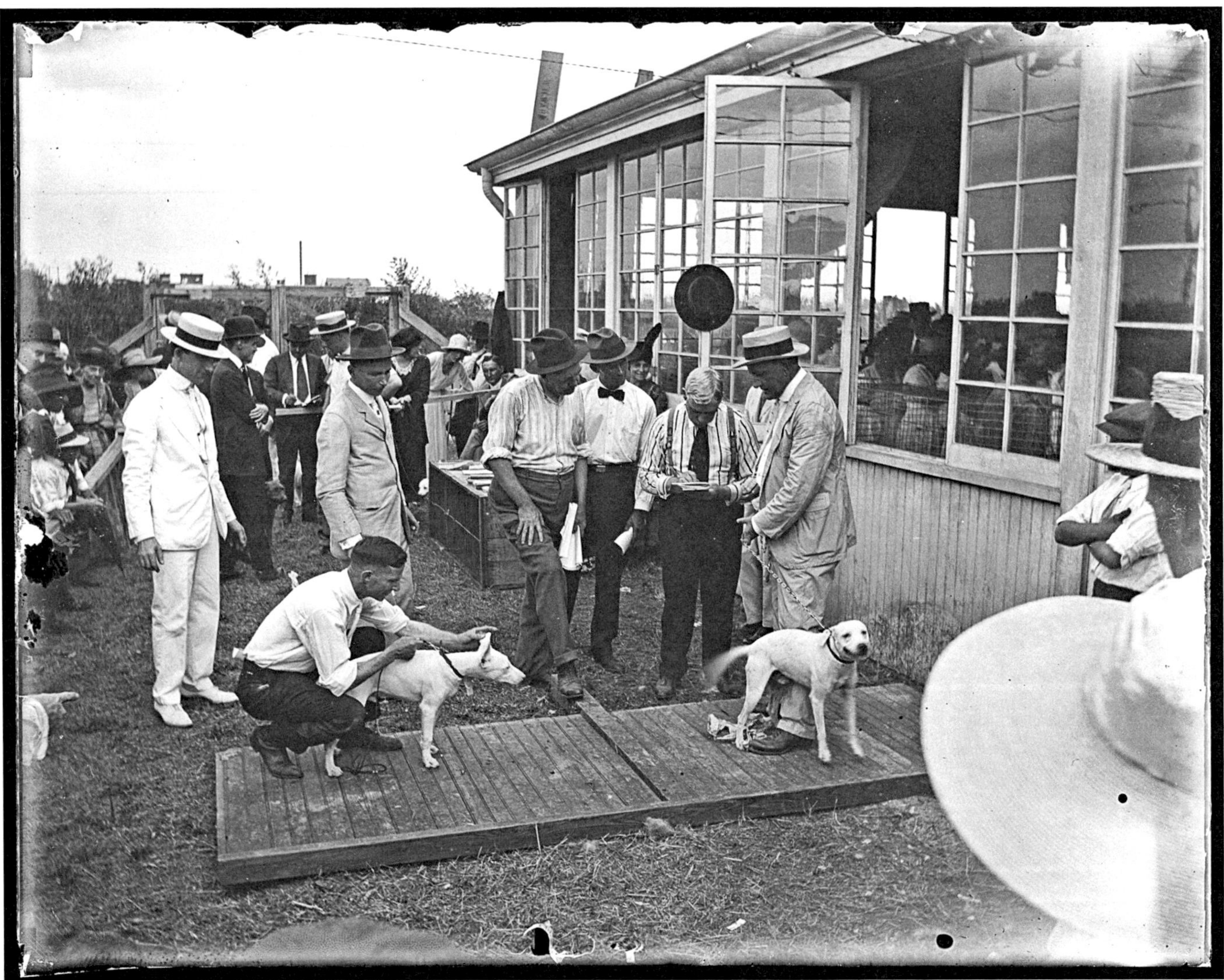

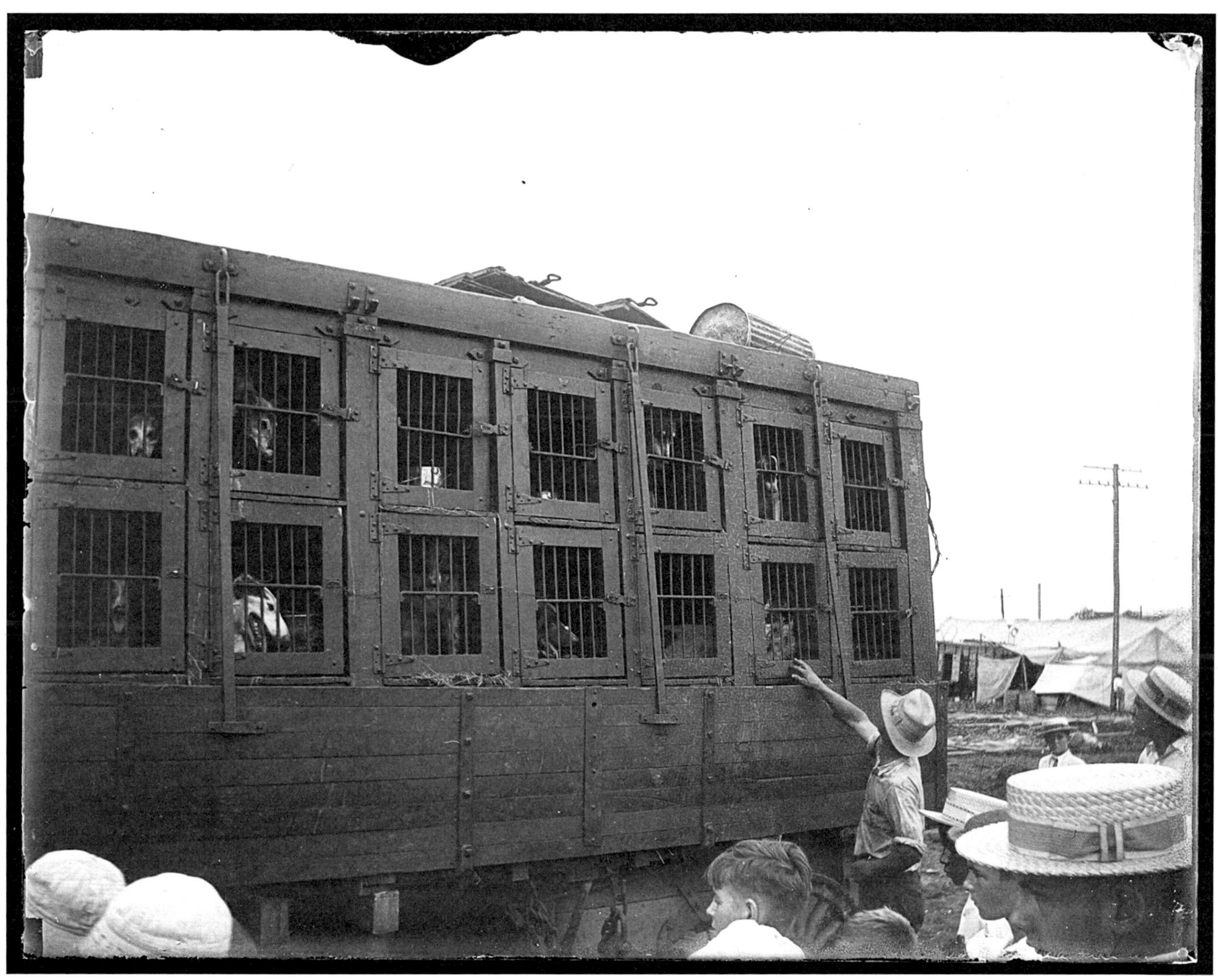

Small Animal Cages. Barnes Show 1

2003.182.360
August 1928

The only ones that gave to me an unselfish, honest, and true love was my beloved Mother, and all of Our dogs. When death took them away from me I lost everything worth-while on this earth. I am just a tired "Old Man," as I called myself when speaking to all of the "Dogs In My Life" now wanting only Peace, and Quiet.

- *Dogs in My Life*, 127

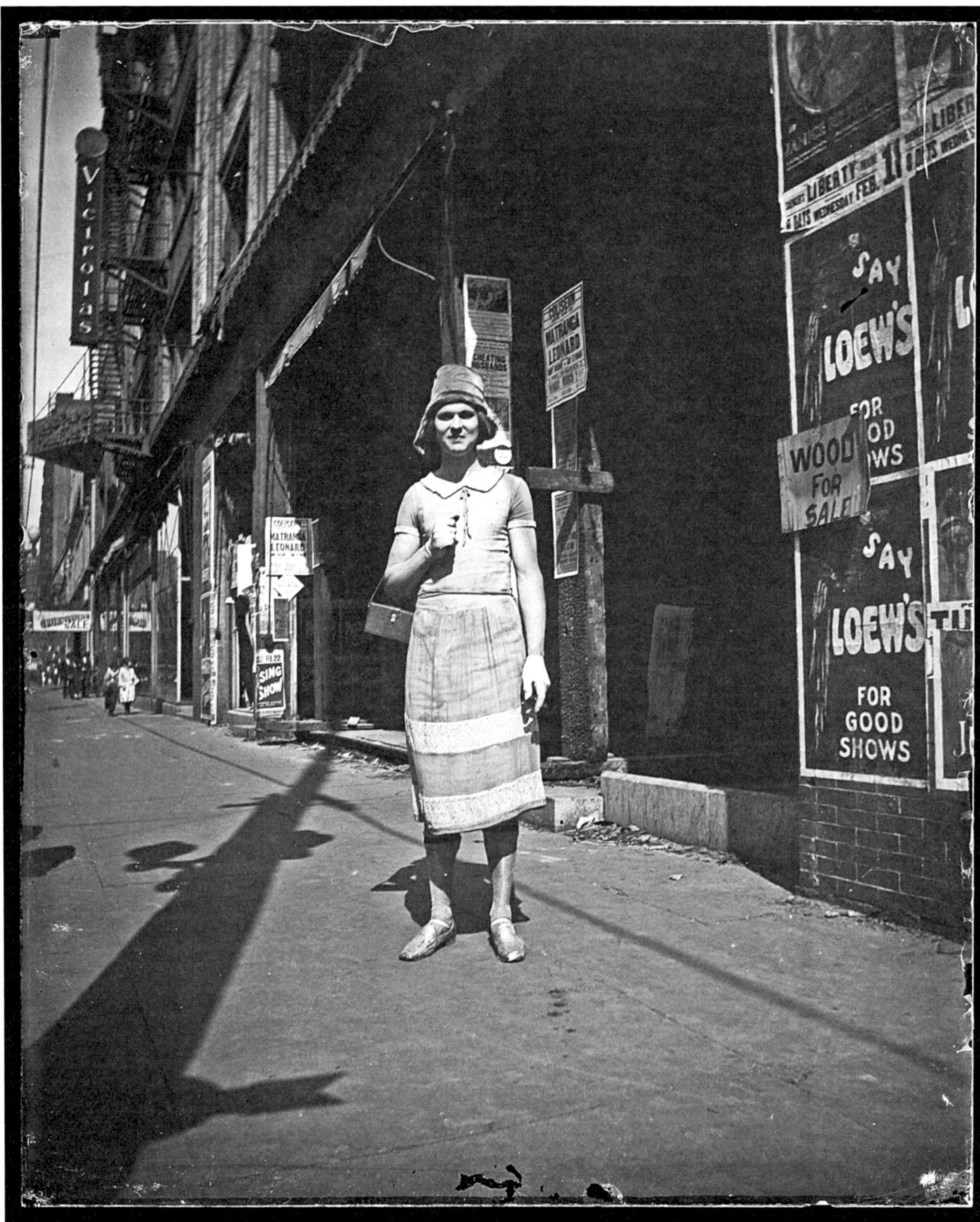

Female
Impersonator

2003.182.353
February 24, 1925

[Uncaptioned]

2003.182.482
[ca. 1921]

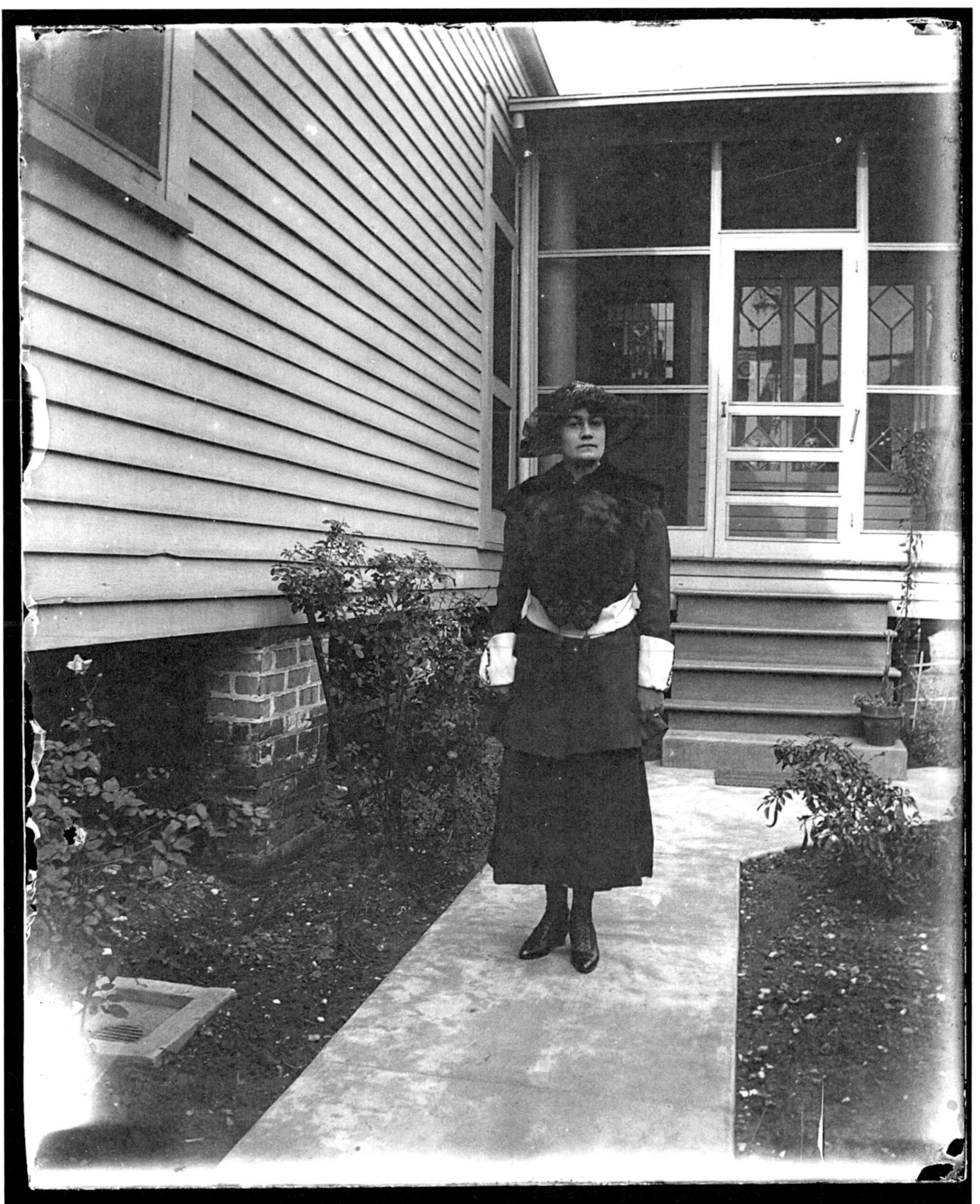

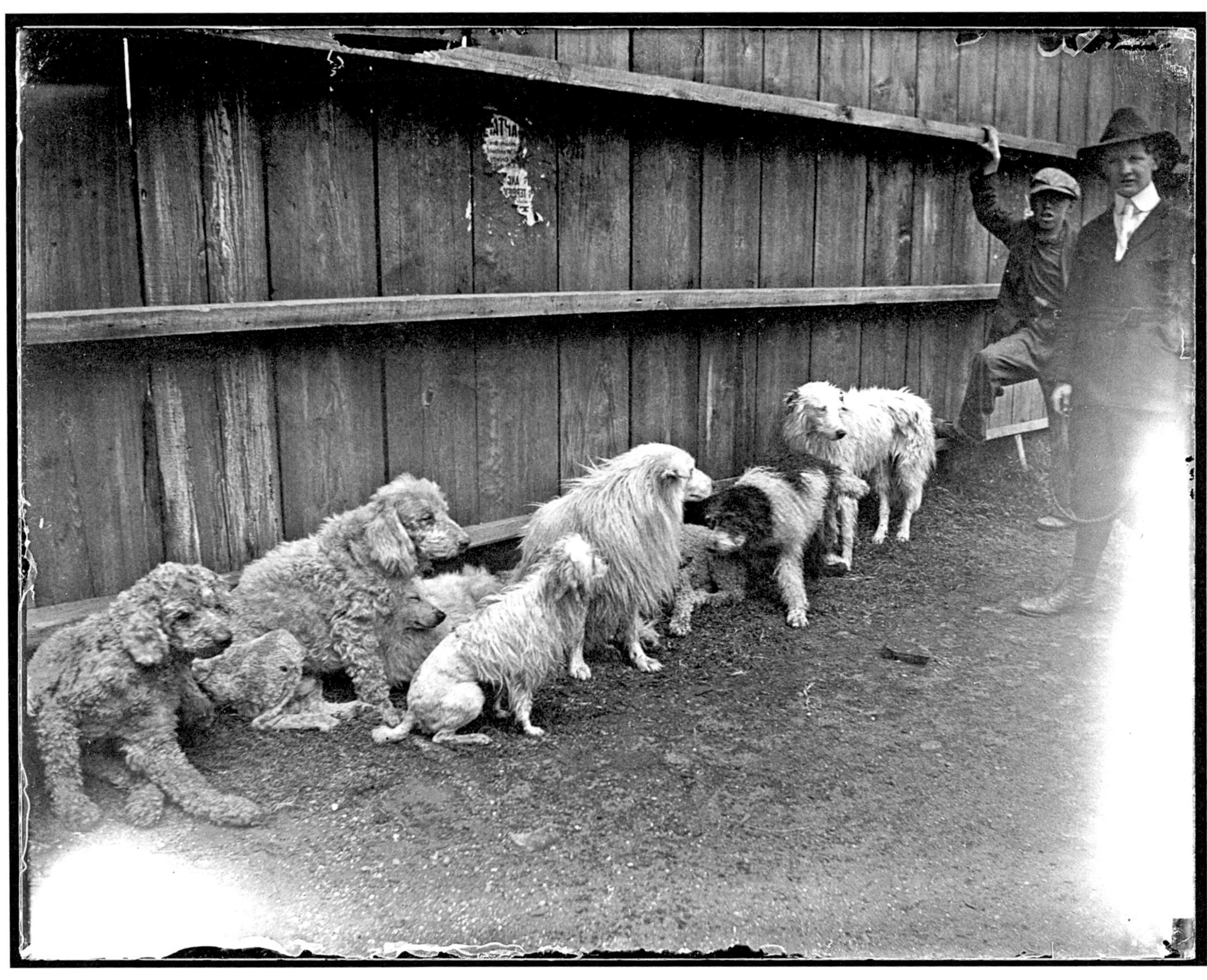

Gentry Bros. Shows. Dogs— with small boy (one of their keepers)

2003.182.191
April 21, 1919

Former King Manuel
when he was a child
From photo that appeared in the
Litery Digest of Oct. 29th 1910

2003.182.566
Copied in March 1920

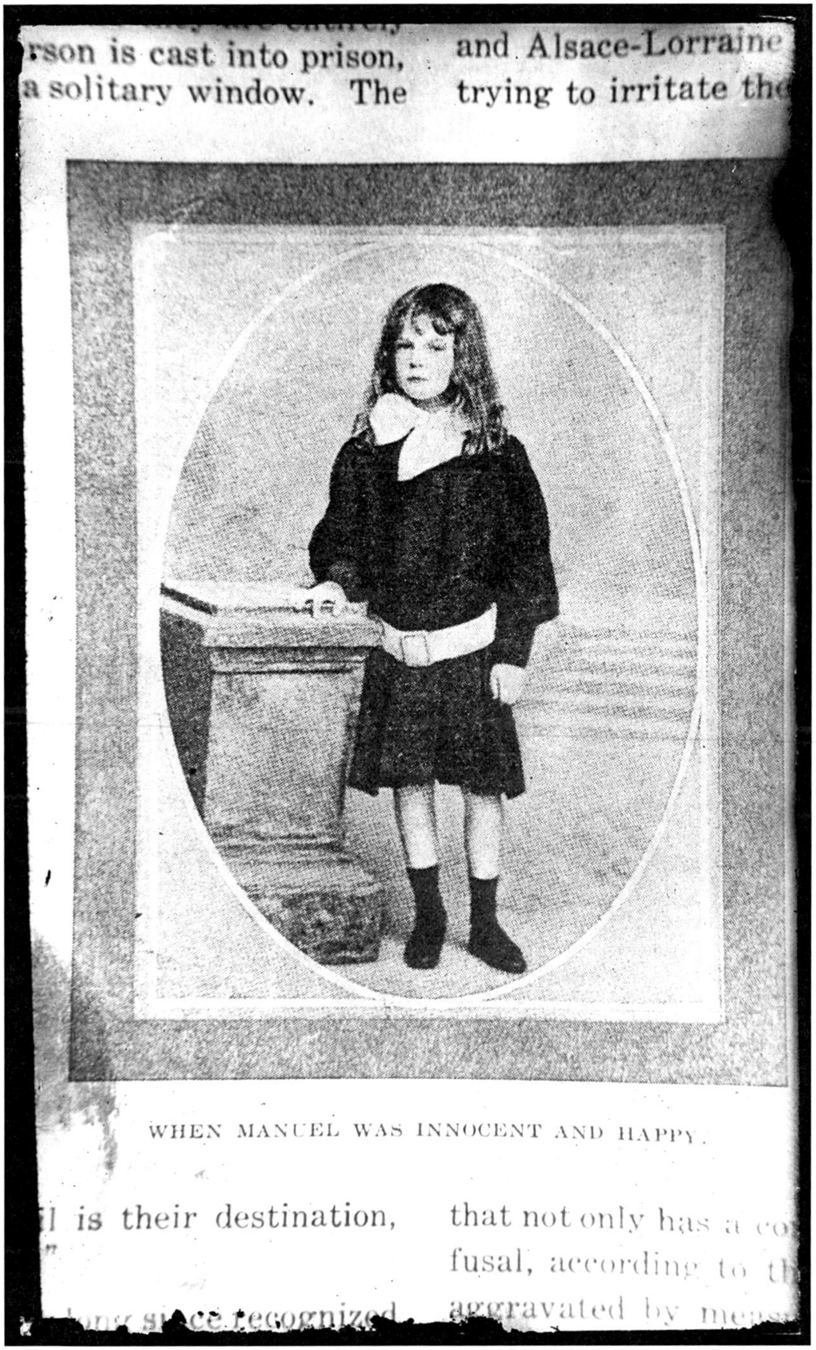

WHEN MANUEL WAS INNOCENT AND HAPPY.

Before me as I write are two photographs of what appears to be two small "girls," both clad in dresses a little below the knees, stocking clad legs, and high button shoes. Both "girls" have long hair in curls, and the curls on one of those "girls" are thick. Both are standing, an expression of innocence is on their pretty childish faces. Their age seems to be about seven years. One of those "girls" grew up to become king of his native land, and the other "girl" is the writer of this book. People of today cannot understand the reason why Mothers of long, long ago sometimes kept one of their sons in dresses while the boys were still young. Those boys were "real" boys, and they never did protest. Customs change with times. This man that became a king lived a life as different from the way this writer has lived his life, as a bright sunny day is to the gloom of a dark night. That king, and I were about the very same age, and he died many years ago.

- *Dogs in My Life*, 1

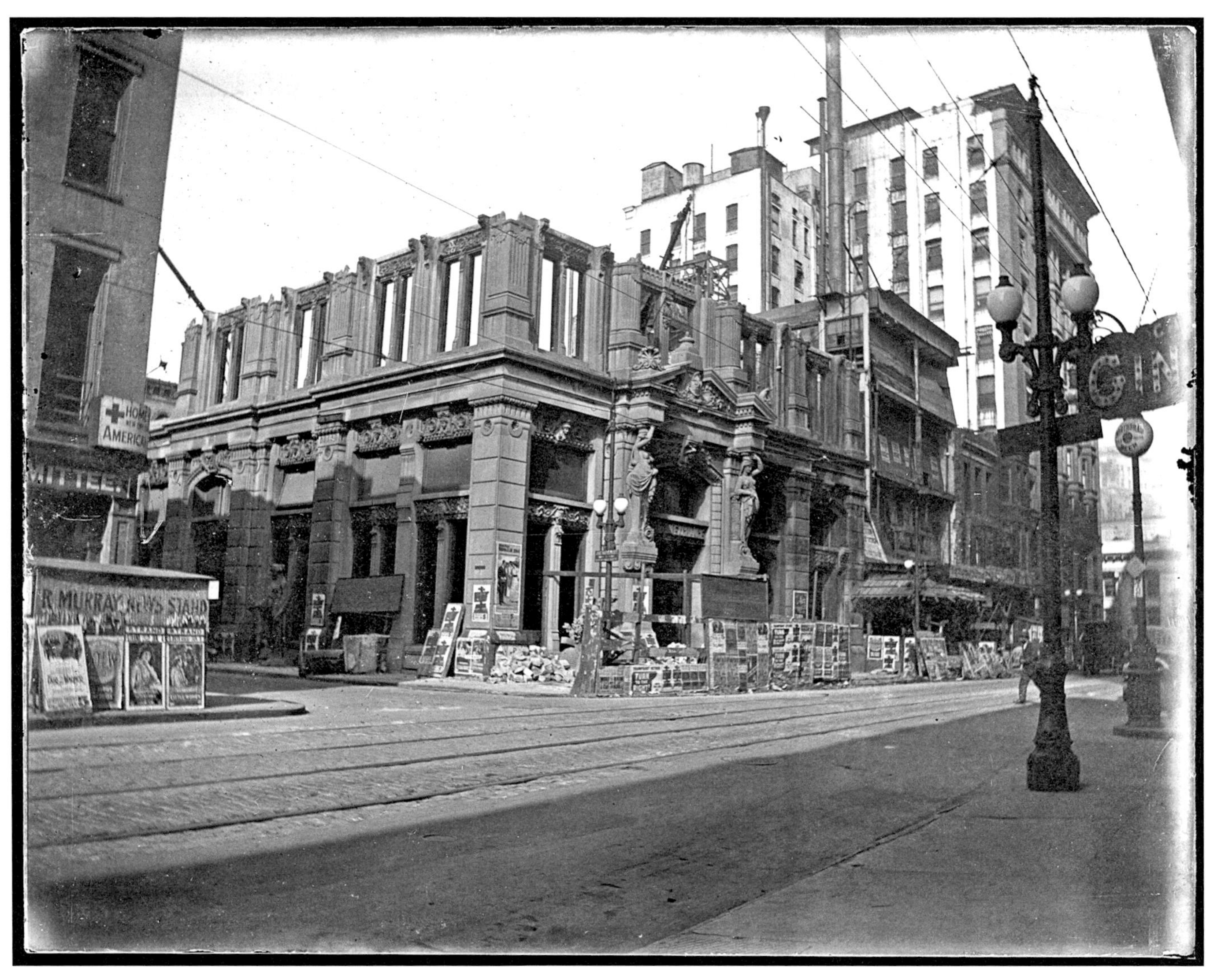

Old Cotton Exchange being demolished

2003.182.138
January 9, 1919

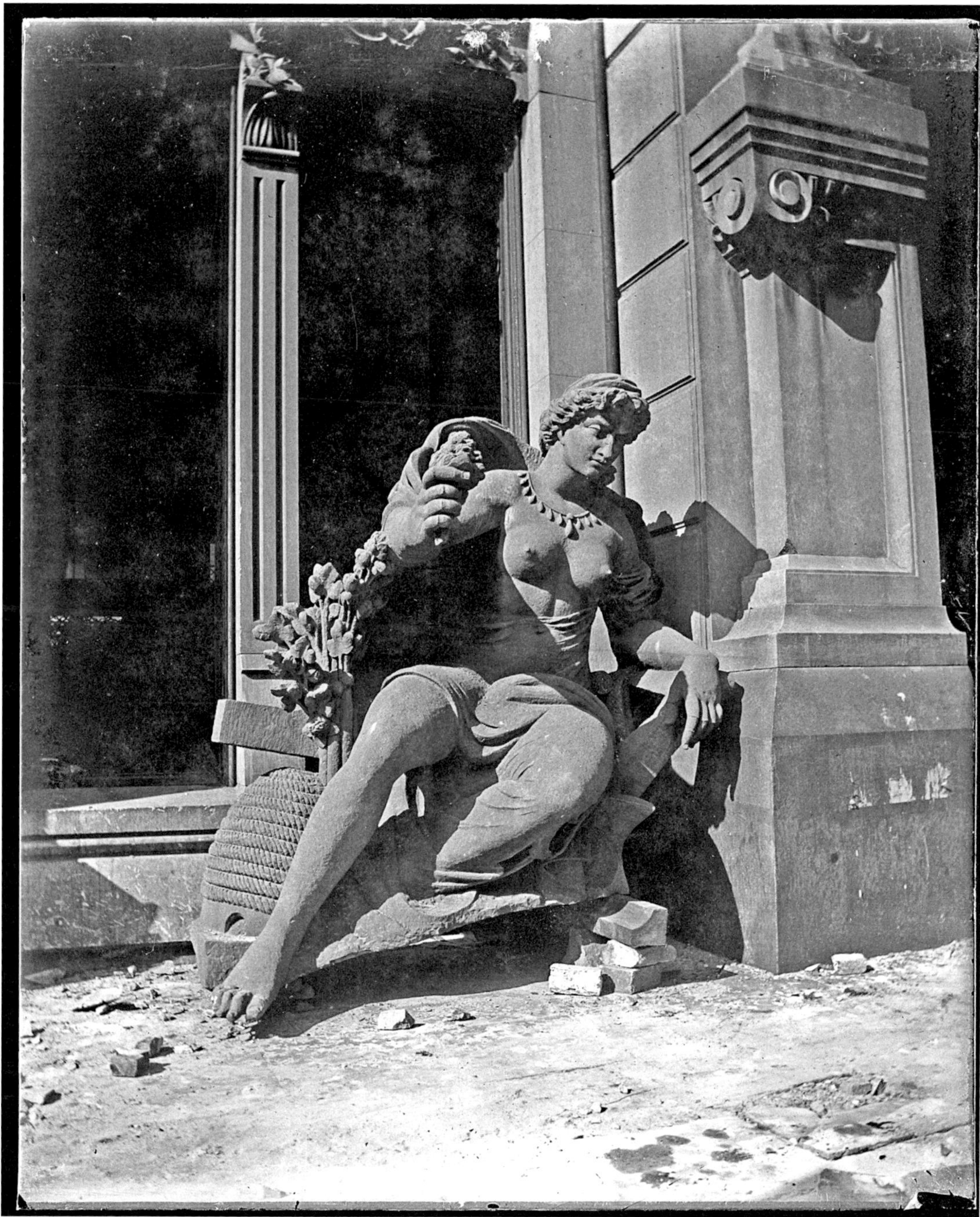

Agriculture from Cotton Exchange

2003.182.122
December 14, 1918

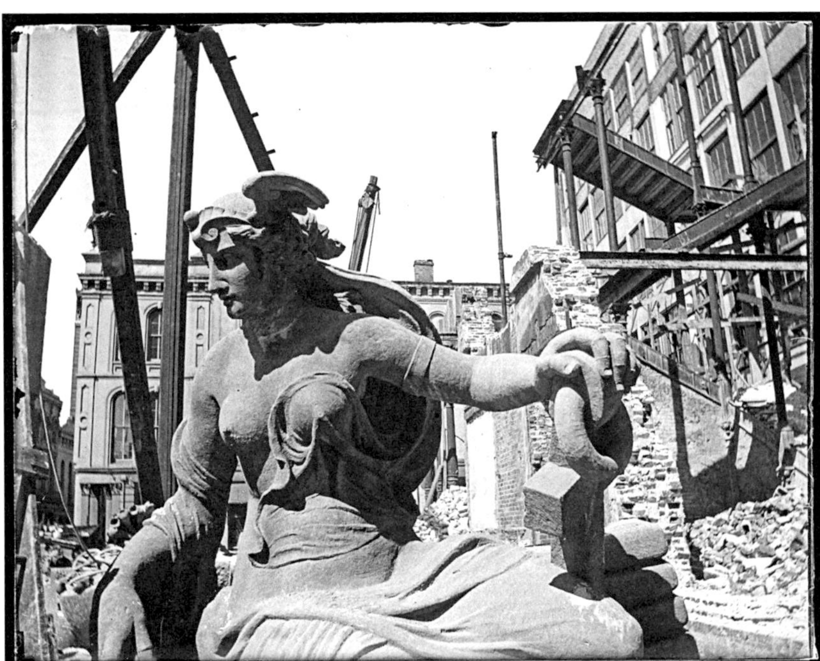

Near view of Industry statuc from old Cotton Exchange (head and bust)

2003.182.165
March 9, 1919

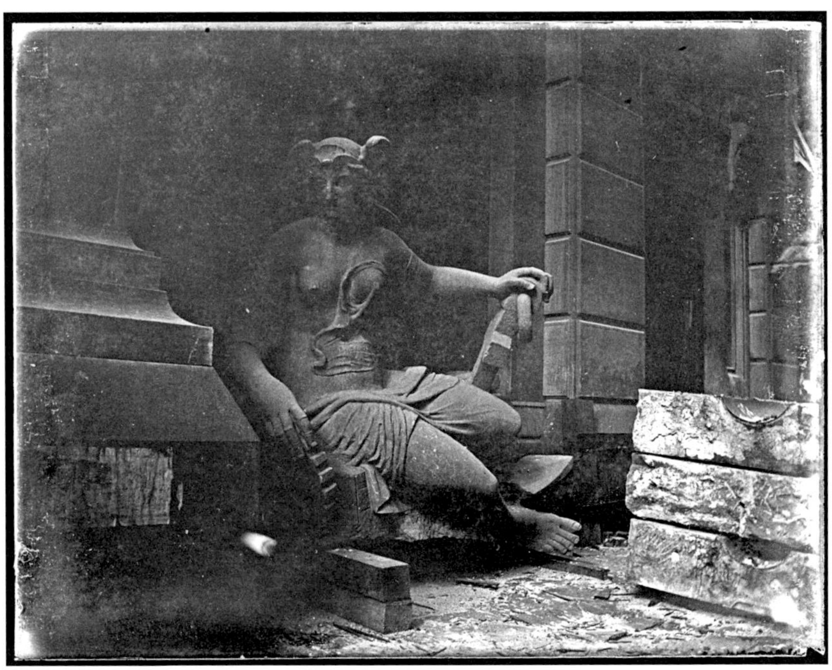

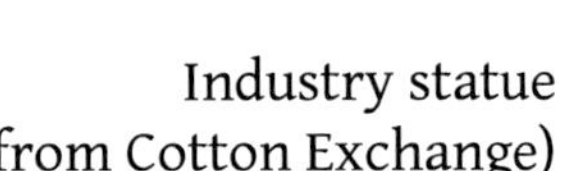

Industry statue
(from Cotton Exchange)

2003.182.184
1919

Peace statue from Old Cotton Exchange

2003.182.167
March 9, 1919

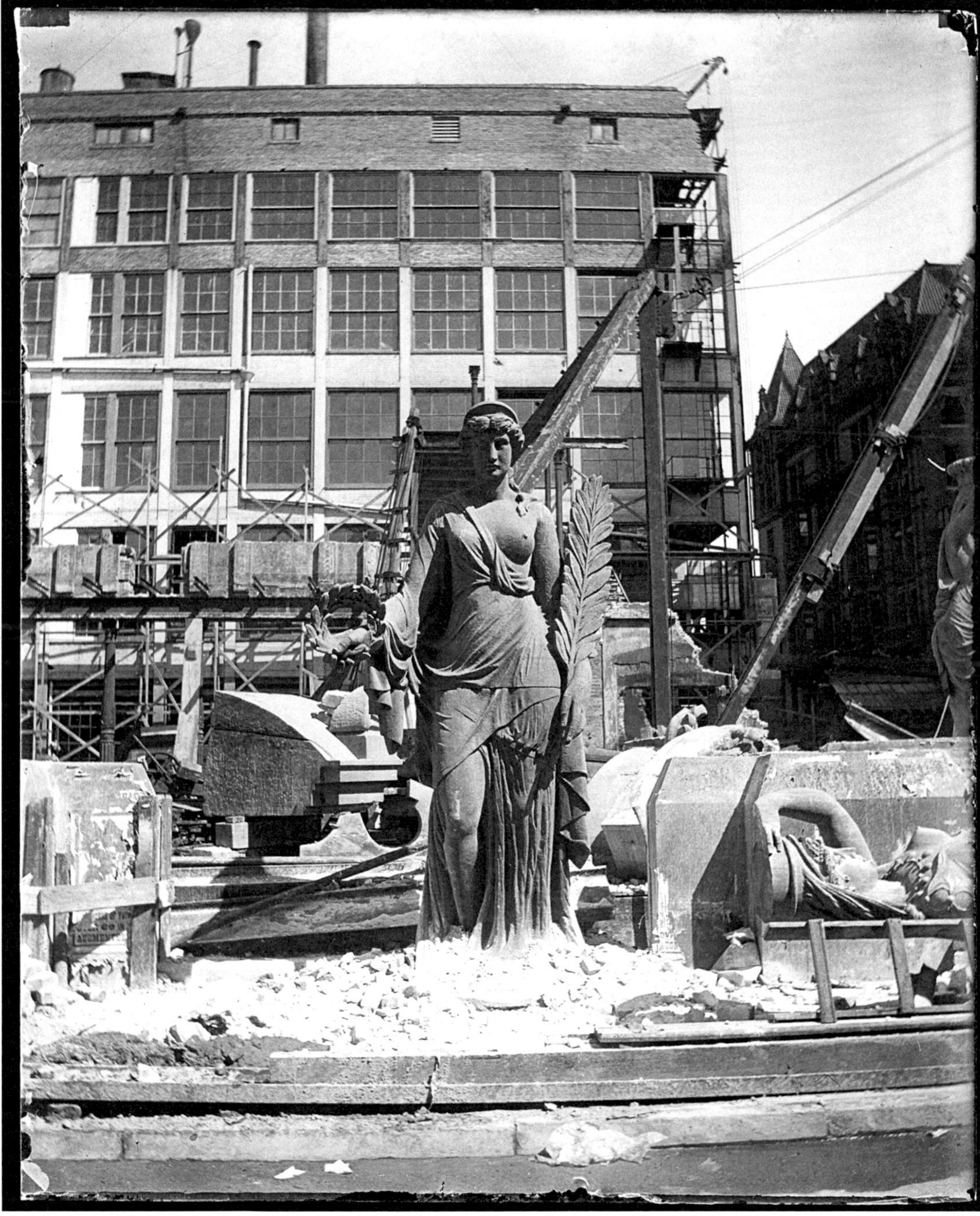

As for this writer I never had any association with any girl other than my own Mother. I have remained a bachelor. I have related all of this because as the reader will learn because I was dressed as a "girl," as a small child that did not handicap me when I went out to earn a living.
- *Dogs in My Life*, 1

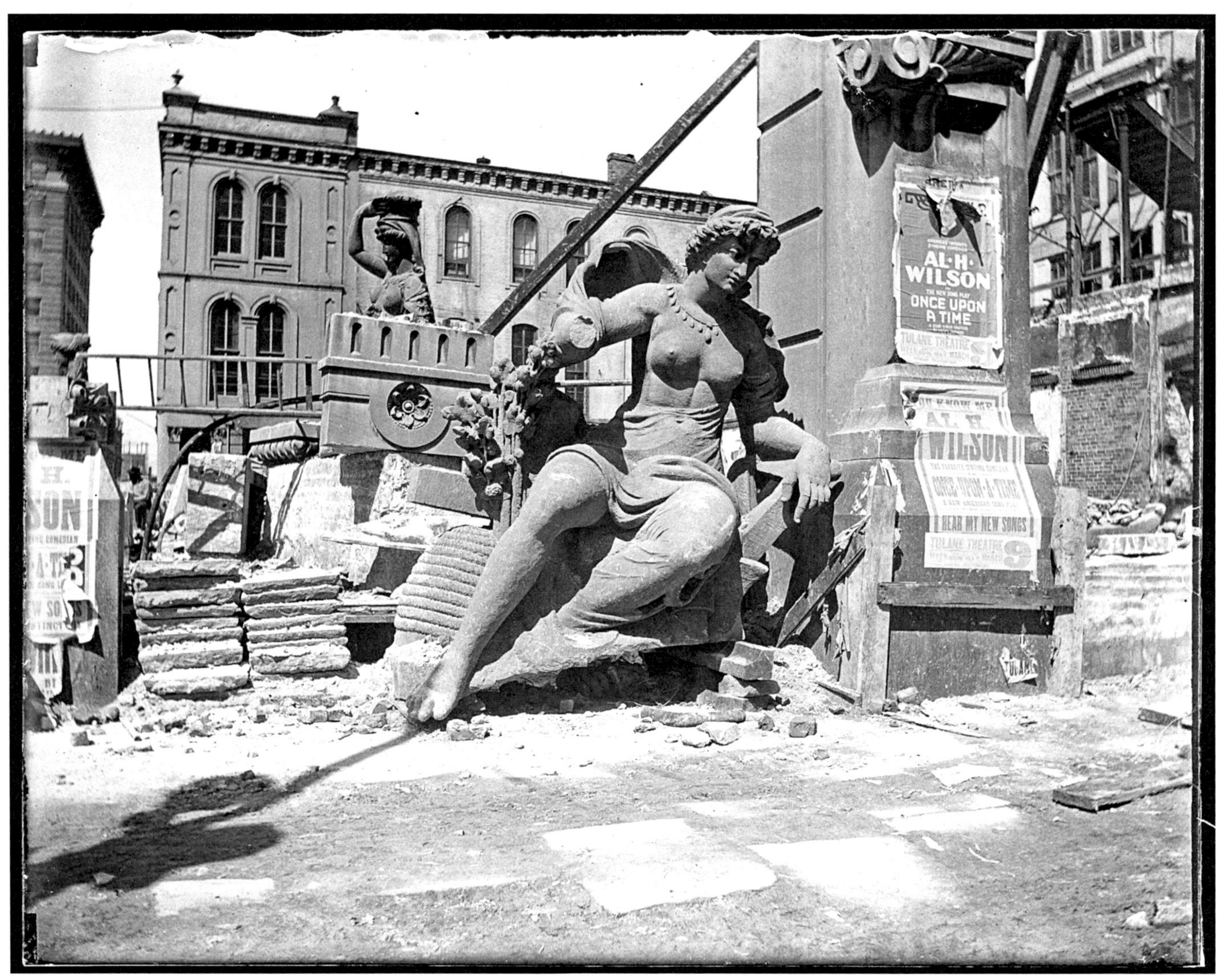

Agriculture showing
hand broken off

2003.182.166
[Between January & March] 1919

Sept. 5th 1949

My 61st Birthday — cloudy.

Took Don for a long walk by way of Hurst Street into the Audubon Park Golf Course, and let him run freely about. Then back home the walk having a total of about 30 blocks.

Breakfast for Don, and I.

Thence to Mother — Sister place in Greenwood — flowers in vases.

Bought some candy, and ice cream for Don, and I Home, good chicken dinner. Look at old Birthday Cards from Mother to me — once such a happy day.

Play with Don. He is a dear dog, and a great comfort to me, and I love him.

Listen to radio play "Saigon". No one remembered me, and the date.

Bed 10 P.M.
J. T. M.

-*Dogs in My Life*, 130

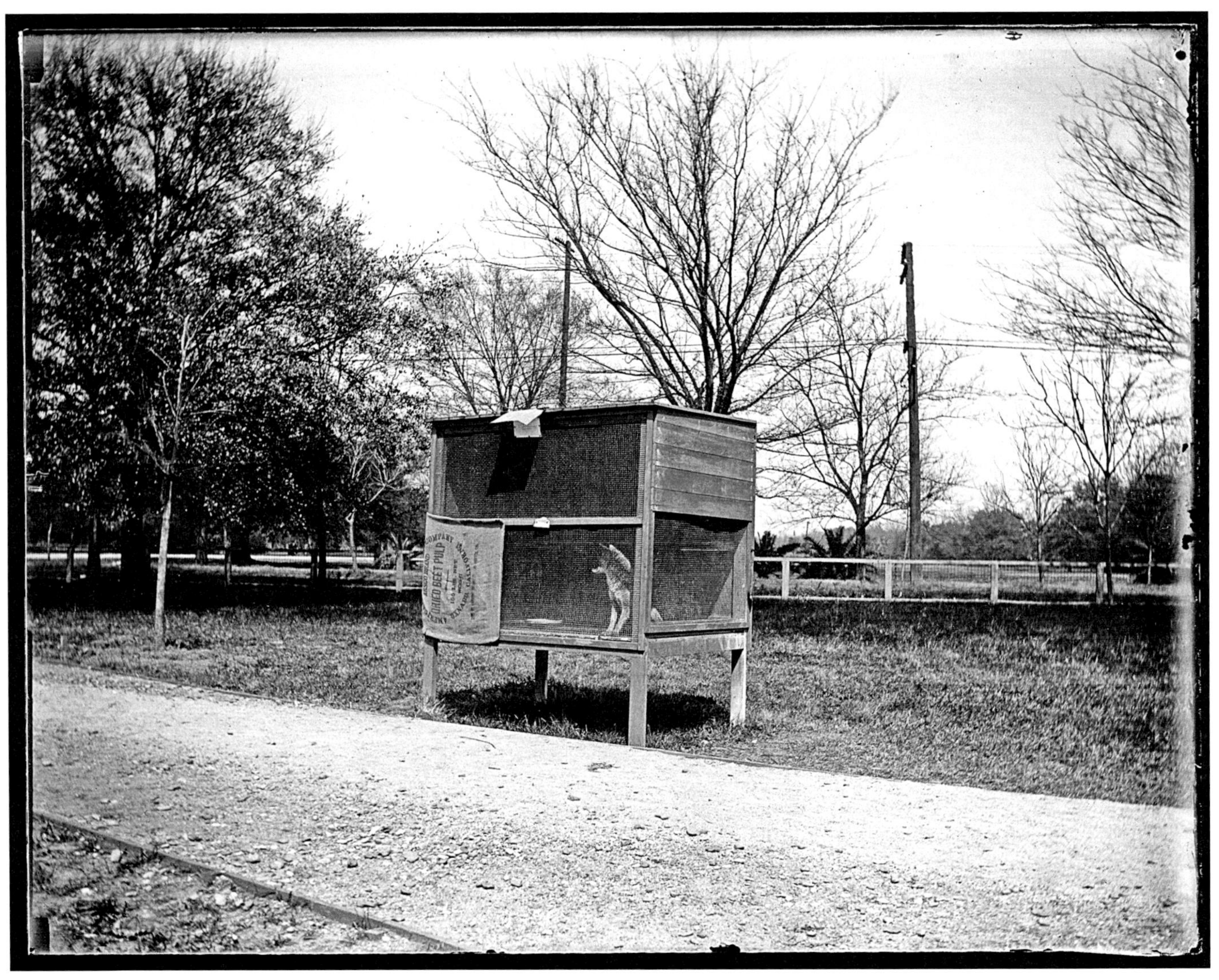

Timber wolf
Audubon Park
Showing manner of cage and surrounding

2003.182.252
March 7, 1920

Also Available from UNO Press:

William Christenberry: Art & Family by J. Richard Gruber (2000)

The El Cholo Feeling Passes by Fredrick Barton (2003)

A House Divided by Fredrick Barton (2003)

Coming Out the Door for the Ninth Ward edited by Rachel Breunlin (2006)

The Change Cycle Handbook by Will Lannes (2008)

Cornerstones: Celebrating the Everyday Monuments & Gathering Places of New Orleans edited by Rachel Breunlin (2008)

A Gallery of Ghosts by John Gery (2008)

Hearing Your Story: Songs of History and Life for Sand Roses by Nabile Farès, translated by Peter Thompson (2008)

The Imagist Poem: Modern Poetry in Miniature edited by William Pratt (2008)

The Katrina Papers: A Journal of Trauma and Recovery by Jerry W. Ward, Jr. (2008)

On Higher Ground: The University of New Orleans at Fifty by Dr. Robert Dupont (2008)

Us Four Plus Four: Eight Russian Poets Conversing translated by Don Mager (2008)

Voices Rising: Stories from the Katrina Narrative Project edited by Rebeca Antoine (2008)

Gravestones (Lápidas) by Antonio Gamoneda, translated by Donald Wellman (2009)

The House of Dance and Feathers: A Museum by Ronald W. Lewis by Rachel Breunlin and Ronald W. Lewis (2009)

I hope it's not over, and good-by: Selected Poems of Everette Maddox by Everette Maddox (2009)

Portraits: Photographs in New Orleans 1998-2009 by Jonathan Traviesa (2009)

Theoretical Killings: Essays & Accidents by Steven Church (2009)

The Fox's Window and Other Stories by Naoko Awa, translated by Toshiya Kamei (2010)

Voices Rising II: More Stories from the Katrina Narrative Project edited by Rebeca Antoine (2010)

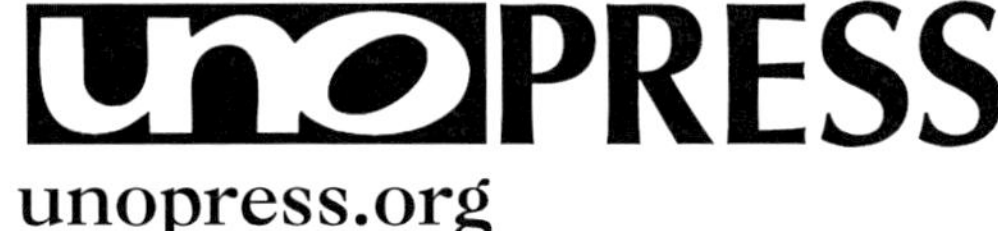

unopress.org